AN

HISTORICAL DISQUISITION

CONCERNING

The Knowledge which the ancients had of INDIA

AN

HISTORICAL DISQUISITION

CONCERNING

The Knowledge which the ancients had of

INDIA;

AND THE

PROGRESS OF TRADE with that COUNTRY

prior to the discovery of the passage to it by the

CAPE OF GOOD HOPE

WILLIAM ROBERTSON, D. D. F. R. S. Ed.

GYAN

Published by

GYAN

Gyan Publishing House
5, Ansari Road
Daryaganj, New Delhi-110002
Phone: 011-47034999, 9811692060
E-mail: books@gyanbooks.com

Distribution Network
gyanbooks.com
India, USA, Canada, UK, Australia, France

ISBN: 978-81-212-9382-2 (PB)
First Published, 1791

2nd Impression 2023

Printed at: Gyan Press, Delhi.

AN HISTORICAL DISQUISITION CONCERNING THE KNOWLEDGE WHICH THE ANCIENTS HAD OF INDIA

AUTHOR: WILLIAM ROBERTSON

AN

HISTORICAL DISQUISITION

CONCERNING

ANCIENT INDIA.

AN

HISTORICAL DISQUISITION

CONCERNING

The Knowledge which the *Ancients* had of

INDIA;

AND THE

PROGRESS of TRADE with that COUNTRY prior to the Discovery of the Passage to it by the *CAPE OF GOOD HOPE.*

With an APPENDIX,

CONTAINING

Observations on the Civil Policy—the Laws and Judicial Proceedings—the Arts—the Sciences—and Religious Institutions, of the *INDIANS*.

By WILLIAM ROBERTSON, D. D. F. R. S. Ed.

PRINCIPAL OF THE UNIVERSITY, AND HISTORIOGRAPHER TO HIS MAJESTY FOR SCOTLAND.

LONDON:

PRINTED FOR A. STRAHAN, AND T. CADELL IN THE STRAND; AND E. BALFOUR AT EDINBURGH.

M DCC XCI.

PREFACE.

THE perusal of Major Rennell's Memoir for illustrating his Map of Indostan, one of the most valuable geographical treatises that has appeared in any age or country, gave rise to the following work. It suggested to me the idea of examining more fully than I had done in the Introductory Book to my History of America, into the knowledge which the Ancients had of India, and of considering what is certain, what is obscure, and what is fabulous, in the accounts of that country which they have handed down to us. In undertaking this inquiry, I had originally no other object than my own amusement and instruction:

a But

But in carrying it on, and consulting with care the authors of antiquity, some facts, hitherto unobserved, and many which had not been examined with proper attention, occurred; new views opened; my ideas gradually extended and became more interesting; until, at length, I imagined that the result of my researches might prove amusing and instructive to others, by exhibiting such a view of the various modes in which intercourse with India had been carried on from the earliest times, as might shew how much that great branch of commerce has contributed, in every age, to increase the wealth and power of the nations which possessed it.

THUS the Historical Disquisition which I now lay before the Reader was begun and completed. What degree of merit it possesses, the Public must determine. My grateful recollection of the favourable manner in which my other works have been received, naturally increases the solicitude with which I wait for its decision concerning this which I now publish.

WHEN

When I first turned my thoughts to this subject, I was so fully aware of the disadvantage under which I laboured in undertaking to describe countries of which I had not any local knowledge, that I have been at the utmost pains to guard against any errors which this might occasion. I have consulted, with persevering industry, the works of all the authors I could procure, who have given any account of India; I have never formed any decided opinion, which was not supported by respectable authority; and as I have the good fortune to reckon among the number of my friends some Gentlemen who have filled important stations, civil and military, in India, and who have visited many different parts of it, I had recourse frequently to them, and from their conversation learned things which I could not have found in books. Were it proper to mention their names, the Public would allow that by their discernment and abilities they are fully entitled to the confidence which I have placed in them.

In the progreſs of the work, I became ſenſible of my own deficiency with reſpect to another point. In order to give an accurate idea of the imperfection both of the theory and practice of navigation among the Ancients, and to explain with ſcientific preciſion, the manner in which they aſcertained the poſition of places, and calculated their longitude and latitude, a greater portion of mathematical knowledge was requiſite, than my attention to other ſtudies had permitted me to acquire. What I wanted, the friendſhip of my ingenious and reſpectable Colleague, Mr. Playfair, Profeſſor of Mathematics, has ſupplied, and I have been enabled by him to elucidate all the points I have mentioned, in a manner which, I am confident, will afford my Readers complete ſatisfaction. To him, likewiſe, I am indebted for the conſtruction of two maps neceſſary for illuſtrating this Diſquiſition, which without his aſſiſtance I could not have undertaken.

I HAVE adhered, in this work, to an arrangement I followed in my former compoſitions, and to which the Public has been long accuſtomed. I have kept hiſtorical narrative as much ſeparate as poſſible from ſcientific and critical diſcuſſions, by reſerving the latter for Notes and Illuſtrations. I flatter myſelf that I may claim, without preſumption, the merit of having examined with diligence what I ſubmit to public inſpection, and of having referred, with ſcrupulous accuracy, to the authors from whom I have derived information.

College of Edinburgh,
May 10th, 1791.

CONTENTS.

SECTION I.

Page

INtercourse with India, from the earliest Times, until the Conquest of Egypt by the Romans. 1

SECTION II.

Intercourse with India, from the Establishment of the Roman Dominion in Egypt, to the Conquest of that Kingdom by the Mahomedans. 43

SECTION III.

Intercourse with India, from the Conquest of Egypt by the Mahomedans, to the Discovery of the Passage by the Cape of Good Hope, and the Establishment of the Portuguese Dominion in the East. - - - 91

SECTION IV.

Page

General Observations. - - 149

NOTES *and* ILLUSTRATIONS. - 180

APPENDIX. - - 255

NOTES *to the* APPENDIX. - 337

AN

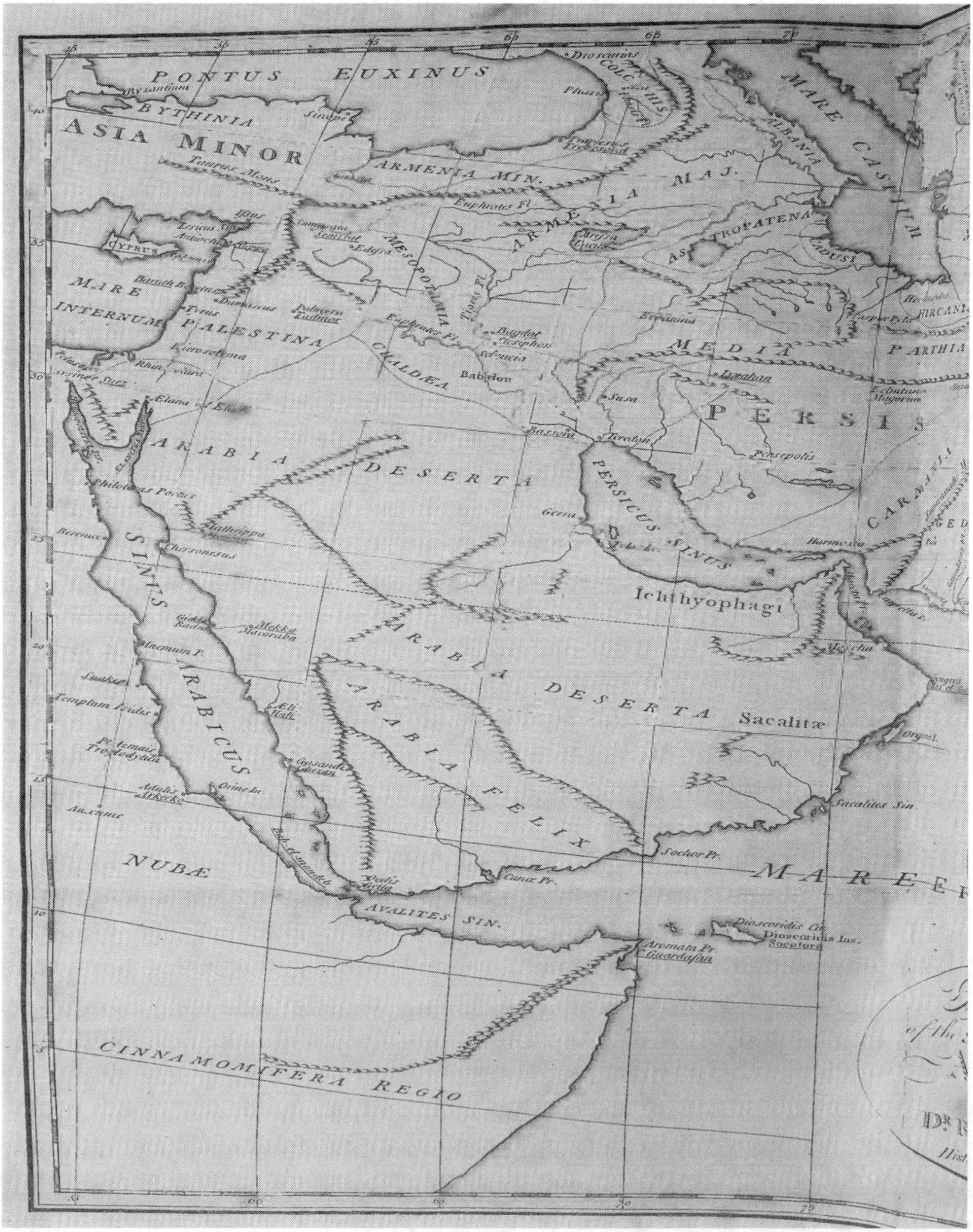
PONTUS EUXINUS
ASIA MINOR
BYTHINIA
Byzantium
Sinope
Taurus Mons
ARMENIA MIN.
ARMENIA MAJ.
ALBANIA
MARE CASPIUM
Euphrates Fl.
ATROPATENA
CYPRUS
Antiochia
Issus
Samosata
Edessa
MESOPOTAMIA
MARE INTERNUM
Tyrus
Damascus
Palmyra
Tadmor
PALESTINA
Hierosolyma
Tigris Fl.
Bagdat
Ctesiphon
Seleucia
Babylon
CHALDÆA
MEDIA
PARTHIA
HIRCANIA
Ecbatana
Susa
PERSIS
Persepolis
Bassora
ARABIA DESERTA
Gerra
PERSICUS SINUS
CARMANIA
Harmozia
Ichthyophagi
Chersonesus
Philoteras Portus
Berenice
Jathrippa
Mekka
Macoraba
SINUS ARABICUS
ARABIA DESERTA
Sacalitæ
Templum Isidis
Ptolemais
Troglodytica
Adulis
Arkeeko
Auxume
ARABIA FELIX
Sacalites Sin.
Socher Pr.
NUBÆ
Cana Pr.
AVALITES SIN.
Dioscoridis Ins.
Socotora
Aromata Pr.
C. Guardafan
MARE E
CINNAMOMIFERA REGIO

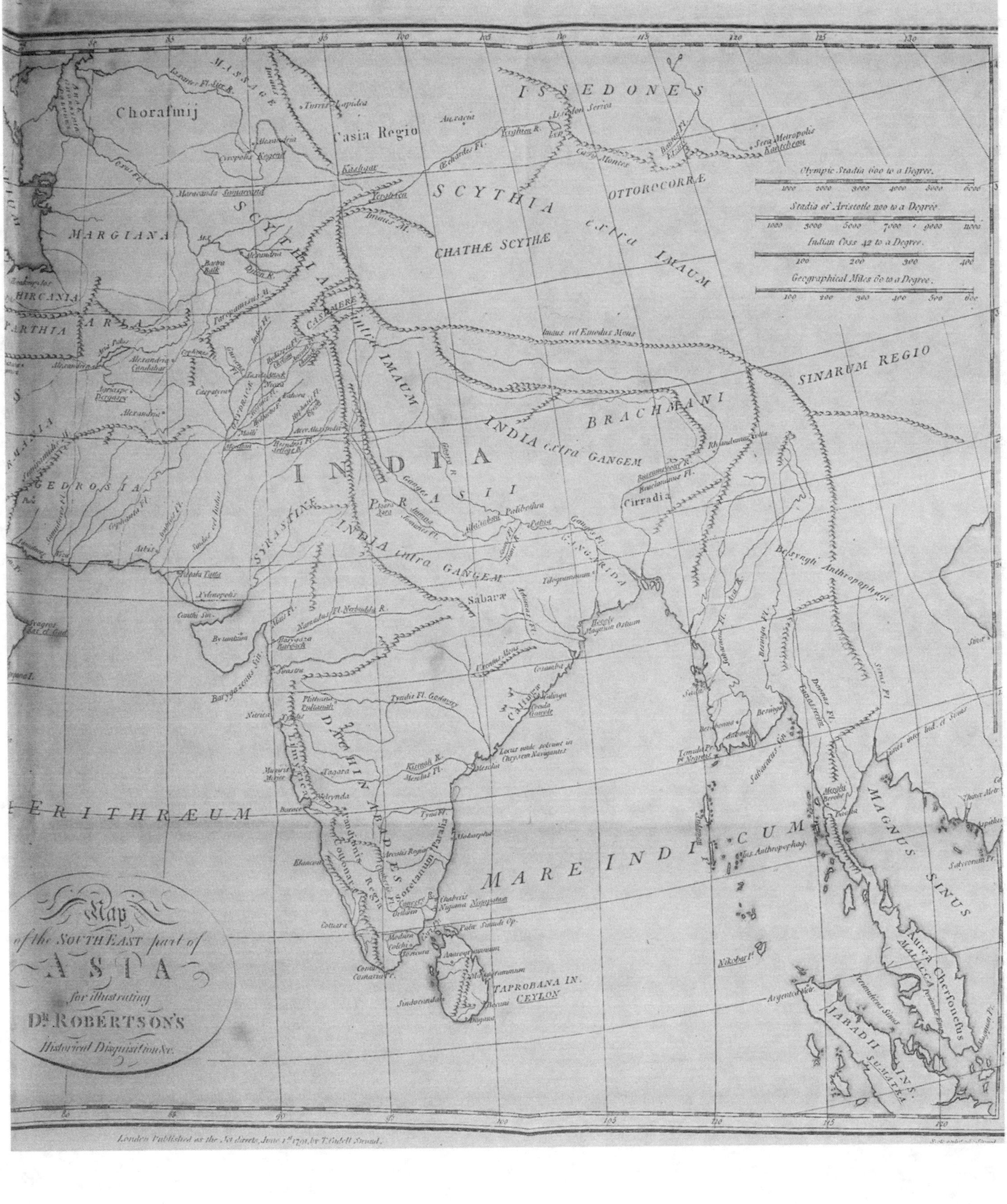
Map
of the SOUTH EAST part of
ASIA
for illustrating
Dr. ROBERTSON'S
Historical Disquisition &c.
Chorafmij
Casia Regio
ISSEDONES
SCYTHIA
extra IMAUM
OTTOROCORRÆ
CHATHÆ SCYTHÆ
MARGIANA
HIRCANIA
PARTHIA
ARIA
CASSIMERE
IMAUM
SINARUM REGIO
BRACHMANI
INDIA extra GANGEM
INDIA
GEDROSIA
Cirradia
SYRASTINE
INDIA intra GANGEM
Sabaræ
MAGNUS SINUS
MARE INDICUM
TAPROBANA IN.
CEYLON
Aurea Cherfonefus
MALACCA
JABADII INS.
SUMATRA
Olympic Stadia 600 to a Degree.
Stadia of Aristotle 1100 to a Degree.
Indian Coss 42 to a Degree.
Geographical Miles 60 to a Degree.

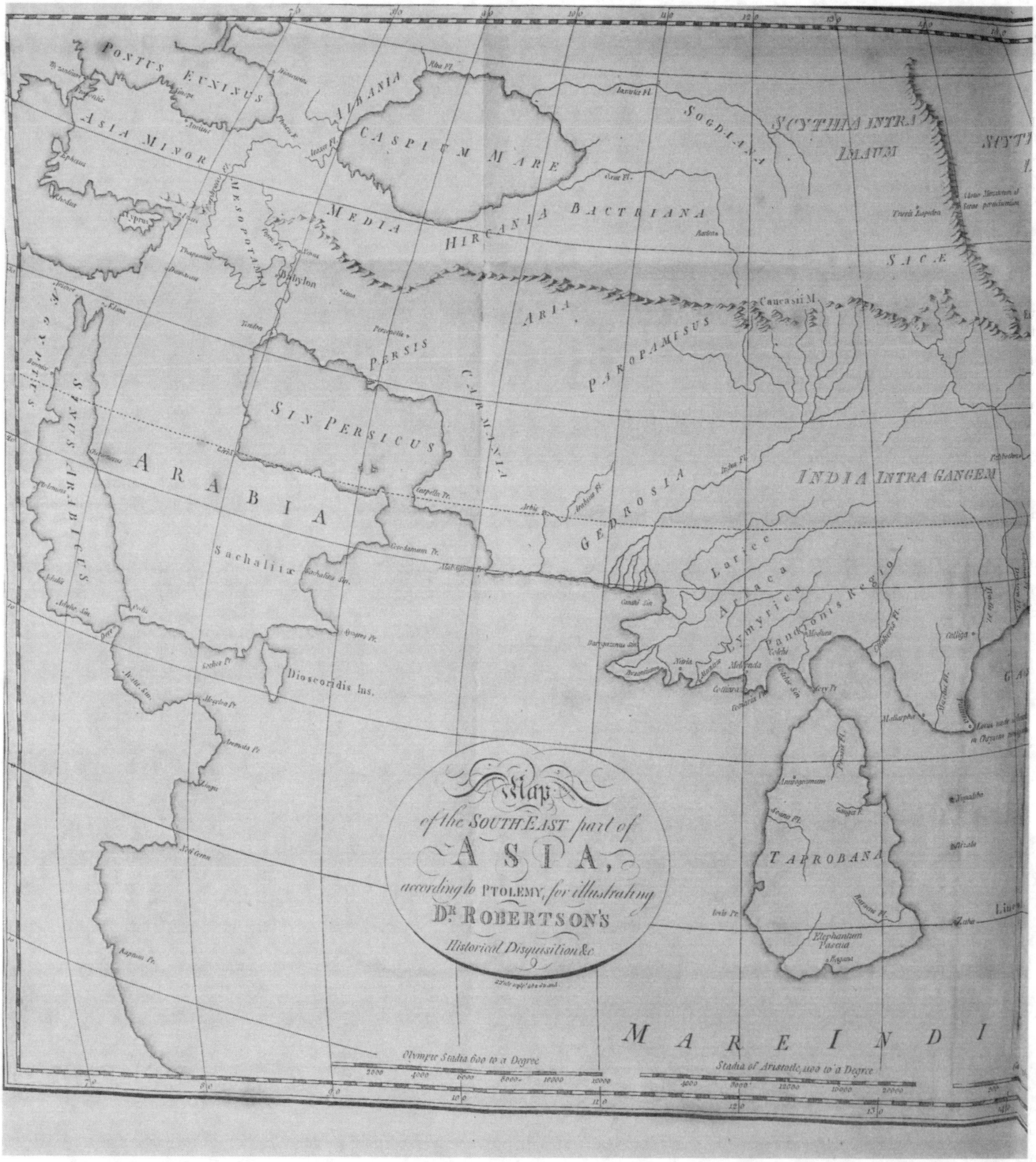
Map
of the SOUTH EAST part of
ASIA,
according to PTOLEMY, for illustrating
Dr ROBERTSON'S
Historical Disquisition &c.
PONTUS EUXINUS
ASIA MINOR
ALBANIA
CASPIUM MARE
SOGDIANA
SCYTHIA INTRA IMAUM
MEDIA
HIRCANIA
BACTRIANA
MESOPOTAMIA
Babylon
SACÆ
Caucasii M.
ARIA
PERSIS
PAROPAMISUS
CARMANIA
SIN PERSICUS
SINUS ARABICUS
ARABIA
GEDROSIA
INDIA INTRA GANGEM
Sachalitæ
Larice
Ariaca
Limyrica
Pandionis Regio
Dioscoridis Ins.
TAPROBANA
Elephantum Pascua
MARE INDI
Olympic Stadia 600 to a Degree
Stadia of Aristotle, 400 to a Degree

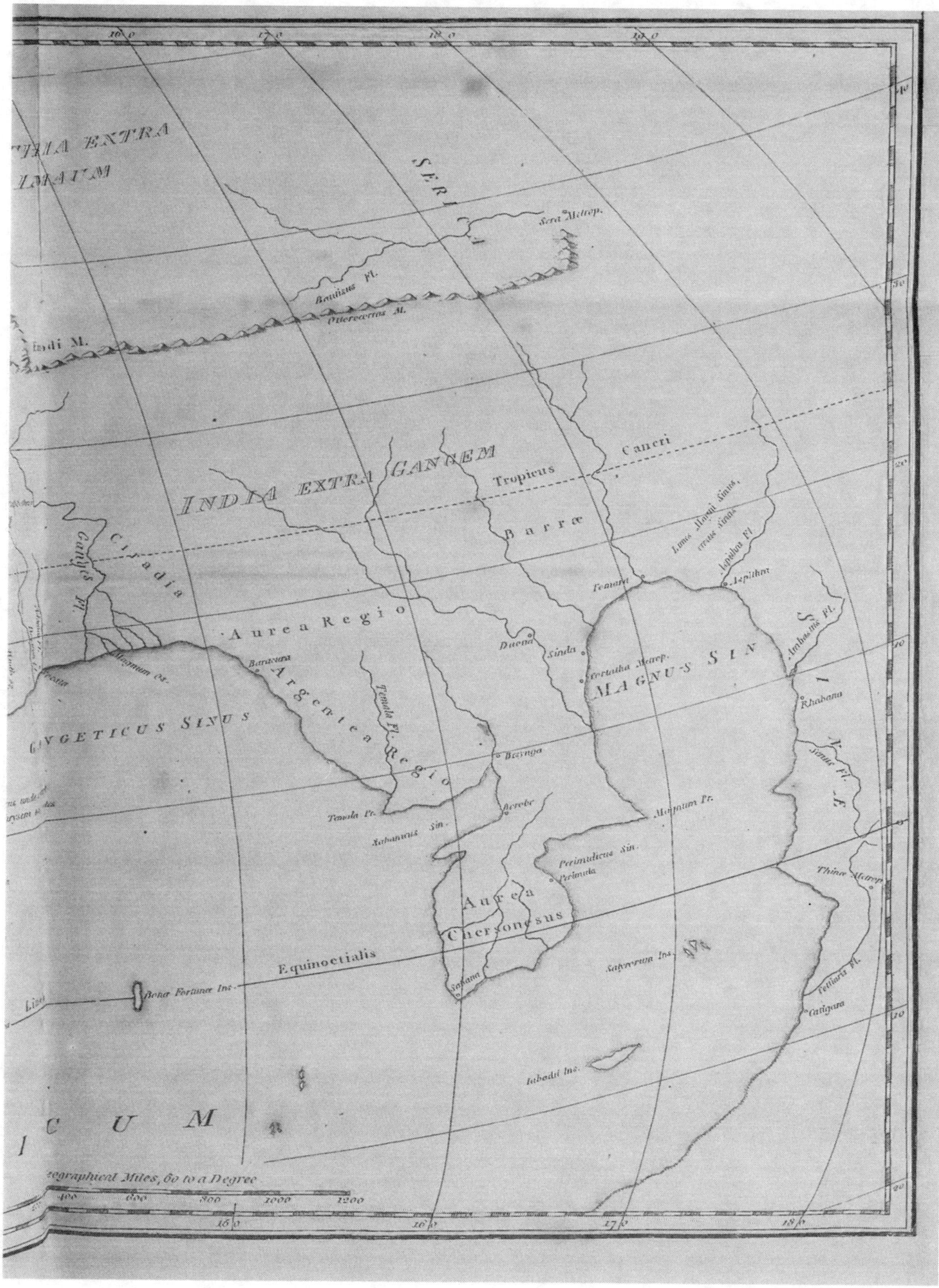
INDIA EXTRA GANGEM
Tropicus
Cancri
Barræ
Aurea Regio
Argentea Regio
Aurea
Chersonesus
Equinoctialis
Bona Fortunæ Ins.
MAGNUS SIN
Sera Metrop.
Tamala Pt.
Magnum Pr.
Cattigara
Rhabana
Sinda
Satyrorum Ins.

AN

HISTORICAL DISQUISITION

CONCERNING

ANCIENT INDIA.

SECTION I.

Intercourse with India, from the earlieſt Times, until the Conqueſt of Egypt by the Romans.

SECT. I.

WHOEVER attempts to trace the operations of men in remote times, and to mark the various ſteps of their progreſs in any line of exertion, will ſoon have the mortification to find, that the period of authentic hiſtory is extremely limited. It is little more than three thouſand years ſince the Books of Moſes, the moſt ancient and only genuine record of what paſſed in the early ages of the world, were

B composed.

SECT. I. composed. Herodotus, the most ancient Heathen historian whose works have reached us, flourished a thousand years later. If we push our inquiries concerning any point beyond the æra where written history commences, we enter upon the region of conjecture, of fable, and of uncertainty. Upon that ground I will neither venture myself, nor endeavour to conduct my readers. In my researches concerning the intercourse between the Eastern and Western regions of the earth, and concerning the progress of that great branch of trade, which, in every age, has contributed so conspicuously towards raising the people who carried it on, to wealth and power, I shall confine myself within the precincts I have marked out. Whereever the inspired writers, intent upon higher objects, mention occasionally any circumstance that tends to illustrate the subject of my inquiries, I shall attend to it with reverence. Whatever other writers relate, I shall examine with freedom, and endeavour to ascertain the degree of credit to which they are entitled.

THE original station allotted to man by his Creator, was in the mild and fertile regions of the East. There the human race began its career of improvement; and from the remains of sciences which were anciently cultivated, as well as of arts which were anciently exercised in India, we may conclude it to be one of the first countries in which men made any considerable progress in that career. The wisdom of the East was early celebrated [a], and its productions were early in re-

[a] 1 Kings, iv. 30.

quest

queſt among diſtant nations [b]. The intercourſe, however, between different countries was carried on at firſt entirely by land. As the people of the Eaſt appear ſoon to have acquired complete dominion over the uſeful animals [c], they could early undertake the long and toilſome journies which it was neceſſary to make, in order to maintain this intercourſe; and by the provident bounty of Heaven, they were furniſhed with a beaſt of burden, without whoſe aid it would have been impoſſible to accompliſh them. The Camel, by its perſevering ſtrength, by its moderation in the uſe of food, and the ſingularity of its internal ſtructure, which enables it to lay in a ſtock of water ſufficient for ſeveral days, put it in their power to convey bulky commodities through thoſe deſerts, which muſt be traverſed by all who travel from any of the countries weſt of the Euphrates towards India. Trade was carried on in this manner, particularly by the nations near to the Arabian Gulf, from the earlieſt period to which hiſtorical information reaches. Diſtant journies, however, would be undertaken at firſt only occaſionally, and by a few adventurers. But by degrees, from attention to their mutual ſafety and comfort, numerous bodies of merchants aſſembled at ſtated times, and forming a temporary aſſociation (known afterwards by the name of a Caravan), governed by officers of their own choice, and ſubject to regulations of which experience had taught them the utility, they performed journies of ſuch extent and duration, as appear aſtoniſhing to nations not accuſtomed to this mode of carrying on commerce.

[b] Gen. xxxvii. 25.

[c] Ibid. xii. 16. xxiv. 10, 11.

SECT. I.

But notwithstanding every improvement that could be made in the manner of conveying the productions of one country to another by land, the inconveniences which attended it were obvious and unavoidable. It was often dangerous; always expensive, and tedious, and fatiguing. A method of communication more easy and expeditious was sought, and the ingenuity of man gradually discovered, that the rivers, the arms of the sea, and even the ocean itself, were destined to open and facilitate intercourse with the various regions of the earth, between which they appear, at first view, to be placed as insuperable barriers. Navigation, however, and ship-building, (as I have observed in another work[d]) are arts so nice and complicated, that they require the talents, as well as experience of many successive ages, to bring them to any degree of perfection. From the raft or canoe, which first served to carry a savage over the river that obstructed him in the chace, to the construction of a vessel capable of conveying a numerous crew, or a considerable cargo of goods, to a distant coast, the progress of improvement is immense. Many efforts would be made, many experiments would be tried, and much labour as well as ingenuity would be employed, before this arduous and important undertaking could be accomplished.

Even after some improvement was made in ship-building, the intercourse of nations with each other by sea was far from being extensive. From the accounts of the earliest historians, we learn that navigation made its first efforts in the Mediter-

[d] Hist. of America, vol. i. p. 2.

ranean

ranean and the Arabian Gulf, and in them the firſt active operations of commerce were carried on. From an attentive inſpection of the poſition and form of theſe two great inland ſeas, theſe accounts appear to be highly probable. Theſe ſeas lay open the continents of Europe, Aſia, and Africa, and ſpreading to a great extent along the coaſts of the moſt fertile and moſt early civilized countries in each, ſeem to have been deſtined by nature to facilitate their communication with one another. We find, accordingly, that the firſt voyages of the Egyptians and Phenicians, the moſt ancient navigators mentioned in hiſtory, were made in the Mediterranean. Their trade, however, was not long confined to the countries bordering upon it. By acquiring early poſſeſſion of ports on the Arabian Gulf, they extended the ſphere of their commerce, and are repreſented as the firſt people of the Weſt who opened a communication by ſea with India.

In that account of the progreſs of navigation and diſcovery which I prefixed to the Hiſtory of America, I conſidered with attention the maritime operations of the Egyptians and Phenicians; a brief review of them here, as far as they relate to their connection with India, is all that is requiſite for illuſtrating the ſubject of my preſent inquiries. With reſpect to the former of theſe people, the information which hiſtory affords is ſlender, and of doubtful authority. The fertile ſoil and mild climate of Egypt produced the neceſſaries and comforts of life in ſuch profuſion, as to render its inhabitants ſo independent of other countries, that it became early an eſtabliſhed maxim in their policy, to renounce all intercourſe with foreigners. In

2 conſequence

SECT. I. consequence of this, they held all sea-faring persons in detestation, as impious and profane; and fortifying their harbours, they denied strangers admission into them [e].

The enterprising ambition of Sesostris, disdaining the restraints imposed upon it by these contracted ideas of his subjects, prompted him to render the Egyptians a commercial people; and in the course of his reign, he so completely accomplished this, that (if we may give credit to some Historians) he was able to fit out a fleet of four hundred ships in the Arabian Gulf, which conquered all the countries stretching along the Erythrean sea to India. At the same time, his army, led by himself, marched through Asia, and subjected to his dominion every part of it as far as to the banks of the Ganges; and, crossing that river, advanced to the Eastern Ocean [f]. But these efforts produced no permanent effect, and appear to have been so contrary to the genius and habits of the Egyptians, that, on the death of Sesostris, they resumed their ancient maxims, and many ages elapsed before the commercial connection of Egypt with India came to be of such importance as to merit any notice in this Disquisition [g].

The history of the early maritime operations of Phenicia are not involved in the same obscurity with those of Egypt. Every circumstance in the character and situation of the Phenicians,

[e] Diodor. Sicul. lib. i. p. 78. edit. Wesselingi. Amst. 1746. Strab. Geog. lib. xvii. p. 1142. A. edit. Casaub. Amst. 1707.

[f] Diod. Sic. lib. i. p. 64.

[g] See NOTE I.

7 was

was favourable to the commercial ſpirit. The territory which they poſſeſſed, was neither large nor fertile. It was from commerce only, that they could derive either opulence or power. Accordingly, the trade carried on by the Phenicians of Sidon and Tyre, was extenſive and adventurous; and, both in their manners and policy, they reſemble the great commercial ſtates of modern times, more than any people in the ancient world. Among the various branches of their commerce, that with India may be regarded as one of the moſt conſiderable and moſt lucrative. As by their ſituation on the Mediterranean, and the imperfect ſtate of navigation, they could not attempt to open a direct communication with India by ſea; the enterprizing ſpirit of commerce prompted them to wreſt from the Idumæans ſome commodious harbours towards the bottom of the Arabian Gulf. From theſe they held a regular intercourſe with India, on the one hand, and with the Eaſtern and Southern coaſts of Africa on the other. The diſtance, however, from the Arabian Gulf to Tyre was conſiderable, and rendered the conveyance of goods to it by land carriage ſo tedious and expenſive, that it became neceſſary for them to take poſſeſſion of Rhinocolura, the neareſt port in the Mediterranean to the Arabian Gulf. Thither all the commodities brought from India, were conveyed over land by a route much ſhorter, and more practicable than that by which the productions of the Eaſt were carried at a ſubſequent period from the oppoſite ſhore of the Arabian Gulf to the Nile[h]. At Rhinocolura, they were reſhipped, and tranſported by an eaſy navigation to Tyre, and diſtributed

[h] Diod. Sic. lib. i. p. 70. Strab. lib. xvi. p. 1128. A.

through

SECT. I.

through the world. This, as it is the earlieſt route of communication with India, of which we have any authentic deſcription, had ſo many advantages over any ever known before the modern diſcovery of a new courſe of navigation to the Eaſt, that the Phenicians could ſupply other nations with the productions of India in greater abundance, and at a cheaper rate, than any people of antiquity. To this circumſtance, which, for a conſiderable time, ſecured to them a monopoly of that trade, was owing, not only the extraordinary wealth of individuals, which rendered the "merchants of Tyre, Princes, "and her traffickers the Honourable of the Earth[i];" but the extenſive power of the ſtate itſelf, which firſt taught mankind to conceive what vaſt reſources a commercial people poſſeſs, and what great exertions they are capable of making[k].

THE Jews, by their vicinity to Tyre, had ſuch an opportunity of obſerving the wealth which flowed into that city from the lucrative commerce carried on by the Phenicians from their ſettlements on the Arabian Gulf, as incited them to aim at obtaining ſome ſhare of it. This they effected under the proſperous reigns of David and Solomon, partly by the conqueſts which they made of a ſmall diſtrict in the land of Edom, that gave them poſſeſſion of the harbours of Elath and Eſiongeber on the Red Sea, and partly by the friendſhip of Hiram, king of Tyre; who enabled Solomon to fit out fleets, which, under the direction of Phenician pilots, ſailed to Tarſhiſh and Ophir[l]. In what region of the earth we ſhould

[i] Iſaiah, xxiii. 8. [k] See NOTE II. [l] Kings, ix. 26. x. 22.

ſearch

ſearch for theſe famous ports which furniſhed the navy of Solomon with the various commodities enumerated by the ſacred hiſtorians, is an inquiry that has long exerciſed the induſtry of learned men. They were early ſuppoſed to be ſituated in ſome part of India, and the Jews were held to be one of the nations which traded with that country. But the opinion more generally adopted is, that Solomon's fleets, after paſſing the ſtraits of Babelmandeb, held their courſe along the ſouth-weſt coaſt of Africa, as far as the kingdom of Sofala; a country celebrated for its rich mines of gold and ſilver, (from which it has been denominated the Golden Sofala by Oriental writers [m],) and abounding in all the other articles which compoſed the cargoes of the Jewiſh ſhips. This opinion, which the accurate reſearches of M. D'Anville rendered highly probable [n], ſeems now to be eſtabliſhed with the utmoſt certainty by a late learned traveller; who, by his knowledge of the monſoons in the Arabian Gulf, and his attention to the ancient mode of navigation, both in that ſea and along the African coaſt, has not only accounted for the extraordinary length of time which the fleets of Solomon took in going and returning, but has ſhewn, from circumſtances mentioned concerning the voyage, that it was not made to any place in India [o]. The Jews, then, we may conclude, have no title to be reckoned among the nations which carried on intercourſe with India by ſea; and if, from deference to the ſentiments of ſome reſpectable authors, their claim were to be admitted,

[m] Notices des MSS. du Roi, tom. ii. p. 40.

[n] Diſſert. ſur le Pays d'Ophir, Mem. de Literat. tom. xxx. p. 83, &c.

[o] Bruce's Travels, book ii. ch. 4.

C we

SECT. I. we know with certainty, that the commercial effort which they made in the reign of Solomon was merely a tranſient one, and that they quickly returned to their former ſtate of unſocial ſecluſion from the reſt of mankind.

FROM collecting the ſcanty information which hiſtory affords, concerning the moſt early attempts to open a commercial intercourſe with India, I now proceed, with more certainty and greater confidence, to trace the progreſs of communication with that country, under the guidance of authors who recorded events nearer to their own times, and with reſpect to which, they had received more full and accurate intelligence.

THE firſt eſtabliſhment of any foreign power in India, which can be aſcertained by evidence, meriting any degree of credit, is that of the Perſians; and even of this we have only a very general and doubtful account. Darius, the ſon of Hyſtaſpes, though raiſed to the throne of Perſia by chance or by artifice, poſſeſſed ſuch active and enterprizing talents, as rendered him worthy of that high ſtation. He examined the different provinces of his kingdom more diligently than any of his predeceſſors, and explored regions of Aſia formerly little known[p]. Having ſubjected to his dominion many of the countries which ſtretch ſouth-eaſt from the Caſpian ſea towards the river Oxus, his curioſity was excited to acquire a more excluſive and accurate knowledge of India, on which they bordered. With this view he appointed Scylax of Caryandra to take the command of a ſquadron fitted out at

[p] Herodoti, lib. iv. c. 44.

Caſpatyrus,

Caſpatyrus, in the country of Pactya, [the modern Pehkely,] towards the upper part of the navigable courſe of the river Indus, and to fall down its ſtream until he ſhould reach the ocean. This Scylax performed, though it ſhould ſeem with much difficulty, and notwithſtanding many obſtacles; for he ſpent no leſs than two years and ſix months in conducting his ſquadron from the place where he embarked, to the Arabian Gulf[q]. The account which he gave of the populouſneſs, fertility, and high cultivation of that region of India through which his courſe lay, rendered Darius impatient to become maſter of a country ſo valuable. This he ſoon accompliſhed; and though his conqueſts in India ſeem not to have extended beyond the diſtrict watered by the Indus, we are led to form an high idea of its opulence, as well as of the number of its inhabitants, in ancient times, when we learn, that the tribute which he levied from it, was near a third part of the whole revenue of the Perſian monarchy[r]. But neither this voyage of Scylax, nor the conqueſts of Darius, to which it gave riſe, diffuſed any general knowledge of India. The Greeks, who were the only enlightened people at that time in Europe, paid but little attention to the tranſactions of the people whom they conſidered as Barbarians, eſpecially in countries far remote from their own; and Scylax had embelliſhed the narrative of his voyage with ſo many circumſtances, manifeſtly fabulous[s], that he ſeems to have met with the juſt puniſhment, to which perſons who have a notorious propenſity to what is marvellous, are often

[q] Herod. iv. c. 42. 44. [r] Herod. lib. iii. c. 90—96. See NOTE III.

[s] Philoſtr. Vita Apoll. lib. iii. c. 47. and Note 3d of Olearius Tzetzet. Chiliad. vii. verſ. 630.

SECT. I. ſubjected, of being liſtened to with diſtruſt, even when they relate what is exactly true.

About an hundred and ſixty years after the reign of Darius Hyſtaſpes, Alexander the Great undertook his expedition into India. The wild ſallies of paſſion, the indecent exceſſes of intemperance, and the oſtentatious diſplays of vanity too frequent in the conduct of this extraordinary man, have ſo degraded his character, that the pre-eminence of his merit, either as a conqueror, a politician, or a legiſlator, has ſeldom been juſtly eſtimated. The ſubject of my preſent inquiry leads me to conſider his operations only in one light, but it will enable me to exhibit a ſtriking view of the grandeur and extent of his plans. He ſeems, ſoon after his firſt ſucceſſes in Aſia, to have formed the idea of eſtabliſhing an univerſal monarchy, and aſpired to the dominion of the ſea, as well as of the land. From the wonderful efforts of the Tyrians in their own defence, when left without any ally or protector, he conceived an high opinion of the reſources of maritime power, and of the wealth to be derived from commerce, eſpecially that with India, which he found engroſſed by the citizens of Tyre. With a view to ſecure this commerce, and to eſtabliſh a ſtation for it, preferable in many reſpects to that of Tyre, as ſoon as he completed the conqueſt of Egypt, he founded a city near one of the mouths of the Nile, which he honoured with his own name; and with ſuch admirable diſcernment was the ſituation of it choſen, that Alexandria ſoon became the greateſt trading city in the ancient world; and, notwithſtanding many ſucceſſive revolutions in empire, continued, during

during eighteen centuries, to be the chief ſeat of commerce with India [t]. Amidſt the military operations to which Alexander was ſoon obliged to turn his attention, the deſire of acquiring the lucrative commerce which the Tyrians had carried on with India, was not relinquiſhed. Events ſoon occurred, that not only confirmed and added ſtrength to his deſire, but opened to him a proſpect of obtaining the ſovereignty of thoſe regions which ſupplied the reſt of mankind with ſo many precious commodities.

After his final victory over the Perſians, he was led in purſuit of the laſt Darius, and of Beſſus, the murderer of that unfortunate monarch, to traverſe that part of Aſia which ſtretches from the Caſpian ſea beyond the river Oxus. He advanced towards the eaſt as far as Maracanda [u], then a city of ſome note, and deſtined, in a future period, under the modern name of Samarcand, to be the capital of an empire not inferior to his own in extent or power. In a progreſs of ſeveral months, through provinces hitherto unknown to the Greeks, in a line of march often approaching near to India, and among people accuſtomed to much intercourſe with it, he learned many things concerning the ſtate of a country [x] that had been long the object of his thoughts and wiſhes [y], which increaſed his deſire of invading it. Deciſive and prompt in all his reſolutions, he ſet out from Bactria, and croſſed that ridge of mountains which, under various denominations, forms the

[t] Hiſt. of America, vol. i. p. 20.

[u] Arrian, iii. c. 30.

[x] Strab. xv. p. 1021. A.

[y] Arrian, iv. c. 15.

Stony

SECT. I. Stony Girdle (if I may use an expression of the Oriental geographers) which encircles Asia, and constitutes the northern barrier of India.

The most practicable avenue to every country, it is obvious, must be formed by circumstances in its natural situation, such as the defiles which lead through mountains, the course of rivers, and the places where they may be passed with the greatest ease and safety. In no place of the earth is this line of approach marked and defined more conspicuously, than on the northern frontier of India; insomuch that the three great invaders of this country, Alexander, Tamerlane, and Nadir Shah, in three distant ages, and with views and talents extremely different, advanced by the same route, with hardly any deviation. Alexander had the merit of having first discovered the way. After passing the mountains, he encamped at Alexandria Paropamisana, on the same site with the modern city Candahar; and having subdued or conciliated the nations seated on the north-west bank of the Indus, he crossed the river at Taxila, now Attock, the only place where its stream is so tranquil that a bridge can be thrown over it [z].

After passing the Indus, Alexander marched forward in the road which leads directly to the Ganges, and the opulent provinces to the south-east, now comprehended under the general name of Indostan. But, on the banks of the Hydaspes, known in modern times by the name of the Betah or Chelum,

[z] Rennell Mem. p. 92.

he

he was oppoſed by Porus, a powerful monarch of the country, at the head of a numerous army. The war with Porus, and the hoſtilities in which he was ſucceſſively engaged with other Indian princes, led him to deviate from his original route, and to turn more towards the ſouth-weſt. In carrying on theſe operations, Alexander marched through one of the richeſt and beſt peopled countries of India, now called the Panjab, from the five great rivers by which it is watered; and as we know that this march was performed in the rainy ſeaſon, when even Indian armies cannot keep the field, it gives an high idea both of Alexander's perſevering ſpirit, and of the extraordinary vigour and hardineſs of conſtitution which ſoldiers, in ancient times, derived from the united effects of gymnaſtic exerciſe and military diſcipline. In every ſtep of his progreſs, objects no leſs ſtriking than new preſented themſelves to Alexander. The magnitude of the Indus, even after he had ſeen the Nile, the Euphrates, and the Tigris, muſt have filled him with ſurpriſe [a]. No country he had hitherto viſited was ſo populous and well cultivated, or abounded in ſo many valuable productions of nature and of art, as that part of India through which he had led his army. But when he was informed in every place, and probably with exaggerated deſcription, how much the Indus was inferior to the Ganges, and how far all that he had hitherto beheld was ſurpaſſed in the happy regions through which that great river flows, it is not wonderful that his eagerneſs to view and to take poſſeſſion of them ſhould have prompted him to aſſemble his ſoldiers, and to propoſe that

[a] Strab. lib. xv. p. 1027. C. & note 5. Cauſab.

SECT. I. they ſhould reſume their march towards that quarter where wealth, dominion, and fame awaited them. But they had already done ſo much, and had ſuffered ſo greatly, eſpecially from inceſſant rains and extenſive inundations, that their patience as well as ſtrength were exhauſted [b], and with one voice they refuſed to advance farther. In this reſolution they perſiſted with ſuch ſullen obſtinacy, that Alexander, though poſſeſſed in the higheſt degree of every quality that gains an aſcendant over the minds of military men, was obliged to yield, and to iſſue orders for marching back to Perſia [c].

The ſcene of this memorable tranſaction was on the banks of the Hyphaſis, the modern Beyah, which was the utmoſt limit of Alexander's progreſs in India. From this it is manifeſt, that he did not traverſe the whole extent of the Panjab. Its ſouth-weſt boundary is formed by a river anciently known by the name of Hyſudrus, and now by that of the Setlege, to which Alexander never approached nearer than the ſouthern bank of the Hyphaſis, where he erected twelve ſtupendous altars, which he intended as a monument of his exploits, and which (if we may believe the biographer of Apollonius Tyanæus) were ſtill remaining, with legible inſcriptions, when that fantaſtic ſophiſt viſited India, three hundred and ſeventy-three years after Alexander's expedition [d]. The breadth of the Panjab, from Ludhana on the Setlege to Attock on the Indus, is computed to be two hundred and fifty-nine geographical

[b] See NOTE IV. [c] Arrian, v. c. 24, 25.

[d] Philoſtr. Vita Apollon. lib. ii. c. 43. edit. Olear. Lipſ. 1709.

5 miles,

miles, in a ſtraight line; and Alexander's march, computed in the ſame manner, did not extend above two hundred miles. But, both as he advanced and returned, his troops were ſo ſpread over the country, and often acted in ſo many ſeparate diviſions, and all his movements were ſo exactly meaſured and delineated by men of ſcience, whom he kept in pay for the purpoſe, that he acquired a very extenſive and accurate knowledge of that part of India [e].

When, upon his return, he reached the banks of the Hydaſpes, he found that the officers to whom he had given it in charge to build and collect as many veſſels as poſſible, had executed his orders with ſuch activity and ſucceſs that they had aſſembled a numerous fleet. As amidſt the hurry of war, and the rage of conqueſt, he never loſt ſight of his pacific and commercial ſchemes, the deſtination of this fleet was to ſail down the Indus to the ocean, and from its mouth to proceed to the Perſian Gulf, that a communication by ſea might be opened with India and the centre of his dominions.

The conduct of this expedition was committed to Nearchus, an officer equal to that important truſt. But as Alexander was ambitious to acquire fame of every kind, and fond of engaging in new and ſplendid undertakings, he himſelf accompanied Nearchus in his navigation down the river. The armament was, indeed, ſo great and magnificent, as deſerved to be commanded by the conqueror of Aſia. It was compoſed of an

[e] Plin. Nat. Hiſt. lib. vi. c. 17.

D army

SECT. I. army of a hundred and twenty thousand men, and two hundred elephants, and of a fleet of near two thousand vessels, various in burden and form [f]; on board of which one-third of the troops embarked, while the remainder marching in two divisions, one on the right, and the other on the left, of the river, accompanied them in their progress. As they advanced, the nations on each side were either compelled or persuaded to submit. Retarded by the various operations in which this engaged him, as well as by the slow navigation of such a fleet as he conducted, Alexander was above nine months before he reached the ocean [g].

ALEXANDER's progress in India, in this line of direction, was far more considerable than that which he made by the route we formerly traced; and when we attend to the various movements of his troops, the number of cities which they took, and the different states which they subdued, he may be said not only to have viewed, but to have explored, the countries through which he passed. This part of India has been so little frequented by Europeans in later times, that neither the position of places, nor their distances, can be ascertained with the same accuracy as in the interior provinces, or even in the Panjab. But from the researches of Major Rennell, carried on with no less discernment than industry, the distance of that place on the Hydaspes, where Alexander fitted out his fleet from the ocean, cannot be less than a thousand British miles. Of this extensive region

[f] See NOTE V.

[g] Strabo, lib. xv. p. 1014.

a cona conſiderable portion, particularly the upper Delta, ſtretching from the capital of the ancient Malli, now Moultan, to Patala, the modern Tatta, is diſtinguiſhed for its fertility and population [h].

SOON after he reached the ocean, Alexander, ſatisfied with having accompliſhed this arduous undertaking, led his army by land back to Perſia. The command of the fleet, with a conſiderable body of troops on board of it, he left to Nearchus, who, after a coaſting voyage of ſeven months, conducted it ſafely up the Perſian Gulf into the Euphrates [i].

IN this manner did Alexander firſt open the knowledge of India to the people of Europe, and an extenſive diſtrict of it was ſurveyed with greater accuracy than could have been expected from the ſhort time he remained in that country. Fortunately an exact account, not only of his military operations, but of every thing worthy of notice in the countries where they were carried on, was recorded in the Memoirs or Journals of three of his principal officers, Ptolemy the ſon of Lagus, Ariſtobulus, and Nearchus. The two former have not indeed reached our times, but it is probable that the moſt important facts which they contained, are preſerved, as Arrian profeſſes to have followed them as his guides in his Hiſtory of the Expedition of Alexander [k]; a work which, though compoſed long after Greece had loſt its liberty, and in an age when

[h] Rennell Mem. 68, &c.

[i] Plin. Nat. Hiſt. lib. vi. c. 23. See NOTE VI.

[k] Arrian, lib. i. in proemio.

SECT. I. genius and taste were on the decline, is not unworthy the purest times of Attic literature.

WITH respect to the general state of India, we learn from these writers, that in the age of Alexander, though there was not established in it any powerful empire, resembling that which in modern times stretched its dominion from the Indus almost to Cape Comorin, it was even then formed into monarchies of considerable extent. The king of the Prasij was prepared on the banks of the Ganges to oppose the Macedonians, with an army of twenty thousand cavalry, two thousand armed chariots, and a great number of elephants [l]. The territory of which Alexander constituted Porus the sovereign, is said to have contained no fewer than two thousand towns [m]. Even in the most restricted sense that can be given to the vague indefinite appellations of *nations* and *towns*, an idea is conveyed of a very great degree of population. As the fleet sailed down the river, the country on each side was found to be in no respect inferior to that of which the government was committed to Porus.

IT was likewise from the Memoirs of the same officers that Europe derived its first authentic information concerning the climate, the soil, the productions, and the inhabitants of India; and in a country where the manners, the customs, and even the dress of the people are almost as permanent and invariable as the face of nature itself, it is wonderful how exactly the descriptions given by Alexander's officers delineate what we now behold in India, at the distance of two thousand years.

[l] Diod. Sicul. lib. xvii. p. 232.

[m] Arrian, lib. vi. c. 2.

The

The stated change of seasons, now known by the name of *Monsoons;* the periodical rains; the swelling of the rivers; the inundations which these occasion; the appearance of the country during their continuance; are particularly mentioned and described. No less accurate are the descriptions which they have given of the inhabitants, their delicate and slender form, their dark complexion, their black uncurled hair, their garments of cotton, their living entirely upon vegetable food, their division into separate tribes or *casts*, the members of which never intermarry, the custom of wives burning themselves with their deceased husbands, and many other particulars, in all which they perfectly resemble the modern Hindoos. To enter into any detail with respect to these in this place would be premature; but as the subject, though curious and interesting, will lead unavoidably into discussions not well suited to the nature of an historical work, I shall reserve my ideas concerning it for an Appendix, which I purpose to annex to this Disquisition; and hope they may contribute to throw some additional light upon the origin and nature of the commerce with India. SECT. I.

MUCH as the Western world was indebted for its knowledge of India to the expedition of Alexander, it was only a small portion of that vast continent which he explored. His operations did not extend beyond the modern province of Lahor, and the countries on the banks of the Indus from Moultan to the sea. These, however, were surveyed with that degree of accuracy which I have already described; and it is a circumstance not unworthy of notice, that this district of India which Europeans

first

SECT. I. first entered, and with which they were best acquainted in ancient times, is now less known than almost any part of that continent[n], neither commerce nor war, to which, in every age, geography is chiefly indebted for its improvement, having led any nation of Europe to frequent or explore it.

If an untimely death had not put a period to the reign of the Macedonian hero, India, we have reason to think, would have been more fully explored by the ancients, and the European dominion would have been established there two thousand years sooner. When Alexander invaded India, he had something more in view than a transient incursion. It was his object to annex that extensive and opulent country to his empire, and though the refractory spirit of his army obliged him, at that time, to suspend the prosecution of his plan, he was far from relinquishing it. To exhibit a general view of the measures which he adopted for this purpose, and to point out their propriety and probable success, is not foreign from the subject of this Disquisition, and will convey a more just idea than is usually entertained, of the original genius and extent of political wisdom which distinguished this illustrious man.

When Alexander became master of the Persian empire, he early perceived, that with all the power of his hereditary dominions, re-inforced by the troops which the ascendant he had acquired over the various states of Greece might enable him to raise there, he could not hope to retain in subjection territories so extensive and populous; that to render his authority

[n] Rennell Mem. 114.

secure

fecure and permanent, it muft be eftablifhed in the affection of the nations which he had fubdued, and maintained by their arms; and that in order to acquire this advantage, all diftinctions between the victors and vanquifhed muft be abolifhed, and his European and Afiatic fubjects muft be incorporated, and become one people, by obeying the fame laws, and by adopting the fame manners, inftitutions, and difcipline.

LIBERAL as this plan of policy was, and well adapted to accomplifh what he had in view, nothing could be more repugnant to the ideas and prejudices of his countrymen. The Greeks had fuch an high opinion of the pre-eminence to which they were raifed by civilization and fcience, that they feem hardly to have acknowledged the reft of mankind to be of the fame fpecies with themfelves. To every other people they gave the degrading appellation of Barbarians, and, in confequence of their own boafted fuperiority, they afferted a right of dominion over them, in the fame manner as the foul has over the body, and men have over irrational animals. Extravagant as this pretenfion may now appear, it found admiffion, to the difgrace of ancient philofophy, into all the fchools. Ariftotle, full of this opinion, in fupport of which he employs arguments more fubtle than folid [o], advifed Alexander to govern the Greeks like fubjects, and the Barbarians as flaves; to confider the former as companions, the latter as creatures of an inferior nature [p]. But the fentiments of the pupil were more enlarged

[o] Ariftot. Polit. i. c. 3—7.

[p] Plut. de Fortuna Alex. Orat. i. p. 302. vol. vii. edit. Reifke. Strab. lib. i. p. 116. A.

2 than

SECT. I.

than thoſe of his maſter, and his experience in governing men taught the monarch what the ſpeculative ſcience of the philoſopher did not diſcover. Soon after the victory at Arbela, Alexander himſelf, and by his perſuaſion many of his officers, aſſumed the Perſian dreſs, and conformed to ſeveral of their cuſtoms. At the ſame time he encouraged the Perſian nobles to imitate the manners of the Macedonians, to learn the Greek language, and to acquire a reliſh for the beauties of the elegant writers in that tongue, which were then univerſally ſtudied and admired. In order to render the union more complete, he reſolved to marry one of the daughters of Darius, and choſe wives for a hundred of his principal officers in the moſt illuſtrious Perſian families. Their nuptials were celebrated with great pomp and feſtivity, and with high exultation of the conquered people. In imitation of them, above ten thouſand Macedonians of inferior rank married Perſian women, to each of whom Alexander gave nuptial preſents, as a teſtimony of his approbation of their conduct[q].

But aſſiduouſly as Alexander laboured to unite his European and Aſiatic ſubjects by the moſt indiſſoluble ties, he did not truſt entirely to the ſucceſs of that meaſure for the ſecurity of his new conqueſts. In every province which he ſubdued, he made choice of proper ſtations, where he built and fortified cities, in which he placed garriſons, compoſed partly of ſuch of the natives as conformed to the Grecian manners and diſcipline, and partly of ſuch of his European ſubjects, as were worn out

[q] Arrian, lib. vii. c. 4. Plut. de Fort. Alex. p. 304. See NOTE VII.

5 with

with the fatigues of ſervice, and wiſhed-for repoſe, and a permanent eſtabliſhment. Theſe cities were numerous, and ſerved not only as a chain of poſts to keep open the communication between the different provinces of his dominions, but as places of ſtrength to over-awe and curb the conquered people. Thirty thouſand of his new ſubjects who had been diſciplined in theſe cities, and armed after the European faſhion, appeared before Alexander in Suſa, and were formed by him into that compact ſolid body of infantry, known by the name of the Phalanx, which conſtituted the ſtrength of a Macedonian army. But in order to ſecure entire authority over this new corps, as well as to render it more effective, he appointed that every officer in it entruſted with command, either ſuperior or ſubaltern, ſhould be European. As the ingenuity of mankind naturally has recourſe in ſimilar ſituations to the ſame expedients, the European powers, who now in their Indian territories employ numerous bodies of the natives in their ſervice, have, in forming the eſtabliſhment of theſe troops, adopted the ſame maxims; and, probably without knowing it, have modelled their battalions of Seapoys upon the ſame principles as Alexander did his Phalanx of Perſians.

THE farther Alexander puſhed his conqueſts from the banks of the Euphrates, which may be conſidered as the center of his dominions, he found it neceſſary to build and to fortify a greater number of cities. Several of theſe to the Eaſt and South of the Caſpian ſea are mentioned by ancient authors; and in India itſelf, he founded two cities on the banks of the Hydaſpes, and a third on the Aceſines, both navigable rivers, which, after

SECT. I. uniting their ſtreams, fall into the Indus [p]. From the choice of ſuch ſituations, it is obvious that he intended, by means of theſe cities, to keep open a communication with India, not only by land, but by ſea. It was chiefly with a view to the latter of theſe objects, (as I have already obſerved,) that he examined the navigation of the Indus with ſo much attention. With the ſame view, on his return to Suſa, he, in perſon, ſurveyed the courſe of the Euphrates and Tigris, and gave directions to remove the cataracts or dams, with which the ancient monarchs of Perſia, induced by a peculiar precept of their religion, which enjoined them to guard with the utmoſt care againſt defiling any of the elements, had conſtructed near the mouths of theſe rivers, in order to ſhut out their ſubjects from any acceſs to the ocean [q]. By opening the navigation in this manner, he propoſed, that the valuable commodities of India ſhould be conveyed from the Perſian Gulf into the interior parts of his Aſiatic dominions, while by the Arabian Gulf they ſhould be carried to Alexandria, and diſtributed to the reſt of the world.

GRAND and extenſive as theſe ſchemes were, the precautions employed, and the arrangements made for carrying them into execution, were ſo various and ſo proper, that Alexander had good reaſon to entertain ſanguine hopes of their proving ſucceſsful. At the time when the mutinous ſpirit of his ſoldiers obliged him to relinquiſh his operations in India, he was not thirty years of age complete. At this enterprizing period of life, a prince, of a ſpirit ſo active, perſevering, and indefati-

[p] See NOTE VIII.

[q] Arrian, lib. vi. c. 7. Strab. lib. xvi. p. 1074. &c. See NOTE IX.

2 gable,

gable, muſt have ſoon found means to reſume a favourite meaſure on which he had been long intent. If he had invaded India a ſecond time, he would not, as formerly, have been obliged to force his way through hoſtile and unexplored regions, oppoſed at every ſtep by nations and tribes of Barbarians, whoſe names had never reached Greece. All Aſia, from the ſhores of the Ionian ſea to the banks of the Hyphaſis, would then have been ſubject to his dominion; and through that immenſe ſtretch of country he had eſtabliſhed ſuch a chain of cities, or fortified ſtations [r], that his armies might have continued their march with ſafety, and have found a regular ſucceſſion of magazines provided for their ſubſiſtence. Nor would it have been difficult for him to bring into the field forces ſufficient to have atchieved the conqueſt of a country ſo populous and extenſive as India. Having armed and diſciplined his ſubjects in the Eaſt like Europeans, they would have been ambitious to imitate and to equal their inſtructors, and Alexander might have drawn recruits, not from his ſcanty domains in Macedonia and Greece, but from the vaſt regions of Aſia, which, in every age, has covered the earth, and aſtoniſhed mankind with its numerous armies. When at the head of ſuch a formidable power he had reached the confines of India, he might have entered it under circumſtances very different from thoſe in his firſt expedition. He had ſecured a firm footing there, partly by means of the garriſons which he left in the three cities which he had built and fortified, and partly by his alliance with Taxiles and Porus. Theſe two Indian princes, won by Alexander's humanity and beneficence, which, as they were

[r] See NOTE X.

virtues

SECT. I. virtues ſeldom diſplayed in the ancient mode of carrying on war, excited of courſe an higher degree of admiration and gratitude, had continued ſteady in their attachment to the Macedonians. Re-inforced by their troops, and guided by their information as well as by the experience which he had acquired in his former campaigns, Alexander muſt have made rapid progreſs in a country, where every invader, from his time to the preſent age, has proved ſucceſsful.

BUT this and all his other ſplendid ſchemes were terminated at once by his untimely death. In conſequence of that, however, events took place, which illuſtrate and confirm the juſtneſs of the preceding ſpeculations and conjectures by evidence the moſt ſtriking and ſatisfactory. When that great empire, which the ſuperior genius of Alexander had kept united and in ſubjection, no longer felt his ſuperintending controul, it broke into pieces, and its various provinces were ſeized by his principal officers, and parcelled out among them. From ambition, emulation, and perſonal animoſity, they ſoon turned their arms againſt one another; and as ſeveral of the leaders were equally eminent for political abilities and for military ſkill, the conteſt was maintained long, and carried on with frequent viciſſitudes of fortune. Amidſt the various convulſions and revolutions which theſe occaſioned, it was found that the meaſures of Alexander for the preſervation of his conqueſts had been concerted with ſuch ſagacity, that upon the final reſtoration of tranquillity, the Macedonian dominion continued to be eſtabliſhed in every part of Aſia, and not one province had ſhaken off the yoke. Even India, the moſt remote

mote of Alexander's conquests, quietly submitted to Pytho the son of Agenor, and afterwards to Seleucus, who successively obtained dominion over that part of Asia. Porus and Taxiles, notwithstanding the death of their benefactor, neither declined submission to the authority of the Macedonians, nor made any attempt to recover independence. SECT. I.

DURING the contests for power and superiority among the successors of Alexander, Seleucus, who, in every effort of enterprising ambition, was inferior to none of them, having rendered himself master of all the provinces of the Persian empire comprehended under the name of Upper Asia, considered those countries of India which had been subdued by Alexander, as belonging to that portion of the Macedonian empire of which he was now the sovereign. Seleucus, like all the officers formed under Alexander, entertained such high ideas of the advantages which might be derived from a commercial intercourse with India, as induced him to march into that country, partly with a view of establishing his own authority there, and partly in order to curb Sandracottus, who having lately acquired the sovereignty of the Prasij, a powerful nation on the banks of the Ganges, threatened to attack the Macedonians, whose Indian territories bordered on his dominions. Unfortunately, no account of this expedition, which seems to have been splendid and successful, has reached our times. All we know of it is, that he advanced considerably beyond the utmost boundary of Alexander's progress in India [s], and would probably have proceeded much farther if he had not been constrained to stop

[s] See NOTE XI.

11 short

SECT. I. ſhort in his career in order to oppoſe Antigonus, who was preparing to invade his dominions at the head of a formidable army. Before he begun his march towards the Euphrates, he concluded a treaty with Sandracottus; in conſequence of which, that monarch quietly retained the kingdom he had acquired. But the power and poſſeſſions of the Macedonians ſeem to have remained unimpaired during the reign of Seleucus, which terminated forty-two years after the death of Alexander.

WITH a view of cultivating a friendly intercourſe with Sandracottus, Seleucus made choice of Megaſthenes, an officer, who, from his having accompanied Alexander in his expedition into India, had ſome knowledge of the ſtate of the country, and the manners of its inhabitants, and ſent him as his ambaſſador to Palibothra [t]. In this famous capital of the Praſij, ſituated on the banks of the Ganges, Megaſthenes reſided ſeveral years, and was probably the firſt European who ever beheld that mighty river, far ſuperior to any of the ancient continent in magnitude [u], and no leſs diſtinguiſhed by the fertility of the countries through which it flows. This journey of Megaſthenes to Palibothra made Europeans acquainted with a large extent of country, of which they had not hitherto any knowledge; for Alexander did not advance farther towards the ſouth-eaſt, than that part of the river Hydraotes or Raûvee, where the modern city of Lahore is ſituated, and Palibothra, the ſite of which, as it is a capital poſition in the geography of ancient India, I have inveſtigated with the utmoſt attention, appears

[t] Strabo, lib. ii. p. 121, &c. Arrian, Hiſt. Ind. paſſim.
[u] See NOTE XII.

to

SECT. I.

to me the same with that of the modern city of Allahabad, at the confluence of the two great rivers, Jumna and Ganges [x]. As the road from Lahore to Allahabad runs through some of the most cultivated and opulent provinces of India, the more the country was explored the idea of its value rose higher. Accordingly, what Megasthenes observed during his progress to Palibothra, and his residence there, made such an impression upon his own mind, as induced him to publish an ample account of India, in order to make his countrymen more thoroughly acquainted with its importance. From his writings the ancients seem to have derived almost all their knowledge of the interior state of India, and from comparing the three most ample accounts of it, by Diodorus Siculus, Strabo, and Arrian, they appear manifestly, from their near resemblance, to be a transcript of his words. But, unfortunately, Megasthenes was so fond of the marvellous, that he mingled with the truths which he related many extravagant fictions; and to him may be traced up the fabulous tales of men with ears so large that they could wrap themselves up in them, of others with a single eye, without mouths, without noses, with long feet, and toes turned backwards, of people only three spans in height, of wild men with heads in the shape of a wedge, of ants as large as foxes that dug up gold, and many other things no less wonderful [y]. The extracts from his narrative which have been transmitted to us by Strabo, Arrian, and other writers, seem not to be entitled to credit, unless when they are supported by internal evidence, and confirmed by the testimony of other ancient authors, or when they coincide with the experience of modern times. His account, however, of the dimensions and geo-

[x] See NOTE XIII.

[y] Strabo, lib. xx. 1032. A. 1037. C.

graphy

SECT. I.

graphy of India, is curious and accurate. His description of the power and opulence of the Prasij perfectly resembles that which might have been given of some of the greater states in the modern Indostan, before the establishment of the Mahomedan or European power in India, and is consonant to the accounts which Alexander had received concerning that people. He was informed that they were ready to oppose him on the banks of the Ganges, with an army consisting of twenty thousand cavalry, two hundred thousand infantry, and two thousand armed chariots [z]; and Megasthenes relates, that he had an audience of Sandracottus in a place where he was encamped with an army of four hundred thousand men [a]. The enormous dimensions which he assigns to Palibothra, of no less than ten miles in length, and two in breadth, and surrounded by walls in which there were five hundred and seventy towers, and sixty-four gates, would probably have been ranked by Europeans among the wonders which he delighted to relate, if they were not now well acquainted with the rambling manner in which the cities of India are built, and did not know with certainty that, both in former and in the present times, it might boast of cities still more extensive [b].

This embassy of Megasthenes to Sandracottus, and another of Daimachus to his son and successor Allitrochidas, are the last transactions of the Syrian monarchs with India, of which we have any account [c]. Nor can we either fix with accuracy the

[z] Diod. Sicul. lib. xvii. p. 232. Q. Curt. lib. ix. c. 2.

[a] Strabo, lib. xv. p. 1035. C. [b] Rennell Mem. 49, 50.

[c] See NOTE XIV.

time,

time, or deſcribe the manner in which their poſſeſſions in India were wreſted from them. It is probable that they were obliged to abandon that country ſoon after the death of Seleucus [c]. SECT. I.

But though the great monarchs of Syria loſt, about this period, thoſe provinces in India which had been ſubject to their dominion, the Greeks in a ſmaller kingdom, compoſed of ſome fragments of Alexander's empire, ſtill maintained an intercourſe with India, and even made ſome conſiderable acquiſition of territory there. This was the kingdom of Bactria, originally ſubject to Seleucus, but wreſted from his ſon or grandſon, and rendered an independent ſtate, about ſixty-nine years after the death of Alexander. Concerning the tranſactions of this kingdom, we muſt reſt ſatisfied with gleaning a few imperfect hints in ancient authors. From them we learn that its commerce with India was great; that the conqueſts of the Bactrian kings in that country were more extenſive than thoſe of Alexander himſelf, and particularly that they recovered poſſeſſion of the diſtrict near the mouth of the Indus, which he had ſubdued [d]. Each of the ſix princes who reigned in Bactria, carried on military operations in India with ſuch ſucceſs, that they penetrated far into the interior part of the country, and proud of the conqueſts which they had made, as well as of the extenſive dominions over which they reigned, ſome of them

[c] Juſtin. lib. xv. c. 4.

[d] Strabo, lib. xi. 785. D. lib. xv. 1006. B. Juſtin. lib. xli. c. 4. Bayer Hiſt. Regni Græcor. Bactriani, paſſim.

F aſſumed

SECT. I.

aſſumed the lofty title of *Great King*, which diſtinguiſhed the Perſian monarchs in the days of their higheſt ſplendor. But we ſhould not have known how long this kingdom of Bactria ſubſiſted, or in what manner it terminated, if M. de Guignes had not called in the hiſtorians of China to ſupply the defects of the Greek and Roman writers. By them we are informed, that about one hundred and twenty-ſix years before the Chriſtian æra, a powerful horde of Tartars, puſhed from their native ſeats on the confines of China, and obliged to move towards the weſt by the preſſure of a more numerous body that rolled on behind them, paſſed the Jaxartes, and pouring in upon Bactria, like an irreſiſtible torrent, overwhelmed that kingdom, and put an end to the dominion of the [e] Greeks there, after it had been eſtabliſhed near one hundred and thirty years [f].

From this time until the cloſe of the fifteenth century, when the Portugueſe, by doubling the Cape of Good Hope, opened a new communication with the Eaſt, and carried their victorious arms into every part of India, no European power acquired territory, or eſtabliſhed its dominion there. During this long period, of more than ſixteen hundred years, all ſchemes of conqueſt in India ſeem to have been totally relinquiſhed, and nothing more was aimed at by any nation, than to ſecure an intercourſe of trade with that opulent country.

It was in Egypt that the ſeat of this intercourſe was eſtabliſhed; and it is not without ſurpriſe that we obſerve how

[e] Mem. de Literat. tom. xxv. p. 17, &c.

[f] See NOTE XV.

ſoon

ſoon and how regularly the commerce with the Eaſt came to be carried on by that channel, in which the ſagacity of Alexander deſtined it to flow. Ptolemy, the ſon of Lagus, as ſoon as he took poſſeſſion of Egypt, eſtabliſhed the ſeat of government in Alexandria. By ſome exertions of authority, and many acts of liberality, but chiefly by the fame of his mild and equal adminiſtration, he drew ſuch a number of inhabitants to this favourite reſidence, that it ſoon became a populous and wealthy city. As Ptolemy deſerved and had poſſeſſed the confidence of Alexander more perfectly than any of his officers, he knew well that his chief object in founding Alexandria was to ſecure the advantages ariſing from the trade with India. A long and proſperous reign was favourable to the proſecution of that object, and though ancient authors have not enabled us to trace the ſteps which the firſt Ptolemy took for this purpoſe, we have a ſtriking evidence of his extraordinary attention to naval affairs, in his erecting the light-houſe on the iſland of Pharos, at the mouth of the harbour of Alexandria [g], a work of ſuch magnificence as to be reckoned one of the ſeven wonders of the world. With reſpect to the commercial arrangements of his ſon Ptolemy Philadelphus, we have more perfect information. In order to bring the trade with India (which began to revive at Tyre, its ancient ſtation [h],) to centre in Alexandria, he ſet about forming a canal, an hundred cubits in breadth, and thirty cubits in depth, between Arſinoe on the Red Sea, not far from the ſituation of the modern Suez, and the Peluſiac or eaſtern branch of the Nile, by means of which the productions of India might have been conveyed to that capital wholly by

g Strabo, lib. xvii. p. 1140. C.

h Ibid. lib. xvi. 1089. A.

water.

SECT. I. water. But either on account of ſome danger apprehended from completing it, that work was never finiſhed; or from the ſlow and dangerous navigation towards the northern extremity of the Red Sea, this canal was found to be of ſo little uſe, that in order to facilitate the communication with India, he built a city on the weſt coaſt of that ſea, almoſt under the Tropic, to which he gave the name of Berenice [i]. This new city ſoon became the ſtaple of the trade with India [k]. From Berenice the goods were tranſported by land to Coptos, a city three miles diſtant from the Nile, but which had a communication with that river by a navigable canal, of which there are ſtill ſome remains [l], and thence carried down the ſtream to Alexandria. The diſtance between Berenice and Coptos was, according to Pliny, two hundred and fifty-eight Roman miles, and the road lay through the deſart of Thebais, almoſt entirely deſtitute of water. But the attention of a powerful monarch made proviſion for ſupplying this want, by ſearching for ſprings, and wherever theſe were found he built inns, or more probably in the eaſtern ſtile caravanſeras, for the accommodation of merchants [m]. In this channel the intercourſe between the Eaſt and Weſt continued to be carried on during two hundred and fifty years, as long as Egypt remained an independent kingdom.

The ſhips deſtined for India took their departure from Berenice, and ſailing, according to the ancient mode of navi-

[i] Strabo, lib. xvii. 1156. D. Plin. Nat. Hiſt. lib. vi. c. 29.

[k] See NOTE XVI.

[l] D'Anville Mem. de l' Egypte, p. 21.

[m] Strabo, lib. xvii. p. 1157. D. 1169.

gation,

gation, along the Arabian ſhore, to the promontory Syagrus (now Cape Raſalgate), held their courſe along the coaſt of Perſia, either directly to Pattala (now Tatta) at the head of the lower Delta of the Indus, or to ſome other emporium on the weſt coaſt of India. To this part of India which Alexander had viſited and ſubdued, the commerce under the protection of the Egyptian monarchs ſeems to have been confined for a conſiderable time. Afterwards a more convenient courſe was followed, and from Cape Raſalgate veſſels ſailed in a direct courſe to Zizerus. This, according to M. de Monteſquieu [n], was the kingdom of Sigertis, on the ſea coaſt adjacent to the mouth of the Indus, conquered by the Greek monarchs of Bactria; according to Major Rennell [o], it was a port on the northern part of the Malabar coaſt. Ancient authors have not conveyed ſuch information as will enable us to pronounce with certainty, which of theſe two oppoſite opinions is beſt founded. Nor can we point out with accuracy, what were the other ports in India which the merchants from Berenice frequented, when that trade was firſt opened. As they ſailed in veſſels of ſmall burden, which crept timidly along the coaſt, it is probable that their voyages were circumſcribed within very narrow limits, and that under the Ptolemies no conſiderable progreſs was made in the diſcovery of India [p].

FROM this monopoly of the commerce by ſea between the eaſt and weſt, which Egypt long enjoyed, it derived that

[n] L'Eſprit des Loix, lib. xxi. c. 7.

[o] Introduct. p. xxxvii.

[p] See NOTE XVII.

extra-

SECT. I.

extraordinary degree of opulence and power for which it was conſpicuous. In modern times, acquainted with the vigilant and enterprizing activity of commercial rivalſhip, there is hardly any circumſtance in ancient ſtory which appears more ſurpriſing, than that the ſovereigns of Egypt ſhould have been permitted to engroſs this lucrative trade without competition, or any attempt to wreſt it out of their hands; eſpecially as the powerful monarchs of Syria might, from the Perſian Gulf, have carried on an intercourſe with the ſame parts of India, by a ſhorter and ſafer courſe of navigation. Different conſiderations ſeem to have induced them ſo tamely to relinquiſh all the obvious advantages of this commerce. The kings of Egypt, by their attention to maritime affairs, had formed a powerful fleet, which gave them ſuch decided command of the ſea, that they could have cruſhed with eaſe any rival in trade. No commercial intercourſe ſeems ever to have been carried on by ſea between Perſia and India. The Perſians had ſuch an inſuperable averſion to that element, or were ſo much afraid of foreign invaſion, that their monarchs (as I have already obſerved) obſtructed the navigation of the great rivers, which gave acceſs to the interior parts of the country, by artificial works. As their ſubjects, however, were no leſs deſirous than the people around them, to poſſeſs the valuable productions and elegant manufactures of India, theſe were conveyed to all the parts of their extenſive dominions by land-carriage.[1] The commodities deſtined for the ſupply of the northern provinces, were tranſported on camels from the banks of the Indus to thoſe of the Oxus, down the ſtream of which they were carried to the Caſpian ſea, and diſtributed,

4 partly

SECT. I.

partly by land-carriage, and partly by navigable rivers, through the different countries, bounded on one hand by the Caſpian, and on the other by the Euxine, ſea [q]. The commodities of India intended for the ſouthern and interior provinces, proceeded by land from the Caſpian gates to ſome of the great rivers, by which they were circulated through every part of the country. This was the ancient mode of intercourſe with India, while the Perſian empire was governed by its native princes; and it has been obſerved in every age, that when any branch of commerce has got into a certain channel, although it may be neither the moſt proper nor the moſt commodious one, it requires long time, and conſiderable efforts, to give it a different direction [r].

To all theſe reaſons for ſuffering the monarchs of Egypt to continue in the undiſturbed poſſeſſion of the trade with India by ſea, another may be added. Many of the ancients, by an error in geography extremely unaccountable, and in which they perſiſted, notwithſtanding repeated opportunities of obtaining more accurate information, believed the Caſpian ſea to be a branch of the great Northern Ocean, and the kings of Syria might hope by that means to open a communication with Europe, and to circulate through it the valuable productions of the Eaſt, without intruding into thoſe ſeas, the navigation of which the Egyptian monarchs ſeemed to conſider as their excluſive right. This idea had been early formed by the Greeks, when they became maſters of Aſia. Seleucus Nicator,

[q] Strabo, lib. xii. 776. D. Plin. Nat. Hiſt. lib. vi. c. 17.

[r] See NOTE XVIII.

the

SECT. I. the firſt and moſt ſagacious of the Syrian kings, at the time when he was aſſaſſinated, entertained thoughts of forming a junction between the Caſpian and Euxine ſeas by a canal[1], and if this could have been effected, his ſubjects, beſides the extenſion of their trade in Europe, might have ſupplied all the countries in the North of Aſia, on the coaſt of the Euxine ſea, as well as many of thoſe which ſtretch eaſtward from the Caſpian, with the productions of India. As thoſe countries, though now thinly inhabited by a miſerable race of men, deſtitute of induſtry and of wealth, were in ancient times extremely populous, and filled with great and opulent cities, this muſt have been conſidered as a branch of commerce of ſuch magnitude and value, as to render the ſecuring of it an object worthy the attention of the moſt powerful monarch.

But while the monarchs of Egypt and Syria laboured with emulation and ardour to ſecure to their ſubjects all the advantages of the Indian trade, a power aroſe in the Weſt which proved fatal to both. The Romans, by the vigour of their military inſtitutions, and the wiſdom of their political conduct, having rendered themſelves maſters of all Italy and Sicily, ſoon overturned the rival republic of Carthage, ſubjected Ma-
A. C. 65. cedonia and Greece, extended their dominion over Syria, and at laſt turned their victorious arms againſt Egypt, the only kingdom remaining of thoſe eſtabliſhed by the ſucceſſors of Alexander the Great. After a ſeries of events, which belong not to the ſubject of this Diſquiſition, Egypt was annexed

[1] Plin. Nat. Hiſt. lib. vi. c. 11.

6 to

to the Roman empire, and reduced into the form of a Roman province by Auguſtus. Aware of its great importance, he, with that provident ſagacity which diſtinguiſhes his character, not only reſerved it as one of the provinces ſubject immediately to Imperial authority, but by various precautions, well known to every ſcholar, provided for its ſecurity. This extraordinary ſolicitude ſeems to have proceeded not only from conſidering Egypt as one of the chief granaries on which the capital depended for ſubſiſtence, but as the ſeat of that lucrative commerce which had enabled its ancient monarchs to amaſs ſuch enormous wealth, as excited the admiration and envy of other princes, and produced, when brought into the treaſury of the empire, an alteration in the value of property, and the ſtate of manners, in Rome itſelf.

SECT. I.

A. C. 30.

G

A N

HISTORICAL DISQUISITION

CONCERNING

ANCIENT INDIA.

SECTION II.

Interccurſe with India, from the Eſtabliſhment of the Roman Dominion in Egypt, to the Conqueſt of that Kingdom by the Mahomedans.

UPON the conqueſt of Egypt by the Romans, and the reduction of that kingdom to a province of their empire, the trade with India continued to be carried on in the ſame mode, under their powerful protection: Rome, enriched with the ſpoils and the tribute of almoſt all the known world, had acquired a taſte for luxuries of every kind. Among people of this deſcription, the productions of India have SECT. II.

G 2 always

SECT. II.

always been held in the higheſt eſtimation. The capital of the greateſt empire ever eſtabliſhed in Europe, filled with citizens who had now no occupation, but to enjoy and diſſipate the wealth accumulated by their anceſtors, demanded every thing elegant, rare, or coſtly, which that remote region could furniſh, in order to ſupport its pomp, or heighten its pleaſures. To ſupply this demand, new and extraordinary efforts became requiſite, and the commerce with India increaſed to a degree, which (as I have obſerved in another place [a]) will appear aſtoniſhing even to the preſent age, in which that branch of trade has been extended far beyond the practice or conception of any former period.

Besides the Indian commodities imported into the capital of the empire from Egypt, the Romans received an additional ſupply of them by another mode of conveyance. From the earlieſt times, there ſeems to have been ſome communication between Meſopotamia, and other provinces on the banks of the Euphrates, and thoſe parts of Syria and Paleſtine, which lay near the Mediterranean. The migration of Abram from Ur, of the Chaldees to Sichem in the land of Canaan, is an inſtance of this [b]. The journey through the deſart, which ſeparated theſe countries, was much facilitated by its affording a ſtation abounding with water, and capable of cultivation. As the intercourſe increaſed, the poſſeſſion of this ſtation became an object of ſo much importance, that Solomon, when he turned his attention towards the extenſion of commerce among his

[a] Hiſt. of America, vol. i. p. 25.

[b] Geneſ. xi. and xii.

ſubjects,

SECT. II.

ſubjects, built a fenced city there[c]. Its Syrian name of *Tadmor* in the wilderneſs, and its Greek one of *Palmyra*, are both deſcriptive of its ſituation in a ſpot adorned with palm-trees. This is plentifully ſupplied with water, and ſurrounded by a portion of fertile land, which (though of no great extent) render it a delightful habitation in the midſt of barren ſands and an inhoſpitable deſart. Its happy poſition, at the diſtance of little more than ſixty miles from the river Euphrates, and of two hundred and three miles from the neareſt coaſt of the Mediterranean, induced its inhabitants to enter with ardour into the trade of conveying commodities from one of theſe to the other. As the moſt valuable productions of India, brought up the Euphrates from the Perſian Gulf, are of ſuch ſmall bulk as to bear the expence of a long land-carriage, this trade ſoon became ſo conſiderable that the opulence and power of Palmyra increaſed rapidly. Its government was of the form which is beſt ſuited to the genius of a commercial city, republican; and from the peculiar advantages of its ſituation, as well as the ſpirit of its inhabitants, it long maintained its independence, though ſurrounded by powerful and ambitious neighbours. Under the Syrian monarchs deſcended from Seleucus it attained to its higheſt degree of ſplendour and wealth, one great ſource of which ſeems to have been the ſupplying their ſubjects with Indian commodities. When Syria ſubmitted to the irreſiſtible arms of Rome, Palmyra continued upwards of two centuries a free ſtate, and its friendſhip was courted with emulation and ſolicitude by the Romans, and their rivals for empire, the Parthians. That it traded with both, particularly that from it the capital, as well as other parts

[c] 1 Kings. ix. 18. 2 Chron. viii. 4.

of

SECT. II. of the empire received the productions of India, we learn from Appian, an author of good credit[d]. But in tracing the progress of the commerce of the ancients with the East, I should not have ventured, upon his single testimony, to mention this among the channels of note in which it was carried on, if a singular discovery, for which we are indebted to the liberal curiosity and enterprizing spirit of our own countrymen, did not confirm and illustrate what he relates. Towards the close of the last century, some gentlemen of the English factory at Aleppo, incited by what they heard in the East concerning the wonderful ruins of Palmyra, ventured, notwithstanding the fatigue and danger of a journey through the desart, to visit them. To their astonishment they beheld a fertile spot of some miles in extent, arising like an island out of a vast plain of sand, covered with the remains of temples, porticoes, aqueducts, and other public works, which in magnificence and splendour, and some of them in elegance, were not unworthy of Athens or of Rome in their most prosperous state. Allured by their description of them, about sixty years thereafter, a party of more enlightened travellers, having reviewed the ruins of Palmyra with greater attention and more scientific skill, declared that what they beheld there exceeded the most exalted ideas which they had formed concerning it[e].

FROM both these accounts, as well as from recollecting the extraordinary degree of power to which Palmyra had attained,

[d] Appian. de Bello Civil. lib. v. p. 1076. edit. Tollii.

[e] Wood's Ruins of Palmyra, p. 37.

when

when Egypt, Syria, Mesopotamia, and a considerable part of Asia Minor were conquered by its arms; when Odenatus, its chief magistrate, was decorated with the Imperial purple, and Zenobia contended for the dominion of the East with Rome under one of its most warlike Emperors, it is evident, that a state which could derive little importance from its original territory, must have owed its aggrandizement to the opulence acquired by extensive commerce. Of this the Indian trade was undoubtedly the most considerable, and most lucrative branch. But it is a cruel mortification, in searching for what is instructive in the history of past times, to find that the exploits of conquerors who have desolated the earth, and the freaks of tyrants who have rendered nations unhappy, are recorded with minute and often disgusting accuracy, while the discovery of useful arts, and the progress of the most beneficial branches of commerce, are passed over in silence, and suffered to sink into oblivion. SECT. II.

AFTER the conquest of Palmyra by Aurelian, trade never revived there. At present a few miserable huts of beggarly Arabs are scattered in the courts of its stately temples, or deform its elegant porticoes; and exhibit an humiliating contrast to its ancient magnificence.

BUT while the merchants of Egypt and Syria exerted their activity in order to supply the increasing demands of Rome for Indian commodities, and vied with each other in their efforts, the eagerness of gain (as Pliny observes) brought India itself nearer to the rest of the world. In the course of their voyages to that country, the Greek and Egyptian pilots could not fail

6 to

SECT. II. to obſerve the regular ſhifting of the periodical winds or monſoons, and how ſteadily they continued to blow during one part of the year from the Eaſt, and during the other from the Weſt. Encouraged by attending to this circumſtance, Hippalus, the commander of a ſhip engaged in the Indian trade, ventured, about four-ſcore years after Egypt was annexed to the Roman empire, to relinquiſh the ſlow and circuitous courſe which I have deſcribed, and ſtretching boldly from the mouth of the Arabian Gulf acroſs the ocean, was carried by the weſtern monſoon to Muſiris, a harbour in that part of India, now known by the name of the Malabar coaſt.

THIS route to India was held to be a diſcovery of ſuch importance, that in order to perpetuate the memory of the inventor, the name of Hippalus was given to the wind which enabled him to perform the voyage[f]. As this was one of the greateſt efforts of navigation in the ancient world, and opened the beſt communication by ſea between the Eaſt and Weſt that was known for fourteen hundred years, it merits a particular deſcription. Fortunately Pliny has enabled us to give it with a degree of accuracy, which can ſeldom be attained in tracing the naval or commercial operations of the ancients. From Alexandria (he obſerves) to Juliopolis is two miles; there the cargo deſtined for India is embarked on the Nile, and is carried to Coptos, which is diſtant three hundred and three miles, and the voyage is uſually accompliſhed in twelve days. From Coptos goods are conveyed to Berenice on the Arabian Gulf, halting

[f] Perip. Mar. Erythr. p. 32.

5 at

at different ſtations regulated according to the conveniency of watering. The diſtance between theſe cities is two hundred and fifty-eight miles. On account of the heat, the caravan travels only during the night, and the journey is finiſhed on the twelfth day. From Berenice, ſhips take their departure about midſummer, and in thirty days reach Ocelis (Gella) at the mouth of the Arabian Gulf, or Cane (Cape Fartaque) on the coaſt of Arabia Felix. Thence they ſail in forty days to Muſiris, the firſt emporium in India. They begin their voyage homewards early in the Egyptian month Thibi, which anſwers to our December; they ſail with a north-eaſt wind, and when they enter the Arabian Gulf meet with a ſouth or ſouth-weſt wind, and thus complete the voyage in leſs than a year [g].

THE account which Pliny gives of Muſiris, and of Barace, another harbour not far diſtant, which was likewiſe frequented by the ſhips from Berenice, as being both ſo incommodious for trade on account of the ſhallowneſs of the ports, that it became neceſſary to diſcharge and take in the cargoes in ſmall boats, does not enable us to fix their poſition with perfect accuracy. This deſcription applies to many ports on the Malabar coaſt, but from two circumſtances mentioned by him; one, that they are not far diſtant from Cottonara, the country which produces pepper in great abundance; and the other, that in ſailing towards them the courſe lay near Nitrias, the ſtation of the pirates; I adopt the opinion of Major Rennell, that they were ſituated ſomewhere between Goa and Tellicherry, and that probably

[g] Plin. Nat. Hiſt. lib. vi. c. 23. See NOTE XIX.

SECT. II. the modern Meerzaw or Merjec is the Mufiris of the ancients, and Barcelore their Barace[h].

As in thefe two ports was the principal ftaple of the trade between Egypt and India, when in its moft flourifhing ftate, this feems to be the proper place for inquiring into the nature of the commerce which the ancients, particularly the Romans, carried on with that country, and for enumerating the commodities moft in requeft, which they imported from it. But as the operations of commerce, and the mode of regulating it, were little attended to in thofe ftates of antiquity, of whofe tranfactions we have any accurate knowledge; their hiftorians hardly enter into any detail concerning a fubject of fuch fubordinate importance in their political fyftem, and it is moftly from brief hints, detached facts, and incidental obfervations, that we can gather information concerning it[i].

In every age, it has been a commerce of luxury, rather than of neceffity, which has been carried on between Europe and India. Its elegant manufactures, fpices, and precious ftones, are neither objects of defire to nations of fimple manners, nor are fuch nations poffeffed of wealth fufficient to purchafe them. But at the time the Romans became mafters of the Indian trade, they were not only (as I have already obferved) in that ftage of fociety when men are eager to obtain every thing that can render the enjoyment of life more exquifite, or add to its fplendour, but they had acquired all the fantaftic taftes formed

[h] Introd. p. xxxvii. [i] See NOTE XX.

by

by the caprice and extravagance of wealth. They were of consequence highly delighted with those new objects of gratification with which India supplied them in such abundance. The productions of that country, natural as well as artificial, seem to have been much the same in that age as in the present. But the taste of the Romans in luxury differed in many respects from that of modern times, and of course their demands from India differed considerably from ours.

In order to convey an idea of their demands as complete as possible, I shall in the first place make some observations on the three great articles of general importation from India. 1. Spices and aromatics. 2. Precious stones and pearls. 3. Silk. And then I shall give some account (as far as I can venture to do it from authentic information) of the assortment of cargoes, both outward and homeward bound, for the vessels fitted out at Berenice for different ports of India.

I. Spices and aromatics. From the mode of religious worship in the heathen world; from the incredible number of their deities, and of the temples consecrated to them; the consumption of frankincense and other aromatics which were used in every sacred function, must have been very great. But the vanity of men occasioned a greater consumption of these fragrant substances than their piety. It was the custom of the Romans to burn the bodies of their dead, and they deemed it a display of magnificence, to cover, not only the body but the funeral pile on which it was laid, with the most costly spices. At the funeral of Sylla, two hundred and ten burthens

H 2 of

SECT. II.

of ſpices were ſtrewed upon the pile. Nero is reported to have burnt a quantity of cinnamon and caſſia at the funeral of Pappœa, greater than the countries from which it was imported produced in one year. We conſume in heaps theſe precious ſubſtances with the carcaſes of the dead (ſays Pliny): We offer them to the Gods only in grains [k]. It was not from India, I am aware, but from Arabia, that aromatics were firſt imported into Europe; and ſome of them, particularly frankincenſe, were productions of that country. But the Arabians were accuſtomed, together with ſpices of native growth, to furniſh foreign merchants with others of higher value, which they brought from India, and the regions beyond it. The commercial intercourſe of the Arabians with the Eaſtern parts of Aſia, was not only early (as has been already obſerved) but conſiderable. By means of their trading caravans, they conveyed into their own country all the valuable productions of the Eaſt, among which, ſpices held a chief place. In every ancient account of Indian commodities, ſpices and aromatics of various kinds form a principal article [l]. Some authors aſſert that the greater part of thoſe purchaſed in Arabia were not the growth of that country, but brought from India [m]. That this aſſertion was well-founded, appears from what has been obſerved in modern times. The frankincenſe of Arabia, though reckoned the peculiar and moſt precious production of the country, is much inferior in quality to that imported into it from the Eaſt; and it is chiefly with the latter, that the Arabians at preſent ſupply the extenſive demands of various

[k] Nat. Hiſt. lib. xii. c. 18.

[l] Peripl. Mar. Eryth. p. 22. 28. Strab. lib. ii. p. 156. A. lib. xv. p. 1018. A.

[m] Strab. lib. xvii. p. 1129. C.

provinces

provinces of Asia for this commodity[n]. It is upon good authority, then, that I have mentioned the inportation of spices as one of the most considerable branches of ancient commerce with India.

SECT. II.

II. Precious stones, together with which pearls may be classed, seem to be the article next in value imported by the Romans from the East. As these have no pretension to be of any real use, their value arises entirely from their beauty and their rarity, and even when estimated most moderately is always high. But among nations far advanced in luxury, when they are deemed not only ornaments but marks of distinction, the vain and the opulent vie so eagerly with one another for the possession of them, that they rise in price to an exorbitant and almost incredible height. Diamonds, though the art of cutting them was imperfectly known to the ancients, held an high place in estimation among them as well as among us. The comparative value of other precious stones varied according to the diversity of tastes and the caprice of fashion. The immense number of them mentioned by Pliny, and the laborious care with which he describes and arranges them[o], will astonish, I should suppose, the most skilful lapidary or jeweller of modern times, and shews the high request in which they were held by the Romans.

But among all the articles of luxury, the Romans seem to have given the preference to pearls[p]. Persons of every rank

[n] Niebuhr. Descript. de l'Arabie, tom. i. p. 126.

[o] Nat. Hist. lib. xxxvii.

[p] See NOTE XXI.

purchased

SECT. II. purchased them with eagerness; they were worn on every part of dress; and there is such a difference, both in size and in value, among pearls, that while such as were large and of superior lustre adorned the wealthy and the great, smaller ones, and of inferior quality, gratified the vanity of persons in more humble stations of life. Julius Cæsar presented Servilia, the mother of Brutus, with a pearl, for which he paid forty-eight thousand four hundred and fifty-seven pounds. The famous pearl ear-rings of Cleopatra were in value one hundred and sixty-one thousand four hundred and fifty-eight pounds [q]. Precious stones, it is true, as well as pearls, were found not only in India, but in many different countries, and all were ransacked in order to gratify the pride of Rome. India, however, furnished the chief part, and its productions were allowed to be most abundant, diversified, and valuable.

III. Another production of India in great demand at Rome, was silk; and when we recollect the variety of elegant fabrics into which it may be formed, and how much these have added to the splendour of dress and furniture, we cannot wonder at its being held in such estimation by a luxurious people. The price it bore was exorbitant; but it was deemed a dress too expensive and too delicate for men [r], and was appropriated wholly to women of eminent rank and opulence. This, however, did not render the demand for it less eager, especially after the example of the dissolute Elagabalus introduced the use of it among the other sex, and accustomed men

[q] Plin. Nat. Hist. lib. ix. c. 35. See NOTE XXII.

[r] Tacit. Annal. lib. ii. c. 33.

6 to

to the difgrace (as the feverity of ancient ideas accounted it) of wearing this effeminate garb. Two circumftances concerning the traffic of filk among the Romans merit obfervation. Contrary to what ufually takes place in the operations of trade, the more general ufe of that commodity feems not to have increafed the quantity imported, in fuch proportion as to anfwer the growing demand for it, and the price of filk was not reduced during the courfe of two hundred and fifty years from the time of its being firft known in Rome. In the reign of Aurelian, it ftill continued to be valued at its weight in gold. This, it is probable, was owing to the mode in which that commodity was procured by the merchants of Alexandria. They had no direct intercourfe with China, the only country in which the filk-worm was then reared, and its labour rendered an article of commerce. All the filk which they purchafed in the different ports of India which they frequented, was brought thither in fhips of the country; and either from fome defect of fkill in managing the filk-worm, the produce of its ingenious induftry among the Chinefe was fcanty, or the intermediate dealers found greater advantage in furnifhing the market of Alexandria with a fmall quantity at an high price, than to lower its value by increafing the quantity. The other circumftance which I had in view, is more extraordinary, and affords a ftriking proof of the imperfect communication of the ancients with remote nations, and of the flender knowledge which they had of their natural productions or arts. Much as the manufactures of filk were admired, and often as filk is mentioned by the Greek and Roman authors, they had not for feveral centuries after the ufe of it became common, any certain

SECT. II.

tain knowledge either of the countries to which they were indebted for this favourite article of elegance, or of the manner in which it was produced. By some, silk was supposed to be a fine down adhering to the leaves of certain trees or flowers; others imagined it to be a delicate species of wool or cotton; and even those who had learned that it was the work of an insect, shew, by their descriptions, that they had no distinct idea of the manner in which it was formed[s]. It was in consequence of an event that happened in the sixth century of the Christian æra, of which I shall hereafter take notice, that the real nature of silk became known in Europe.

THE other commodities usually imported from India, will be mentioned in the account, which I now proceed to give, of the cargoes sent out and brought home in the ships employed in that trade. For this we are indebted to the circumnavigation of the Erythræan sea, ascribed to Arrian, a curious though short treatise, less known than it deserves to be, and which enters into some details concerning commerce, to which there is nothing similar in any ancient writer. The first place in India, in which the ships from Egypt, while they followed the ancient course of navigation, were accustomed to trade, was Patala in the river Indus. They imported into it woollen cloth of a slight fabric, linen in chequer work, some precious stones, and some aromatics unknown in India, coral, storax, glass vessels of different kinds, some wrought silver, money, and wine. In return for these, they received spices

[s] See NOTE XXIII.

5 of

of various kinds, ſapphires, and other gems, ſilk ſtuffs, ſilk thread, cotton cloths [t], and black pepper. But a far more conſiderable emporium on the ſame coaſt was Barygaza, and on that account the author, whom I follow here, deſcribes its ſituation, and the mode of approaching it, with great minuteneſs and accuracy. Its ſituation correſponds entirely with that of Baroach, on the great river Nerbuddah, down the ſtream of which, or by land-carriage, from the great city of Tagara acroſs high mountains [u], all the productions of the interior country were conveyed to it. The articles of importation and exportation in this great mart were extenſive and various. Beſides theſe already mentioned, our author enumerates among the former, Italian, Greek, and Arabian wines, braſs, tin, lead, girdles or ſaſhes of curious texture, melilot, white glaſs, red arſenic, black lead, gold and ſilver coin. Among the exports he mentions the onyx, and other gems, ivory, myrrh, various fabrics of cotton, both plain and ornamented with flowers, and long pepper [x]. At Muſiris, the next emporium of note on that coaſt, the articles imported were much the ſame as at Barygaza; but as it lay nearer to the eaſtern parts of India, and ſeems to have had much communication with them, the commodities exported from it were more numerous and more valuable. He ſpecifies particularly pearls in great abundance and of extraordinary beauty, a variety of ſilk ſtuffs, rich perfumes, tortoiſe-ſhell, different kinds of tranſparent gems, eſpecially diamonds, and pepper in large quantities, and of the beſt quality [y].

SECT. II.

[t] See NOTE XXIV.

[u] See NOTE XXV.

[x] Peripl. Mar. Erythr. p. 28.

[y] Ibid. 31, 32.

I THE

SECT. II.

The juſtneſs of the account given by this author of the articles imported from India, is confirmed by a Roman law, in which the Indian commodities ſubject to the payment of duties are enumerated [z]. By comparing theſe two accounts, we may form an idea, tolerably exact, of the nature and extent of the trade with India in ancient times.

As the ſtate of ſociety and manners among the natives of India, in the earlieſt period in which they are known, nearly reſembled what we obſerve among their deſcendants in the preſent age; their wants and demands were, of courſe, much the ſame. The ingenuity of their own artiſts were ſo able to ſupply theſe, that they ſtood little in need of foreign manufactures or productions, except ſome of the uſeful metals, which their own country did not furniſh in ſufficient quantity; and then, as now, it was moſtly with gold and ſilver that the luxuries of the Eaſt were purchaſed. In two particulars, however, our importations from India differ greatly from thoſe of the ancients. The dreſs, both of the Greeks and Romans, was almoſt entirely woollen, which, by their frequent uſe of the warm bath, was rendered abundantly comfortable. Their conſumption of linen and cotton cloths was much inferior to that of modern times, when theſe are worn by perſons in every rank of life. Accordingly, a great branch of modern importation from that part of India with which the ancients were acquainted, is in *piece-goods*; comprehending, under that mercantile term, the immenſe variety of fabrics, which Indian ingenuity has formed of cotton. But, as far as I have obſerved, we have no autho-

[z] Digeſt, lib. xxxix. tit. iv. §. 16. De publicanis et veſtigalibus.

rity

rity that will juſtify us in ſtating the ancient importation of theſe to be in any degree conſiderable.

In modern times, though it continues ſtill to be chiefly a commerce of luxury that is carried on with India, yet, together with the articles that miniſter to it, we import, to a conſiderable extent, various commodities, which are to be conſidered merely as the materials of our domeſtic manufactures. Such are the cotton-wool of Indoſtan, the ſilk of China, and the ſalt-petre of Bengal. But in the accounts of ancient importations from India, raw ſilk and ſilk-thread excepted, I find nothing mentioned that could ſerve as the materials of any home-manufacture. The navigation of the ancients never having extended to China, the quantity of unwrought ſilk with which they were ſupplied, by means of the Indian traders, appears to have been ſo ſcanty, that the manufacture of it could not make an addition of any moment to their domeſtic induſtry.

After this ſuccinct account of the commerce carried on by the ancients in India, I proceed to inquire what knowledge they had of the countries beyond the ports of Muſiris and Barace, the utmoſt boundary towards the Eaſt to which I have hitherto traced their progreſs. The Author of the Circumnavigation of the Erythræan Sea, whoſe accuracy of deſcription juſtifies the confidence with which I have followed him for ſome time, ſeems to have been little acquainted with that part of the coaſt which ſtretches from Barace towards the ſouth. He mentions, indeed, curſorily, two or three different

I 2 ports,

SECT. II. ports, but gives no intimation that any of them were ſtaples of the commerce with Egypt. He haſtens to Comar or Cape Comorin, the ſouthernmoſt point of the Indian peninſula, and his deſcription of it is ſo accurate, and ſo conformable to its real ſtate, as ſhews his information concerning it to have been perfectly authentic [a]. Near to this he places the pearl-fiſhery of Colchos, the modern Kilkare, undoubtedly the ſame with that now carried on by the Dutch in the ſtrait which ſeparates the iſland of Ceylon from the continent. As adjacent to this he mentions three different ports, which appear to have been ſituated on the eaſt ſide of the peninſula now known by the name of the Coromandel coaſt. He deſcribes theſe as *emporia*, or ſtations of trade [b]; but from an attentive conſideration of ſome circumſtances in his account of them, I think it probable that the ſhips from Berenice did not ſail to any of theſe ports, though they were ſupplied, as he informs us, with the commodities brought from Egypt, as well as with the productions of the oppoſite coaſt of the peninſula; but theſe ſeem to have been imported in *country ſhips* [c]. It was likewiſe in veſſels of their own, varying in form and burden, and diſtinguiſhed by different names, ſome of which he mentions, that they traded with the Golden Cherſoneſus, or kingdom of Malacca, and the countries near the Ganges. Not far from the mouth of that river he places an iſland, which he deſcribes as ſituated under the riſing ſun, and as the laſt region in the Eaſt that was inhabited [d]. Of all theſe parts of India,

[a] Peripl. p. 33. D'Anville Ant. de l' Inde, 118, &c.
[b] Peripl. p. 34. [c] τοπικα πλοῖα. [d] Peripl. p. 36.

the

the Author of the Circumnavigation appears to have had very ſlender knowledge, as is manifeſt, not only from what he mentions concerning this imaginary iſland, and from his not attempting to deſcribe them, but from his relating, with the credulity and love of the marvellous, which always accompany and characteriſe ignorance, that theſe remote regions were peopled with cannibals, and men of uncouth and monſtrous forms [e].

I HAVE been induced to beſtow this attention, in tracing the courſe delineated in the Circumnavigation of the Erythræan Sea, becauſe the Author of it is the firſt ancient writer to whom we are indebted for any knowledge of the eaſtern coaſt of the great peninſula of India, or of the countries which lie beyond it. To Strabo, who compoſed his great work on geography in the reign of Auguſtus, India, particularly the moſt eaſtern parts of it, was little known. He begins his deſcription of it with requeſting the indulgence of his readers, on account of the ſcanty information he could obtain with reſpect to a country ſo remote, which Europeans had ſeldom viſited, and many of them tranſiently only, in the functions of military ſervice. He obſerves, that even commerce had contributed little towards an accurate inveſtigation of the country, as few of the merchants from Egypt and the Arabian Gulf had ever ſailed as far as the Ganges; and from men ſo illiterate, intelligence that merited a full degree of confidence could hardly be expected. His deſcriptions of India, particularly its

[e] Peripl. p. 35.

interior

SECT. II. interior provinces, are borrowed almoſt entirely from the Memoirs of Alexander's Officers, with ſome ſlender additions from more recent accounts, and theſe ſo few in number, and ſometimes ſo inaccurate, as to furniſh a ſtriking proof of the ſmall progreſs which the ancients had made, from the time of Alexander, in exploring that country. When an author, poſ-ſeſſed of ſuch diſcernment and induſtry as Strabo, who viſited in perſon ſeveral diſtant regions that he might be able to deſcribe them with greater accuracy, relates, that the Ganges enters the ocean by one mouth [f], we are warranted in conclud-ing, that in his time there was either no direct navigation carried on to that great river, by the traders from the Arabian Gulf, or that this voyage was undertaken ſo ſeldom, that ſcience had not then derived much information from it.

THE next author, in order of time, from whom we receive any account of India, is the elder Pliny, who flouriſhed about fifty years later than Strabo. As in the ſhort deſcription of India given in his Natural Hiſtory, he follows the ſame guides with Strabo, and ſeems to have had no knowledge of the interior country, but what he derived from the officers who ſerved under Alexander and his immediate ſucceſſors, it is unneceſſary to examine his deſcription minutely. He has added, however, two valuable articles, for which he was in-debted to more recent diſcoveries. The one is the account of the new courſe of navigation from the Arabian Gulf to the coaſt of Malabar, the nature and importance of which I have

[f] Strabo, lib. xv. 1011. C.

already

already explained. The other is a deſcription of the iſland of Taprobana, which I ſhall conſider particularly, after enquiring into what Ptolemy has contributed towards our knowledge of the ancient ſtate of India. SECT. II.

THOUGH Ptolemy, who publiſhed his works about fourſcore years after Pliny, ſeems to have been more diſtinguiſhed for his perſevering induſtry, and talent for arrangement, than for an inventive genius; geography has been more indebted to him for its improvement, than to any other philoſopher. Fortunately for that ſcience, in forming his general ſyſtem of geography, he adopted the ideas, and imitated the practice of Hipparchus, who lived near four hundred years before his time. That great philoſopher was the firſt who attempted to make a catalogue of the ſtars. In order to aſcertain their poſition in the heavens with accuracy, he meaſured their diſtance from certain circles of the ſphere, computing it by degrees, either from eaſt to weſt, or from north to ſouth. The former was denominated the longitude of the ſtar, the latter its latitude. This mode he found to be of ſuch utility in his aſtronomical reſearches, that he applied it with no leſs happy effect to geography; and it is a circumſtance worthy of notice, that it was by obſerving and deſcribing the heavens, men were firſt taught to meaſure and delineate the earth with exactneſs. This method of fixing the poſition of places, invented by Hipparchus, though known to the geographers between his time and that of Ptolemy, and mentioned both by Strabo [g], and by Pliny [h], was not employed by any of them.

[g] Lib. ii.

[h] Nat. Hiſt. lib. ii. c. 12. 26. 70.

SECT. II. them. Of this neglect the most probable account seems to be, that, as none of them were astronomers, they did not fully comprehend all the advantages geography might derive from this invention [i]. These Ptolemy, who had devoted a long life to the improvement of astronomy, theoretical as well as practical, perfectly discerned, and, as in both these Hipparchus was his guide, he, in his famous treatise on geography, described the different parts of the earth according to their longitude and latitude. Geography was thus established upon its proper principles, and intimately connected with astronomical observation and mathematical science. This work of Ptolemy soon rose high in estimation among the ancients [k]. During the middle ages, both in Arabia and in Europe, the decisions of Ptolemy, in every thing relative to geography, were submitted to with an assent as implicit, as was yielded to those of Aristotle in all other departments of science. On the revival of a more liberal spirit of inquiry in the sixteenth century, the merit of Ptolemy's improvements in geography was examined and recognized; that scientific language which he first rendered general, continues to be used, and the position of places is still ascertained in the same distinct and compendious manner, by specifying their longitude and latitude.

NOT satisfied with adopting the general principles of Hipparchus, Ptolemy emulated him in the application of them; and, as that philosopher had arranged all the constellations, he ventured upon what was no less arduous, to survey all the regions

[i] See NOTE XXVI. [k] See NOTE XXVII.

of the earth, which were then known, and with minute and bold decision he fixed the longitude and latitude of the most remarkable places in each of them. All his determinations, however, are not to be considered as the result of actual observation, nor did Ptolemy publish them as such. Astronomical science was confined, at that time, to a few countries. A considerable part of the globe was little visited, and imperfectly described. The position of a small number of places only had been fixed with any degree of accuracy. Ptolemy was therefore obliged to consult the itineraries and surveys of the Roman Empire, which the political wisdom of that great state had completed with immense labour and expence [l]. Beyond the precincts of the empire, he had nothing on which he could rely, but the journals and reports of travellers. Upon these all his conclusions were founded; and as he resided in Alexandria at a time when the trade from that city to India was carried on to its utmost extent, this situation might have been expected to afford him the means of procuring ample information concerning it. But either from the imperfect manner in which that country was explored in his time, or from his placing too much confidence in the reports of persons who had visited it with little attention or discernment [m], his general delineation of the form of the Indian continent is the most erroneous that has been transmitted to us from antiquity. By an astonishing mistake, he has made the peninsula of India stretch from the Sinus Barygazenus, or Gulf of Cambay, from west to east, instead of extending, according to

[l] See NOTE XXVIII.

[m] Geogr. lib. i. c. 17.

SECT. II. its real direction, from north to south[n]. This error will appear the more unaccountable, when we recollect that Megasthenes had published a measurement of the Indian peninsula, which approaches near to its true dimensions; and that this had been adopted, with some variations, by Eratosthenes, Strabo, Diodorus Siculus, and Pliny, who wrote prior to the age of Ptolemy[o].

ALTHOUGH Ptolemy was led to form such an erroneous opinion concerning the general dimensions of the Indian continent, his information with respect to the country in detail, and the situation of particular places, was more accurate; and he is the first author possessed of such knowledge as enabled him to trace the sea-coast, to mention the most noted places situated upon it, and to specify the longitude and latitude of each from Cape Comorin eastward, to the utmost boundary of ancient navigation. With regard to some districts, particularly along the east side of the peninsula as far as the mouth of the Ganges, the accounts which he had received seem to have been so far exact, as to correspond more nearly perhaps with the actual state of the country, than the descriptions which he gives of any other part of India. M. D'Anville, with his usual industry and discernment, has considered the principal stations as they are fixed by him, and finds that they correspond to Kilkare, Negapatam, the mouth of the river Cauveri,

[n] See NOTE XXIX.

[o] Strabo, lib. xv. 1010. B. Arrian, Hist. Indic, c. 3, 4. Diod. Sicul. lib. ii. 148. Plin. Nat. Hist. lib. vi. c. 21. See NOTE XXX.

Masulipatam,

Masulipatam, Point Gordeware, &c. It is foreign to the object of this Disquisition, to enter into such a minute detail; but in several instances we may observe, that not only the conformity of position, but the similarity of ancient and modern names, is very striking. The great river Cauveri is by Ptolemy named Chaberis; Arcot, in the interior country, is Arcati Regia; and probably the whole coast has received its present name of Coromandel from *Sor Mandulam*, or the kingdom of Soræ, which is situated upon it [p].

In the course of one hundred and thirty-six years, which elapsed from the death of Strabo to that of Ptolemy, the commercial intercourse with India was greatly extended; the latter geographer had acquired such an accession of new information concerning the Ganges, that he mentions the names of six different mouths of that river, and describes their positions. His delineation, however, of that part of India which lies beyond the Ganges, is not less erroneous in its general form, than that which he gave of the peninsula, and bears as little resemblance to the actual position of those countries. He ventures, nevertheless, upon a survey of them, similar to that which he had made of the other great division of India, which I have already examined. He mentions the places of note along the coast, some of which he distinguishes as *Emporia*; but whether that name was given to them on account of their being staples of trade to the natives, in their traffic carried on from one district of India to another, or whether they were

[p] Ptolem. Geogr. lib. vii. c. 1. D'Anville, Antiq. de l'Inde, 127, &c.

SECT. II.

ports, to which veſſels from the Arabian Gulf reſorted directly, is not ſpecified. The latter I ſhould think to be the idea which Ptolemy means to convey; but theſe regions of India were ſo remote, and, from the timid and ſlow courſe of ancient navigation, were probably ſo little frequented, that his information concerning them is extremely defective, and his deſcriptions more obſcure, more inaccurate, and leſs conformable to the real ſtate of the country, than in any part of his geography. That peninſula to which he gives the name of the Golden Cherſoneſus, he delineates as if it ſtretched directly from north to ſouth, and fixes the latitude of Sabana Emporium, its ſouthern extremity, three degrees beyond the line. To the eaſt of this peninſula he places, what he calls the Great Bay, and in the moſt remote part of it the ſtation of Catigara, the utmoſt boundary of navigation in ancient times, to which he aſſigns no leſs than eight degrees and a half of ſouthern latitude. Beyond this, he declares the earth to be altogether unknown, and aſſerts that the land turns thence to the weſtward, and ſtretches in that direction until it joins the promontory of Praſſum in Ethiopia, which, according to his idea, terminated the continent of Africa to the ſouth [q]. In conſequence of this error, no leſs unaccountable than enormous, he muſt have believed the Erythræan Sea, in its whole extent from the coaſt of Africa to that of Cambodia, to be a vaſt baſon, without any communication with the ocean [r].

[q] Ptolem. Geogr. lib. vii. c. 3. 5. D'Anville, Ant. de l' Inde, 187.

[r] See NOTE XXXI.

OUT

Out of the confusion of those wild ideas, in which the accounts of ignorant or fabulous travellers have involved the geography of Ptolemy, M. D'Anville has attempted to bring order; and, with much ingenuity, he has formed opinions with respect to some capital positions, which have the appearance of being well founded. The peninsula of Malacca is, according to him, the Golden Chersonesus of Ptolemy; but instead of the direction which he has given it, we know that it bends some degrees towards the east, and that Cape de Romania, its southern extremity, is more than a degree to the north of the line. The Gulf of Siam he considers as the Great Bay of Ptolemy, but the position on the east side of that Bay, corresponding to Catigara, is actually as many degrees to the north of the Equator, as he supposed it to be south of it. Beyond this he mentions an inland city, to which he gives the name of Thinæ or Sinæ Metropolis. The longitude which he assigns to it, is one hundred and eighty degrees from his first meridian in the Fortunate Island, and is the utmost point towards the East to which the ancients had advanced by sea. Its latitude he calculates to be three degrees south of the line. If, with M. D'Anville, we conclude the situation of Sin-hoa, in the western part of the kingdom of Cochin-China, to be the same with Sinæ Metropolis, Ptolemy has erred in fixing its position no less than fifty degrees of longitude, and twenty degrees of latitude [s].

[s] Ptolem. Geogr. lib. vii. c. 3. D'Anville, Limites du Monde conudes Anciens au-dela du Gange. Mem. de Literat. xxxii. 604, &c. Ant. de l'Inde, Supplem. i. 161, &c. See NOTE XXXII.

4 THESE

SECT. II.

THESE errors of Ptolemy concerning the remote parts of Aſia, have been rendered more conſpicuous by a miſtaken opinion of modern times ingrafted upon them. Sinæ, the moſt diſtant ſtation mentioned in his geography, has ſuch a near reſemblance in ſound to China, the name by which the greateſt and moſt civilized empire in the Eaſt is known to Europeans, that upon their firſt acquaintance with it, they haſtily concluded them to be the ſame; and of conſequence it was ſuppoſed that China was known to the ancients, though no point ſeems to be more aſcertained, than that they never advanced by ſea beyond that boundary which I have allotted to their navigation.

HAVING thus traced the diſcoveries of India which the ancients made by ſea, I ſhall next examine what additional knowledge of that country they acquired from their progreſs by land. It appears (as I have formerly related) that there was a trade carried on early with India through the provinces that ſtretch along its northern frontier. Its various productions and manufactures were tranſported by land-carriage into the interior parts of the Perſian dominions, or were conveyed, by means of the navigable rivers which flow through the Upper Aſia, to the Caſpian Sea and from that to the Euxine. While the ſucceſſors of Seleucus retained the dominion of the Eaſt, this continued to be the mode of ſupplying their ſubjects with the commodities of India. When the Romans had extended their conqueſts ſo far that the Euphrates was the Eaſtern limit of their empire, they found this trade ſtill eſtabliſhed, and as it opened to them a new communication with the Eaſt, by means of which they received an additional ſupply of luxuries, for which they had

had acquired the higheſt reliſh, it became an object of their policy to protect and encourage it. As the progreſs of the caravans or companies of merchants, which travelled towards the countries whence they received the moſt valuable manufactures, particularly thoſe of ſilk, was often interrupted, and rendered dangerous by the Parthians, who had acquired poſſeſſion of all the provinces which extend from the Caſpian Sea to that part of Scythia or Tartary which borders on China, the Romans endeavoured to render this intercourſe more ſecure by a negociation with one of the monarchs of that great empire. Of this ſingular tranſaction there is, indeed, no veſtige in the Greek or Roman writers; our knowledge of it is derived entirely from the Chineſe hiſtorians, by whom we are informed that An-toun, (the Emperor Marcus Antoninus,) the king of the people of the Weſtern Ocean, ſent an embaſſy with this view to Oun-ti, who reigned over China in the hundred and ſixty-ſixth year of the Chriſtian æra[t]. What was the ſucceſs of this attempt is not known, nor can we ſay whether it facilitated ſuch an intercourſe between theſe two remote nations as contributed towards the ſupply of their mutual wants. The deſign certainly was not unworthy of the enlightened emperor of Rome to whom it is aſcribed.

It is evident, however, that in proſecuting this trade with China, a conſiderable part of the extenſive countries to the eaſt of the Caſpian Sea muſt have been traverſed; and though

[t] Memoire ſur les Liaiſons et le Commerce du Romains, avec les Tartares et les Chinois, par M. de Guignes. Mem. de Literat. xxxii. 355, &c.

6 the

SECT. II. the chief inducement to undertake thoſe diſtant journies was gain, yet, in the courſe of ages, there muſt have mingled among the adventurers, perſons of curioſity and abilities, who could turn their attention from commercial objects to thoſe of more general concern. From them ſuch information was procured, and ſubjected to ſcientific diſcuſſion, as enabled Ptolemy to give a deſcription of thoſe inland and remote regions of Aſia [u], fully as accurate as that of ſeveral countries, of which, from their vicinity, he may have been ſuppoſed to have received more diſtinct accounts. The fartheſt point towards the Eaſt, to which his knowledge of this part of Aſia extended, is Sera Metropolis, which, from various circumſtances, appears to have been in the ſame ſituation with Kant-cheou, a city of ſome note in Chen-ſi, the moſt weſterly province of the Chineſe empire. This he places in the longitude of one hundred and ſeventy-ſeven degrees fifteen minutes, near three degrees to the weſt of Sinæ Metropolis, which he had deſcribed as the utmoſt limit of Aſia diſcovered by ſea. Nor was Ptolemy's knowledge of this diſtrict of Aſia confined only to that part of it through which the caravans may be ſuppoſed to have proceeded directly in their route eaſtward; he had received likewiſe ſome general information concerning various nations towards the north, which, according to the poſition that he gives them, occupied parts of the great plain of Tartary, extending conſiderably beyond Laſſa, the capital of Thibet, and the reſidence of the Dalai Lama.

[u] Lib. vi. c. 11—18.

THE

THE latitudes of ſeveral places in this part of Aſia are fixed by Ptolemy with ſuch uncommon preciſion, that we can hardly doubt of their having been aſcertained by actual obſervation. Out of many inſtances of this, I ſhall ſelect three of places ſituated in very different parts of the country under review. The latitude of Nagara, on the river Cophenes, (the modern Attock,) is, according to Ptolemy, thirty-two degrees and thirty minutes, which co-incides preciſely with the obſervation of an Eaſtern geographer quoted by M. D'Anville [x]. The latitude of Maracanda, or Samarcand, as fixed by him, is thirty-nine degrees fifteen minutes. According to the Aſtronomical Tables of Ulug Beg, the grandſon of Timur, whoſe royal reſidence was in that city, it is thirty-nine degrees thirty-ſeven minutes [y]. The latitude of Sera Metropolis, in Ptolemy, is thirty-eight degrees fifteen minutes; that of Kant-cheou, as determined by the Jeſuit Miſſionaries, is thirty-nine degrees. I have enumerated theſe ſtriking examples of the co-incidence of his calculations with thoſe eſtabliſhed by modern obſervations, for two reaſons: One, becauſe they clearly prove that theſe remote parts of Aſia had been examined with ſome conſiderable degree of attention; the other, becauſe I feel great ſatisfaction, after having been obliged to mention ſeveral errors and defects in Ptolemy's geography, in rendering juſtice to a philoſopher, who has contributed ſo much towards the improvement of that ſcience. The facts which I have produced afford the ſtrongeſt evidence of the extent of his information, as well as the

[x] Eclairciſſemens, &c. Engliſh Tranſlation, p. 10.

[y] Tab. Geogr. ap. Hudſon. Geogr. Minores, iii. 145.

L juſtneſs

SECT. II. justneſs of his concluſions concerning countries with which, from their remote ſituation, we might have ſuppoſed him to be leaſt acquainted.

HITHERTO I have confined my reſearches concerning the knowledge which the ancients had of India, to the continent; I return now to conſider the diſcoveries which they had made, of the iſlands ſituated in various parts of the ocean with which it is ſurrounded, and begin, as I propoſed, with Taprobane, the greateſt and moſt valuable of them. This iſland lay ſo directly in the courſe of navigators who ventured beyond Cape Comorin, eſpecially when, according to the ancient mode of ſailing, they ſeldom ventured far from the coaſt, that its poſition, one ſhould have thought, muſt have been determined with the utmoſt preciſion. There is, however, hardly any point in the geography of the ancients more undecided and uncertain. Prior to the age of Alexander the Great, the name of Taprobane was unknown in Europe. In conſequence of the active curioſity with which he explored every country that he ſubdued or viſited, ſome information concerning it ſeems to have been obtained. From his time, almoſt every writer on geography has mentioned it, but their accounts of it are ſo various, and often ſo contradictory, that we can hardly believe them to be deſcribing the ſame iſland. Strabo, the earlieſt writer now extant, from whom we have any particular account of it, affirms that it was as large as Britain, and ſituated at the diſtance of ſeven days, according to ſome reports, and according to other, of twenty days ſailing from the ſouthern extremity of the Indian peninſula; from which, contrary to what

SECT. II.

what is known to be its real position, he describes it as stretching towards the west above five hundred stadia [z]. Pomponius Mela, the author next in order of time, is uncertain whether he should consider Taprobane as an island, or as the beginning of another world; but as no person, he says, had ever sailed round it, he seems to incline towards the latter opinion [a]. Pliny gives a more ample description of Taprobane, which, instead of bringing any accession of light, involves every thing relating to it in additional obscurity. After enumerating the various and discordant opinions of the Greek writers, he informs us, that ambassadors were sent by a king of that island to the emperor Claudius, from whom the Romans learned several things concerning it, which were formerly unknown; particularly that there were five hundred towns in the island, and that in the centre of it there was a lake three hundred and seventy-five miles in circumference. These ambassadors were astonished at the sight of the Great Bear, and the Pleiades, being constellations which did not appear in their sky; and were still more amazed when they beheld their shadows point towards the north, and the sun rise on their left hand, and set on their right. They affirmed too, that in their country the moon was never seen until the eighth day after the change, and continued to be visible only to the sixteenth [b]. It is surprising to find an author so intelligent as Pliny relating all these circumstances without animadversion, and particularly that he does

[z] Strabo, lib. ii. 124. B. 180. B. 192. A. lib. xv. 1012. B.

[a] De Situ Orbis, lib. iii. c. 7.

[b] Nat. Hist. lib. vi. c. 22.

SECT. II. not take notice, that what the ambaſſadors reported concerning the appearance of the moon, could not take place in any region of the earth.

PTOLEMY, though ſo near to the age of Pliny, ſeems to have been altogether unacquainted with his deſcription of Taprobane, or with the embaſſy to the emperor Claudius. He places that iſland oppoſite to Cape Comorin, at no great diſtance from the continent, and delineates it as ſtretching from north to ſouth no leſs than fifteen degrees, two of which he ſuppoſes to be ſouth of the Equator; and if his repreſentation of its dimenſions had been juſt, it was well intitled from its magnitude to be compared with Britain [c]. Agathemerus, who wrote after Ptolemy, and was well acquainted with his geography, conſiders Taprobane as the largeſt of all iſlands, and aſſigns to Britain only the ſecond place [d].

FROM this diverſity of the deſcriptions given by ancient writers, it is not ſurpriſing that the moderns ſhould have entertained very different ſentiments with reſpect to the iſland in the Indian ocean which was to be conſidered as the ſame with the Taprobane of the Greeks and Romans. As both Pliny and Ptolemy deſcribe it as lying in part to the ſouth of the Equator, ſome learned men maintain Sumatra to be the iſland which correſponds to this deſcription. But the great diſtance of Sumatra from the peninſula of India does not accord with any account

[c] Ptol. lib. vii. c. 4. D'Anville, Ant. de l'Inde, p. 142.

[d] Lib. ii. c. 8. apud Hudſon. Geogr. Minor. vol. ii.

7 which

which the Greek or Roman writers have given of the ſituation of Taprobane, and we have no evidence that the navigation of the ancients ever extended ſo far as Sumatra. The opinion more generally received is, that the Taprobane of the ancients is the iſland of Ceylon; and not only its vicinity to the continent of India, but the general form of the iſland, as delineated by Ptolemy, as well as the poſition of ſeveral places in it, mentioned by him, eſtabliſh this opinion (notwithſtanding ſome extraordinary miſtakes, of which I ſhall afterwards take notice) with a great degree of certainty.

The other iſlands to the eaſt of Taprobane, mentioned by Ptolemy, might be ſhewn (if ſuch a detail were neceſſary) to be the Andaman and Nicobar Iſlands in the Gulf of Bengal.

After this long, and, I am afraid, tedious inveſtigation of the progreſs made by the ancients, in exploring the different parts of India, and after tracing them as far as they advanced towards the Eaſt, either by ſea or land, I ſhall offer ſome general remarks concerning the mode in which their diſcoveries were conducted, and the degree of confidence with which we may rely on the accounts of them, which could not have been offered with the ſame advantage until this inveſtigation was finiſhed.

The art of delineating maps, exhibiting either the figure of the whole earth, as far as it had been explored, or that of particular countries, was known to the ancients; and without the

SECT. II. the uſe of them to aſſiſt the imagination, it was impoſſible to have formed a diſtinct idea either of the one or of the other. Some of theſe maps are mentioned by Herodotus, and other early Greek writers. But no maps prior to thoſe which were formed in order to illuſtrate the geography of Ptolemy, have reached our times, in conſequence of which it is very difficult to conceive what was the relative ſituation of the different places mentioned by the ancient geographers, unleſs when it is preciſely aſcertained by meaſurement [e]. As ſoon, however, as the mode of marking the ſituation of each place by ſpecifying its longitude and latitude was introduced, and came to be generally adopted, every poſition could be deſcribed in compendious and ſcientific terms. But ſtill the accuracy of this new method, and the improvement which geography derived from it, depends upon the mode in which the ancients eſtimated the latitude and longitude of places.

Though the ancients proceeded in determining the latitude and longitude of places upon the ſame principles with the moderns, yet it was by means of inſtruments very inferior in their conſtruction to thoſe now uſed, and without the ſame minute attention to every circumſtance that may affect the accuracy of an obſervation, an attention of which long experience only can demonſtrate the neceſſity. In order to aſcertain the latitude of any place, the ancients obſerved the meridian altitude of the ſun, either by means of the ſhadow of a perpendicular gnomon, or by means of an aſtrolabe, from which it was

[e] See NOTE XXXIII.

easy

eaſy to compute how many degrees and minutes the place of obſervation was diſtant from the Equator. When neither of theſe methods could be employed, they inferred the latitude of any place from the beſt accounts which they could procure of the length of its longeſt day. SECT. II.

WITH reſpect to determining the longitude of any place, they were much more at a loſs, as there was only one ſet of celeſtial phenomena to which they could have recourſe. Theſe were the eclipſes of the moon (for thoſe of the ſun were not ſo well underſtood as to be ſubſervient to the purpoſes of geography): the difference between the time at which an eclipſe was obſerved to begin or to end at two different places, gave immediately the difference between the meridians of thoſe places. But the difficulty of making thoſe obſervations with accuracy, and the impoſſibility of repeating them often, rendered them of ſo little uſe in geography, that the ancients in determining longitudes were obliged, for the moſt part, to have recourſe to actual ſurveys, or to the vague information which was to be obtained from the reckonings of ſailors, or the itineraries of travellers.

BUT though the ancients, by means of the operations which I have mentioned, could determine the poſition of places with a conſiderable degree of accuracy at land, it is very uncertain whether or not they had any proper mode of determining this at ſea. The navigators of antiquity ſeem rarely to have had recourſe to aſtronomical obſervation. They had no inſtruments ſuited to a moveable and unſteady obſervatory;

10 and

SECT. II.

and though by their practice of landing frequently, they might, in some measure, have supplied that defect, yet no ancient author, as far as I know, has given an account of any astronomical observation made by them during the course of their voyages. It seems to be evident from Ptolemy, who employs some chapters in shewing how geography may be improved, and its errors may be rectified, from the reports of navigators [f], that all their calculations were founded solely upon reckoning, and were not the result of observation. Even after all the improvements which the moderns have made in the science of navigation, this mode of computing by reckoning is known to be so loose and uncertain, that, from it alone, no conclusion can be deduced with any great degree of precision. Among the ancients, this inaccuracy must have been greatly augmented, as they were accustomed in their voyages, instead of steering a direct course which might have been more easily measured, to a circuitous navigation along the coast; and were unacquainted with the compass, or any other instrument by which its bearings might have been ascertained. We find, accordingly, the position of many places which we may suppose to have been determined at sea, fixed with little exactness. When, in consequence of an active trade, the ports of any country were much frequented, the reckonings of different navigators may have served in some measure to correct each other, and may have enabled geographers to form their conclusions with a nearer approximation to truth. But in remote countries, which have neither been the seat of military operations,

[f] Lib. i. c. 7—14.

nor

SECT. II.

nor explored by caravans travelling frequently through them, every thing is more vague and undefined, and the resemblance between the ancient descriptions of them, and their actual figure, is often so faint that it can hardly be traced. The latitude of places too, as might be expected, was in general much more accurately known by the ancients than their longitude. The observations by which the former was determined are simple, made with ease, and are not liable to much error. The other cannot be ascertained precisely, without more complex operations, and the use of instruments much more perfect than any that the ancients seem to have possessed[g]. Among the vast number of places, the position of which is fixed by Ptolemy, I know not if he approaches as near to truth in the longitude of any one, as he has done in fixing the latitude of the three cities which I formerly mentioned as a striking, though not singular, instance of his exactness.

THESE observations induce me to adhere to an opinion, which I proposed in another place[h], that the Greeks and Romans, in their commercial intercourse with India, were seldom led, either by curiosity or the love of gain, to visit the more eastern parts of it. A variety of particulars occur to confirm this opinion. Though Ptolemy bestows the appellation of *Emporia* on several places situated on the coast, which stretches from the eastern mouth of the Ganges to the extremity of the Golden Chersonesus, it is uncertain, as I formerly observed, whether from his having given them this name, we are to consider them as harbours frequented by ships from Egypt, or merely by vessels of the country. Beyond the

[g] See NOTE XXXIV.

[h] Hist. of America, vol. i. p. 80. 315.

M Golden

SECT. II.

Golden Cherſoneſus, it is remarkable that he mentions one *Emporium* only [1], which plainly indicates the intercourſe with this region of India to have been very inconſiderable. Had voyages from the Arabian Gulf to thoſe countries of India been as frequent, as to have intitled Ptolemy to ſpecify ſo minutely the longitude and latitude of the great number of places which he mentions, he muſt, in conſequence of this, have acquired ſuch information as would have prevented ſeveral great errors into which he has fallen. Had it been uſual to double Cape Comorin, and to ſail up the Bay of Bengal to the mouth of the Ganges, ſome of the ancient geographers would not have been ſo uncertain, and others ſo widely miſtaken, with reſpect to the ſituation and magnitude of the iſland of Ceylon. If the merchants of Alexandria had often viſited the ports of the Golden Cherſoneſus, and of the Great Bay, Ptolemy's deſcriptions of them muſt have been rendered more correſpondent to their real form, nor could he have believed ſeveral places to lie beyond the line, which are in truth ſome degrees on this ſide of it.

But though the navigation of the ancients may not have extended to the farther India, we are certain that various commodities of that country were imported into Egypt, and thence were conveyed to Rome, and to other parts of the empire. From circumſtances which I have already enumerated, we are warranted in concluding, that theſe were brought in veſſels of the country to Muſiris, and to the other ports on

[1] Lib. vii. c. 2.

the

the Malabar coaſt, which were, at that period, the ſtaples of trade with Egypt. In a country of ſuch extent as India, where the natural productions are various, and greatly diverſified by art and induſtry, an active domeſtic commerce, both by ſea and by land, muſt have early taken place among its different provinces. Of this we have ſome hints in ancient authors; and where the ſources of information are ſo few and ſo ſcanty, we muſt reſt ſatisfied with hints. Among the different claſſes, or caſts, into which the people of India were divided, merchants are mentioned as one [k], from which we may conclude trade to have been one of the eſtabliſhed occupations of men in that country. From the Author of the Circumnavigation of the Erythræan Sea, we learn that the inhabitants of the Coromandel coaſt traded in veſſels of their own with thoſe of Malabar; that the interior trade of Barygaza was conſiderable; and that there was, at all ſeaſons, a number of country ſhips to be found in the harbour of Muſiris [l]. By Strabo we are informed, that the moſt valuable productions of Taprobane were carried to different *Emporia* of India [m]. In this way the traders from Egypt might be ſupplied with them, and thus could finiſh their voyages within the year, which muſt have been protracted much longer if they had extended as far towards the eaſt as is generally ſuppoſed.

FROM all this it appears to be probable, that Ptolemy derived the information concerning the eaſtern parts of India,

[k] Plin. Nat. Hiſt. lib. vi. c. 22.
[l] Perip. Mar. Erythr. 34, 30.
[m] Lib. ii. 124. B.

 upon

SECT. II.

upon which he founds his calculations, not ſo much from any direct and regular intercourſe between Egypt and theſe countries, as from the reports of a few adventurers, whom an enterpriſing ſpirit, or the love of gain, prompted to proceed beyond the uſual limits of navigation.

THOUGH, from the age of Ptolemy, the trade with India continued to be carried on in its former channel, and both Rome, the ancient capital of the empire, and Conſtantinople, the new ſeat of government, were ſupplied with the precious commodities of that country by the merchants of Alexandria, yet, until the reign of the emperor Juſtinian, we have no new information concerning the intercourſe with the Eaſt by ſea, or the progreſs which was made in the diſcovery of its remote regions. Under Juſtinian, Coſmas, an Egyptian merchant, in the courſe of his traffic, made ſome voyages to India, whence he acquired the ſirname of Indicopleuſtes; but afterwards, by a tranſition not uncommon in that ſuperſtitious age, he renounced all the concerns of this life, and aſſumed the monaſtic character. In the ſolitude and leiſure of a cell, he compoſed ſeveral works, one of which, dignified by him with the name of *Chriſtian Topography*, has reached us. The main deſign of it is to combat the opinion of thoſe philoſophers, who aſſert the earth to be of a ſpherical figure, and to prove that it is an oblong plane, of twelve thouſand miles in length from eaſt to weſt, and of ſix thouſand miles in breadth from north to ſouth, surrounded by high walls, covered by the firmament as with a canopy or vault; that the viciſſitude

I I of

SECT. II.

of day and night was occasioned by a mountain of prodigious height, situated in the extremities of the north, round which the sun moved; that when it appeared on one side of this mountain, the earth was illuminated, when concealed on the other side, the earth was left involved in darkness [n]. But amidst those wild reveries, more suited to the credulity of his new profession, than to the sound sense characteristic of that in which he was formerly engaged, Cosmas seems to relate what he himself had observed in his travels, or what he had learned from others, with great simplicity and regard for truth.

He appears to have been well acquainted with the west coast of the Indian peninsula, and names several places situated upon it; he describes it as the chief seat of the pepper trade, and mentions Male, in particular, as one of the most frequented ports on that account [o]. From Male, it is probable that this side of the continent has derived its modern name of Malabar; and the cluster of islands contiguous to it, that of the Maldives. From him too we learn, that the island of Taprobane, which he supposes to lie at an equal distance from the Persian Gulf on the west, and the country of the Sinæ on the east, had become, in consequence of this commodious situation, a great staple of trade; that into it were imported the silk of the Sinæ, and the precious spices of the Eastern countries, which were conveyed thence to all parts of India, to Persia, and to the Arabian Gulf. To this island he

[n] Cosmas ap. Montfaucon Collect. Patrum, ii. 113, &c. 138.

[o] Cosm. lib. ii. p. 138. lib. xi. 337.

gives

SECT. II. gives the name of Sielediba [p], the ſame with that of Selendib, or Serendib, by which it is ſtill known all over the Eaſt.

To Coſmas we are alſo indebted for the firſt information of a new rival to the Romans in trade having appeared in the Indian ſeas. The Perſians, after having overturned the empire of the Parthians, and re-eſtabliſhed the line of their ancient monarchs, ſeem to have ſurmounted entirely the averſion of their anceſtors to maritime exertion, and made early and vigorous efforts in order to acquire a ſhare in the lucrative commerce with India. All its conſiderable ports were frequented by traders from Perſia, who, in return for ſome productions of their own country in requeſt among the Indians, received the precious commodities, which they conveyed up the Perſian Gulf, and by means of the great rivers, Euphrates and Tigris, diſtributed them through every province of their empire. As the voyage from Perſia to India was much ſhorter than that from Egypt, and attended with leſs expence and danger, the intercourſe between the two countries increaſed rapidly. A circumſtance is mentioned by Coſmas which is a ſtriking proof of this. In moſt of the cities of any note in India he found Chriſtian churches eſtabliſhed, in which the functions of religion were performed by prieſts ordained by the archbiſhop of Seleucia, the capital of the Perſian empire, and who continued ſubject to his juriſdiction [q]. India appears to have been more thoroughly explored at this period, than it was in the age of Ptolemy, and a greater number of ſtrangers

[p] Lib. xi. 336.

[q] Coſm. lib. iii. 178.

ſeem

SECT. II.

ſeem to have been ſettled there. It is remarkable, however, that, according to the account of Coſmas, none of theſe ſtrangers were accuſtomed to viſit the eaſtern regions of Aſia, but reſted ſatisfied with receiving their ſilk, their ſpices, and other valuable productions, as they were imported into Ceylon, and conveyed thence to the various marts of India [r].

THE frequency of open hoſtilities between the emperors of Conſtantinople and the monarchs of Perſia, together with the increaſing rivalſhip of their ſubjects in the trade with India, gave riſe to an event which produced a conſiderable change in the nature of that commerce. As the uſe of ſilk, both in dreſs and furniture, became gradually more general in the court of the Greek emperors, who imitated and ſurpaſſed the ſovereigns of Aſia in ſplendour and magnificence; and as China, in which, according to the concurring teſtimony of Oriental writers, the culture of ſilk was originally known [s], ſtill continued to be the only country which produced that valuable commodity; the Perſians, improving the advantages which their ſituation gave them over the merchants from the Arabian Gulf, ſupplanted them in all the marts of India to which ſilk was brought by ſea from the Eaſt. Having it likewiſe in their power to moleſt or to cut off the caravans, which, in order to procure a ſupply for the Greek empire, travelled by land to China, through the northern provinces of the kingdom, they entirely engroſſed that branch of commerce. Conſtantinople was obliged to depend on a rival power for an article which luxury

[r] Lib. xi. 337.

[s] Herbelot Biblioth. Orient. artic. *Harir*.

SECT. II. viewed and desired as essential to elegance. The Persians, with the usual rapacity of monopolists, raised the price of silk to such an exorbitant height[1], that Justinian, eager not only to obtain a full and certain supply of a commodity which was become of indispensable use, but solicitous to deliver the commerce of his subjects from the exactions of his enemies, endeavoured, by means of his ally, the Christian monarch of Abyssinia, to wrest some portion of the silk trade from the Persians. In this attempt he failed; but when he least

A. D. 551. expected it, he, by an unforeseen event, attained, in some measure, the object which he had in view. Two Persian monks having been employed as missionaries in some of the Christian churches, which were established (as we are informed by Cosmas) in different parts of India, had penetrated into the country of the Seres, or China. There they observed the labours of the silk-worm, and became acquainted with all the arts of man in working up its productions into such a variety of elegant fabrics. The prospect of gain, or perhaps an indignant zeal, excited by seeing this lucrative branch of commerce engrossed by unbelieving nations, prompted them to repair to Constantinople. There they explained to the emperor the origin of silk, as well as the various modes of preparing and manufacturing it, mysteries hitherto unknown, or very imperfectly understood in Europe; and encouraged by his liberal promises, they undertook to bring to the capital a sufficient number of those wonderful insects, to whose labours man is so much indebted. This they accomplished by conveying the eggs of the

[1] Procop. Hist. Arcan. c. 25.

silk-

ſilk-worm in a hollow cane. They were hatched by the heat of a dunghill, fed with the leaves of a wild mulberry tree, and they multiplied and worked in the ſame manner as in thoſe climates where they firſt became objects of human attention and care [u]. Vaſt numbers of theſe inſects were ſoon reared in different parts of Greece, particularly in the Peloponeſus. Sicily afterwards undertook to breed ſilk-worms with equal ſucceſs, and was imitated, from time to time, in ſeveral towns of Italy. In all theſe places extenſive manufactures were eſtabliſhed, and carried on, with ſilk of domeſtic production. The demand for ſilk from the Eaſt diminiſhed of courſe, the ſubjects of the Greek emperors were no longer obliged to have recourſe to the Perſians for a ſupply of it, and a conſiderable change took place in the nature of the commercial intercourſe between Europe and India [x].

[u] Procop. de Bello Gothic. lib. iv. c. 17.

[x] See NOTE XXXV.

N

AN

HISTORICAL DISQUISITION

CONCERNING

ANCIENT INDIA.

SECTION III.

Intercourse with India, from the Conquest of Egypt by the Mahomedans, to the Discovery of the Passage by the Cape of Good Hope, and the Establishment of the Portuguese Dominion in the East.

SECT. III.

ABOUT fourscore years after the death of Justinian, an event happened, which occasioned a revolution still more considerable in the intercourse of Europe with the East. Mahomet, by publishing a new religion, seems to have animated his countrymen with a new spirit, and to have called forth

N 2 latent

SECT. III. latent paſſions and talents into exertion. The greateſt part of the Arabs, ſatisfied from the earlieſt times with national independence and perſonal liberty, tended their camels, or reared their palm-trees, within the precincts of their own peninſula, and had little intercourſe with the reſt of mankind, unleſs when they ſallied out to plunder a caravan, or to rob a traveller. In ſome diſtricts, however, they had begun to add the labours of agriculture, and the buſineſs of commerce, to the occupations of paſtoral life. All theſe orders of men, when prompted by the enthuſiaſtic ardour with which the exhortations and example of Mahomet inſpired them, diſplayed, at once, all the zeal of miſſionaries, and the ambition of conquerors. They ſpread the doctrine of their prophet, and extended the dominion of his ſucceſſors, from the ſhores of the Atlantic to the frontier of China, with a rapidity of ſucceſs to which

A. D. 640. there is nothing ſimilar in the hiſtory of mankind. Egypt was one of their earlieſt conqueſts; and as they ſettled in that inviting country, and kept poſſeſſion of it, the Greeks were excluded from all intercourſe with Alexandria, to which they had long reſorted as the chief mart of Indian goods. Nor was this the only effect which the progreſs of the Mahomedan arms had upon the commerce of Europe with India. Prior to their invaſion of Egypt, the Arabians had ſubdued the great kingdom of Perſia, and added it to the empire of their Caliphs. They found their new ſubjects engaged in proſecuting that extenſive trade with India, and the country to the eaſt of it, the commencement and progreſs of which in Perſia I have already mentioned; and they were ſo ſenſible of the great advantages derived from it, that they became deſirous to partake

5 of

of them. As the active powers of the human mind, when roused to vigorous exertions in one line, are most capable of operating with force in other directions; the Arabians, from impetuous warriors, soon became enterprising merchants. They continued to carry on the trade with India in its former channel from the Persian Gulf, but it was with that ardour which characterizes all the early efforts of Mahomet's followers. In a short time they advanced far beyond the boundaries of ancient navigation, and brought many of the most precious commodities of the East directly from the countries which produced them. In order to engross all the profit arising from the sale of them, the Caliph Omar [a], a few years after the conquest of Persia, founded the city of Bassora, on the western banks of the great stream formed by the junction of the Euphrates and Tigris, with a view of securing the command of these two rivers, by which goods imported from India were conveyed into all parts of Asia. With such discernment was the situation chosen, that Bassora soon became a place of trade hardly inferior to Alexandria.

THIS general information with respect to the trade of the Arabians with India, which is all that can be derived from the historians of that period, is confirmed and illustrated by the Relation of a Voyage from the Persian Gulf towards the East, written by an Arabian merchant in the year of the Christian æra eight hundred and fifty-one, about two centuries

[a] Herbel. Biblioth. Orient. artic. *Basrah*.

after

SECT. III. after Persia was subjected to the Caliphs, and explained by the Commentary of another Arabian, who had likewise visited the Eastern parts of Asia [b]. This curious Relation, which enables us to fill up a chasm in the history of mercantile communication with India, furnishes materials for describing more in detail the extent of the Arabian discoveries in the East, and the manner in which they made them.

THOUGH some have imagined that the wonderful property of the magnet, by which it communicates such virtue to a needle or slender rod of iron, as to make it point towards the poles of the earth, was known in the East long before it was observed in Europe, it is manifest, both from the Relation of the Mahometan merchant, and from much concurring evidence, that not only the Arabians, but the Chinese, were destitute of this faithful guide, and that their mode of navigation was not more adventrous than that of the Greeks and Romans [c]. They steered servilely along the coast, seldom stretching out to sea so far as to lose sight of land, and as they shaped their course in this timid manner, their mode of reckoning was defective, and liable to the same errors which I observed in that of the Greeks and Romans [d].

NOTWITHSTANDING these disadvantages, the progress of the Arabians towards the East extended far beyond the Gulf

[b] See NOTE XXXVI. [c] Relation, p. 2. 8, &c.

[d] Renaudot. Inquiry into the Time when the Mahomedans first entered China, p. 143.

7 of

of Siam, the boundary of European navigation. They became acquainted with Sumatra, and the other iſlands of the great Indian Archipelago, and advanced as far as the city of Canton in China. Nor are theſe diſcoveries to be conſidered as the effect of the enterpriſing curioſity of individuals; they were owing to a regular commerce carried on from the Perſian Gulf with China, and all the intermediate countries. Many Mahomedans, imitating the example of the Perſians deſcribed by Coſmas Indicopleuſtes, ſettled in India and the countries beyond it. They were ſo numerous in the city of Canton, that the emperor (as the Arabian authors relate) permitted them to have a Cadi or judge of their own ſect, who decided controverſies among his countrymen by their own laws, and preſided in all the functions of religion [e]. In other places proſelytes were gained to the Mahomedan faith, and the Arabian language was underſtood and ſpoken in almoſt every ſea-port of any note. Ships from China and different places of India traded in the Perſian Gulf [f], and by the frequency of mutual intercourſe, all the nations of the Eaſt became better acquainted with each other [g].

A STRIKING proof of this is the new information concerning China and India we receive from the two authors I have mentioned. They point out the ſituation of Canton, now ſo well known to Europeans, with a conſiderable degree of exactneſs. They take notice of the general uſe of ſilk among the

[e] Relation, p. 7. Remarks, p. 19. Inquiry, p. 171, &c.

[f] See NOTE XXXVII.

[g] Relation, p. 8.

Chineſe.

SECT. III.

Chinese. They are the first who mention their celebrated manufacture of porcelane, which, on account of its delicacy and transparency, they compare to glass. They describe the tea-tree, and the mode of using its leaves; and from the great revenue which was levied (as they inform us) from the consumption of it, tea seems to have been as universally the favourite beverage of the Chinese in the ninth century, as it is at present[h].

Even with respect to those parts of India which the Greeks and Romans were accustomed to visit, the Arabians had acquired more perfect information. They mention a great empire established on the Malabar coast, governed by monarchs whose authority was paramount to that of every power in India. These monarchs were distinguished by the appellation of *Balchara*, a name yet known in India[i], and it is probable that the Samorin, or emperor of Calicut, so frequently mentioned in the accounts of the first voyages of the Portuguese to India, possessed some portion of their dominions. They celebrate the extraordinary progress which the Indians had made in astronomical knowledge, a circumstance which seems to have been unknown to the Greeks and Romans, and assert that in this branch of science they were far superior to the most enlightened nations of the East, on which account their sovereign was denominated the King of Wisdom[k]. Other peculiarities in the political institutions, the mode of judicial

[h] Relation, p. 21. 25.

[i] Herbelot, artic. *Hend.* & *Belhar.*

[k] Relation, p. 37. 53.

proceedings,

proceedings, the paſtimes, and the ſuperſtitions of the Indians, particularly the excruciating mortifications and penances of the faquirs, might be produced as proofs of the ſuperior knowledge which the Arabians had acquired of the manners of that people. SECT. III.

THE ſame commercial ſpirit, or religious zeal, which prompted the Mahomedans of Perſia to viſit the remoteſt regions of the Eaſt, animated the Chriſtians of that kingdom. The Neſtorian churches planted in Perſia, under the protection firſt of its native ſovereigns, and afterwards of its conquerors the Caliphs, were numerous, and governed by reſpectable eccleſiaſtics. They had early ſent miſſionaries into India, and eſtabliſhed churches in different parts of it, particularly, as I have formerly related, in the Iſland of Ceylon. When the Arabians extended their navigation as far as China, a more ample field, both for their commerce and their zeal, opened to their view. If we may rely on the concurring evidence of Chriſtian authors, in the Eaſt as well as in the Weſt, confirmed by the teſtimony of the two Mahomedan travellers, their pious labours were attended with ſuch ſucceſs, that in the ninth and tenth centuries the number of Chriſtians in India and China was very conſiderable [1]. As the churches in both theſe countries received all their eccleſiaſtics from Perſia, where they were ordained by the *Catholicos*, or Neſtorian Primate, whoſe ſupremacy they acknowledged, this became a regular channel of intercourſe and intelligence; and to the combined effect of all theſe circum-

[1] See NOTE XXXVIII.

O ſtances,

SECT. III. ſtances, we are indebted for the information we receive from the two Arabian writers[m], concerning thoſe regions of Aſia which the Greeks and Romans never viſited.

But while both the Mahomedan and Chriſtian ſubjects of the Caliphs continued to extend their knowledge of the Eaſt, the people of Europe found themſelves excluded almoſt entirely from any intercourſe with it. To them the great port of Alexandria was now ſhut, and the new lords of the Perſian Gulf, ſatisfied with ſupplying the demand in their own vaſt dominions for the commodities of the Eaſt, neglected to convey them, by any of the uſual channels, to the trading towns on the Mediterranean. The opulent inhabitants of Conſtantinople, and other great cities of Europe, bore this deprivation of luxuries, to which they had been long accuſtomed, with ſuch impatience, that all the activity of commerce was exerted, in order to find a remedy for an evil which they deemed intolerable. The difficulties which were to be ſurmounted in order to accompliſh this, afford the moſt ſtriking proof of the high eſtimation in which the commodities of the Eaſt were held at that time. The ſilk of China was purchaſed in Chenſi, the weſternmoſt province of that empire, and conveyed thence by a caravan, in a march of eighty or a hundred days, to the banks of the Oxus, where it was embarked, and carried down the ſtream of that river to the Caſpian. After a dangerous voyage acroſs that ſea, and aſcending the river Cyrus as far as it is navigable, it was conducted by a ſhort land-carriage

[m] Relation, p. 39.

of

of five days to the river Phasis[n], which falls into the Euxine or Black Sea. Thence, by an easy and well known course, it was transported to Constantinople. The conveyance of commodities from that region of the East, now known by the name of Indostan, was somewhat less tedious and operose. They were carried from the banks of the Indus, by a route early frequented, and which I have already described, either to the river Oxus, or directly to the Caspian, from which they held the same course to Constantinople.

It is obvious, that only commodities of small bulk, and of considerable value, could bear the expence of such a mode of conveyance; and in regulating the price of those commodities, not only the expence, but the risque and danger of conveying them, were to be taken into account. In their journey across the vast plain extending from Samarcande to the frontier of China, caravans were exposed to the assaults and depredations of the Tartars, the Huns, the Turks, and other roving tribes which infest the north-east of Asia, and which have always considered the merchant and traveller as their lawful prey; nor were they exempt from insult and pillage in their journey from the Cyrus to the Phasis, through the kingdom of Colchis, a country noted, both in ancient and in modern times, for the thievish disposition of its inhabitants. Even under all these disadvantages, the trade with the East was carried on with ardour. Constantinople became a considerable mart of Indian and Chinese commodities, and the wealth which flowed into it

[n] Plin. Nat. Hist. lib. vi. c. 17.

SECT. III. in consequence of this, not only added to the splendour of that great city, but seems to have retarded, for some time, the decline of the empire of which it was the capital.

As far as we may venture to conjecture, from the imperfect information of cotemporary historians, it was chiefly by the mode of conveyance which I have described, perilous and operose as it was, that Europe was supplied with the commodities of the East, during more than two centuries. Throughout that period the Christians and Mahomedans were engaged in almost uninterrupted hostilities; prosecuted with all the animosity which rivalship for power, heightened by religious zeal, naturally excites. Under circumstances which occasioned such alienation, commercial intercourse could hardly subsist, and the merchants of Christendom either did not resort at all to Alexandria, and the ports of Syria, the ancient staples for the commodities of the East, after they were in possession of the Mahomedans, or if the love of gain, surmounting their abhorrence of the Infidels, prompted them to visit the marts which they had long frequented, it was with much caution and distrust.

While the difficulties of procuring the productions of the East were thus augmented, the people of Europe became more desirous of obtaining them. About this time some cities of Italy, particularly Amalphi and Venice, having acquired a greater degree of independence than they formerly possessed, began to cultivate the arts of domestic industry, with an ardour and ingenuity uncommon in the middle ages. The effect of

I I these

these exertions was such an increase of wealth, as created new wants and desires, and formed a taste for elegance and luxury, which induced them to visit foreign countries in order to gratify it. Among men in this stage of their advancement, the productions of India have always been held in high estimation, and from this period they were imported into Italy in larger quantities, and came into more general use. Several circumstances which indicate this revival of a commercial spirit, are collected by the industrious Muratori, and, from the close of the seventh century, an attentive observer may discern faint traces of its progress [o].

Even in enlightened ages, when the transactions of nations are observed and recorded with the greatest care, and the store of historical materials seems to be abundantly ample, so little attention has been paid to the operations of commerce, that every attempt towards a regular deduction of them, has been found an undertaking of the utmost difficulty. The æra, however, to which I have conducted this Disquisition, is one of the periods in the annals of mankind concerning which history furnishes most scanty information. As it was chiefly in the Greek empire, and in some cities of Italy, that any efforts were made to procure the commodities of India, and the other regions of the East, it is only from the Historians of those countries we can expect to find any account of that trade. But from the age of Mahomet, until the time when

[o] Antiquit. Ital. medij Ævi, ii. 400. 408. 410. 883. 885. 894. Rer. Ital. Script. ii. 487.

the

SECT. III. the Comneni aſcended the throne of Conſtantinople, a period of more than four centuries and a half, the Byzantine hiſtory is contained in meagre chronicles, the compilers of which ſeldom extended their views beyond the intrigues in the palace, the factions in the theatre, or the diſputes of theologians. To them the monkiſh annaliſts of the different ſtates and cities of Italy, during the ſame period, are (if poſſible) far inferior in merit, and in the early accounts of thoſe cities which have been moſt celebrated for their commercial ſpirit, we ſearch with little ſucceſs for the origin or nature of that trade by which they firſt roſe to eminence [p]. It is manifeſt, however, from the ſlighteſt attention to the events which happened in the ſeventh and eighth centuries, that the Italian ſtates, while their coaſts were continually infeſted by the Mahomedans, who had made ſome ſettlements there, and had ſubjected Sicily almoſt entirely to their dominion, could not trade with much confidence and ſecurity in Egypt and Syria. With what implacable hatred Chriſtians viewed Mahomedans, as the diſciples of an impoſtor, is well known; and as all the nations which profeſſed the Chriſtian faith, both in the Eaſt and Weſt, had mingled the worſhip of angels and ſaints with that of the Supreme Being, and had adorned their churches with pictures and ſtatues; the true Moſlems conſidered themſelves as the only aſſertors of the unity of God, and beheld Chriſtians of every denomination with abhorrence, as idolaters. Much time was requiſite to ſoften this mutual animoſity, ſo far as to render intercourſe in any degree cordial.

[p] See NOTE XXXIX.

MEAN-

SECT. III.

MEANWHILE a taste for the luxuries of the East continued not only to spread in Italy, but, from imitation of the Italians, or from some improvement in their own situation, the people of Marseilles, and other towns of France on the Mediterranean, became equally fond of them. But the profits exacted by the merchants of Amalphi or Venice, from whom they received those precious commodities, were so exorbitant as prompted them to make some effort to supply their own demands. With this view, they not only opened a trade with Constantinople, but ventured at times to visit the ports of Egypt and Syria [q]. This eagerness of the Europeans, on the one hand, to obtain the productions of India, and, on the other hand, the immense advantages which both the Caliphs and their subjects derived from the sale of them, induced both so far to conceal their reciprocal antipathy, as to carry on a traffic manifestly for their common benefit. How far this traffic extended, and in what mode it was conducted by these new adventurers, the scanty information which can be gathered from contemporary writers, does not enable me to trace with accuracy. It is probable, however, that this communication would have produced insensibly its usual effect, of familiarizing and reconciling men of hostile principles and discordant manners to one another, and a regular commerce might have been established gradually between Christians and Mahometans, upon such equal terms, that the nations of Europe might have received all the luxuries of the East, by the same channels in which they were formerly conveyed to them, first by the

[q] Mem. de Literat. tom. xxxvii. p. 467, &c. 483.

2 Tyrians,

SECT. III. Tyrians, then by the Greeks of Alexandria, next by the Romans, and at last by the subjects of the Constantinopolitan empire.

But whatever might have been the influence of this growing correspondence, it was prevented from operating with full effect by the crusades, or expeditions for the recovery of the Holy Land, which, during two centuries, occupied the professors of the two rival religions, and contributed to alienate them more than ever from each other. I have, in another work[r], contemplated mankind while under the dominion of this frenzy, the most singular, perhaps, and the longest continued, of any that occurs in the history of our species; and I pointed out such effects of it upon government, upon property, upon manners and taste, as were suited to what were then the objects of my enquiry. At present my attention is confined to observe the commercial consequences of the crusades, and how far they contributed to retard, or to promote, the conveyance of Indian commodities into Europe.

To fix an idea of peculiar sanctity to that country, which the Author of our Religion selected as the place of his residence while on earth, and in which he accomplished the redemption of mankind, is a sentiment so natural to the human mind, that, from the first establishment of Christianity, the visiting of the holy places in Judea was considered as an exercise of piety, tending powerfully to awaken and to cherish

[r] Hist. of Charles V. vol. i. p. 26. edit. 1787.

a spirit

a ſpirit of devotion. Through ſucceeding ages, the practice continued, and increaſed in every part of Chriſtendom. When Jeruſalem was ſubjected to the Mahomedan empire, and danger was added to the fatigue and expence of a diſtant pilgrimage, the undertaking was viewed as ſtill more meritorious. It was ſometimes enjoined as a penance to be performed by heinous tranſgreſſors. It was more frequently a duty undertaken with voluntary zeal, and in both caſes it was deemed an expiation for all paſt offences. From various cauſes, which I have elſewhere enumerated [s], theſe pious viſits to the Holy Land multiplied amazingly during the tenth and eleventh centuries. Not only individuals in the lower and middle ranks of life, but perſons of ſuperior condition, attended by large retinues, and numerous caravans of opulent pilgrims, reſorted to Jeruſalem.

In all their operations, however, men have a wonderful dexterity in mingling ſome attention to intereſt with thoſe functions which ſeem to be moſt purely ſpiritual. The Mahomedan caravans which, in obedience to the injunctions of their religion, viſit the holy temple of Mecca, are not compoſed, as I ſhall hereafter explain more fully, of devout pilgrims only, but of merchants, who, both in going and returning, are provided with ſuch an aſſortment of goods, that they carry on a conſiderable traffic [t]. Even the Faquirs of India, whoſe wild enthuſiaſm ſeems to elevate them above all ſolici-

[s] Hiſt. of Charles V. vol. i. p. 27. 285.

[t] Viaggi di Ramuſio, vol. i. p. 151, 152.

P tude

SECT. III.

tude about the concerns of this world, have rendered their frequent pilgrimages ſubſervient to their intereſt, by trading in every country through which they travel[u]. In like manner, it was not by devotion alone that ſuch numerous bands of Chriſtian pilgrims were induced to viſit Jeruſalem. To many of them commerce was the chief motive of undertaking that diſtant voyage, and by exchanging the productions of Europe for the more valuable commodities of Aſia, particularly thoſe of India, which at that time were diffuſed through every part of the Caliphs dominions, they enriched themſelves, and furniſhed their countrymen with ſuch an additional ſupply of Eaſtern luxuries, as augmented their reliſh for them[x].

BUT how faint ſoever the lines may be, which, prior to the cruſades, mark the influence of the frequent pilgrimages to the Eaſt upon commerce, they become ſo conſpicuous after the commencement of theſe expeditions, as to meet the eye of every obſerver. Various circumſtances concurred towards this, from an enumeration of which it will appear, that by attending to the progreſs and effects of the cruſades, conſiderable light is thrown upon the ſubject of my inquiries. Great armies, conducted by the moſt illuſtrious nobles of Europe, and compoſed of men of the moſt enterpriſing ſpirit in all the kingdoms of it, marched towards Paleſtine, through countries far advanced beyond thoſe which they left, in every ſpecies of improvement. They beheld the dawn of proſperity in the

[u] See NOTE XL.

[x] Gul. Tyr. lib. xvii. c. 4. p. 933. ap. Geſta Dei per Francos.

republics

republics of Italy, which had begun to vie with each other in the arts of induſtry, and in their efforts to engroſs the lucrative commerce with the Eaſt. They next admired the more advanced ſtate of opulence and ſplendour in Conſtantinople, raiſed to a pre-eminence above all the cities then known, by its extenſive trade, particularly that which it carried on with India, and the countries beyond it. They afterwards ſerved in thoſe provinces of Aſia through which the commodities of the Eaſt were uſually conveyed, and became maſters of ſeveral cities which had been ſtaples of that trade. They eſtabliſhed the kingdom of Jeruſalem, which ſubſiſted near two hundred years. They took poſſeſſion of the throne of the Greek empire, and governed it above half a century. Amidſt ſuch a variety of events and operations, the ideas of the fierce warriors of Europe gradually opened and improved; they became acquainted with the policy and arts of the people whom they ſubdued; they obſerved the ſources of their wealth, and availed themſelves of all this knowledge. Antioch and Tyre, when conquered by the cruſaders, were flouriſhing cities, inhabited by opulent merchants, who ſupplied all the nations trading in the Mediterranean with the productions of the Eaſt[y], and as far as can be gathered from incidental occurrences, mentioned by the Hiſtorians of the Holy War, who, being moſtly prieſts and monks, had their attention directed to objects very different from thoſe relating to commerce, there is reaſon to believe that both in Conſtantinople, while ſubject

[y] Gul. Tyr. lib. xiii. c. 5. Alb. Aquenſ. Hiſt. Hieroſ. ap. Geſta Dei, vol. i. p. 247.

P 2 to

SECT. III. to the Franks, and in the ports of Syria acquired by the Christians, the long-established trade with the East continued to be protected and encouraged.

But though commerce may have been only a secondary object with the martial leaders of the crusades, engaged in perpetual hostilities with the Turks on one hand, and with the Soldans of Egypt on the other, it was the primary object with the associates, in conjunction with whom they carried on their operations. Numerous as the armies were which assumed the cross, and enterprising as the fanatical zeal was with which they were animated, they could not have accomplished their purpose, or even have reached the seat of their warfare, without securing the assistance of the Italian states. None of the other European powers could either furnish a sufficient number of transports to convey the armies of the crusaders to the coast of Dalmatia, whence they marched to Constantinople, the place of general rendezvous; or were able to supply them with military stores and provisions in such abundance as to enable them to invade a distant country. In all the successive expeditions, the fleets of the Genoese, of the Pisans, or of the Venetians, kept on the coast as the armies advanced by land, and supplying them, from time to time, with whatever was wanting, engrossed all the profits of a branch of commerce which, in every age, has been extremely lucrative. It was with all the interested attention of merchants, that the Italians afforded their aid. On the reduction of any place in which they found it for their interest to settle, they obtained from the crusaders valuable immunities of different kinds; freedom

5 of

of trade; an abatement of the ufual duties paid for what was imported and exported, or a total exemption from them; the property of entire fuburbs in fome cities, and of extenfive ftreets in others; and a privilege granted to every perfon who refided within their precincts, or who traded under their protection, of being tried by their own laws, and by judges of their own appointment [z]. In confequence of fo many advantages, we can trace, during the progrefs of the crufades, a rapid increafe of wealth and of power in all the commercial ftates of Italy. Every port open to trade was frequented by their merchants, who, having now engroffed entirely the commerce of the Eaft, ftrove with fuch active emulation to find new markets for the commodities which it furnifhed, that they extended a tafte for them to many parts of Europe in which they had hitherto been little known.

Two events happened, prior to the termination of the Holy War, which, by acquiring to the Venetians and Genoefe the poffeffion of feveral provinces in the Greek empire, enabled them to fupply Europe more abundantly with all the productions of the Eaft. The firft was the conqueft of Conftantinople, in the year one thoufand two hundred and four, by the Venetians, and the leaders of the fourth crufade. An account of the political interefts and intrigues which formed this alliance, and turned the hallowed arms deftined to deliver the Holy City from the dominion of infidels, againft a Chriftian monarch, is foreign from the defign of this Difquifition.

[z] Hift. of Charles V. vol. i. p. 34.

Conftan-

SECT. III. Conſtantinople was taken by ſtorm, and plundered by the confederates. An earl of Flanders was placed on the Imperial throne. The dominions which ſtill remained ſubject to the ſucceſſors of Conſtantine, were divided into four parts, one of which being allotted to the new emperor, for ſupporting the dignity and expence of government, an equal partition of the other three was made between the Venetians and the chiefs of the cruſade. The former, who, both in concerting and in conducting this enterpriſe, kept their eye ſteadily fixed on what might be moſt for the emolument of their commerce, ſecured the territories of greateſt value to a trading people. They obtained ſome part of the Peloponneſus, at that time the ſeat of flouriſhing manufactures, particularly of ſilk. They became maſters of ſeveral of the largeſt and beſt cultivated iſlands in the Archipelago, and eſtabliſhed a chain of ſettlements, partly military and partly commercial, extending from the Adriatic to the Boſphorus[a]. Many Venetians ſettled in Conſtantinople, and without obſtruction from their warlike aſſociates, little attentive to the arts of induſtry, they engroſſed the various branches of trade which had ſo long enriched that capital. Two of theſe particularly attracted their attention; the ſilk trade, and that with India. From the reign of Juſtinian, it was moſtly in Greece, and ſome of the adjacent iſlands, that ſilk-worms, which he firſt introduced into Europe, were reared. The product of their labours was manufactured into ſtuffs of various kinds in many cities of the empire.

[a] Danduli Chronic. ap. Murat. Script. Rer. Ital. vol. xii. p. 328. Mar. Sanuto Vite de Duchi di Venez. Murat. vol. xxii. p. 532.

But

But it was in Constantinople, the seat of opulence and luxury, that the demand for a commodity of such high price was greatest, and there, of consequence, the commerce of silk naturally centered. In assorting cargoes for the several ports in which they traded, the Venetians had for some time found silk to be an essential article, as it continued to grow more and more into request in every part of Europe. By the residence of so many of their citizens in Constantinople, and by the immunities granted to them, they not only procured silk in such abundance, and on such terms, as enabled them to carry on trade more extensively, and with greater profit than formerly, but they became so thoroughly acquainted with every branch of the silk manufacture, as induced them to attempt the establishment of it in their own dominions. The measures taken for this purpose by individuals, as well as the regulations framed by the state, were concerted with so much prudence, and executed with such success, that in a short time the silk fabrics of Venice vied with those of Greece and Sicily, and contributed both to enrich the republic, and to enlarge the sphere of its commerce. At the same time, the Venetians availed themselves of the influence which they had acquired in Constantinople, in order to improve their Indian trade. The capital of the Greek empire, besides the means of being supplied with the productions of the East, which it enjoyed in common with the other commercial cities of Europe, received a considerable portion of them by a channel peculiar to itself. Some of the most valuable commodities of India and China were conveyed over land, by routes which I have described, to the Black Sea, and thence by a short navigation

to

SECT. III. to Conſtantinople. To this market, the beſt ſtored of any except Alexandria, the Venetians had now eaſy acceſs, and the goods which they purchaſed there, made an addition of great conſequence to what they were accuſtomed to acquire in the ports of Egypt and Syria. Thus while the Latin empire in Conſtantinople ſubſiſted, the Venetians poſſeſſed ſuch advantages over all their rivals, that their commerce extended greatly, and it was chiefly from them every part of Europe received the commodities of the Eaſt.

The other event which I had in view, was the ſubverſion of the dominion of the Latins in Conſtantinople, and the re-eſtabliſhment of the Imperial family on the throne. This was effected after a period of fifty-ſeven years, partly by a tranſient effort of vigour, with which indignation at a foreign yoke animated the Greeks, and partly by the powerful aſſiſtance which they received from the republic of Genoa. The Genoeſe were ſo ſenſible of the advantages which the Venetians, their rivals in trade, derived from their union with the Latin emperors of Conſtantinople, that in order to deprive them of theſe, they ſurmounted the moſt deep-rooted prejudices of their age, and combined with the ſchiſmatic Greeks to dethrone a monarch protected by the Papal power, ſetting at defiance the thunders of the Vatican, which at that time made the greateſt princes tremble. This undertaking, bold and impious as it was then deemed, proved ſucceſsful. In recompence for their ſignal ſervices, the gratitude or weakneſs of the Greek emperor, among other donations, beſtowed upon the Genoeſe Pera, the chief ſuburb of Conſtantinople, to be held as a fief of the empire, together

SECT. III.

together with ſuch exemption from the accuſtomed duties on goods imported and exported, as gave them a decided ſuperiority over every competitor in trade. With the vigilant attention of merchants, the Genoeſe availed themſelves of this favourable ſituation. They ſurrounded their new ſettlement in Pera with fortifications. They rendered their factories on the adjacent coaſts places of ſtrength [b]. They were maſters of the harbour of Conſtantinople more than the Greeks themſelves. The whole trade of the Black Sea came into their hands; and not ſatisfied with this, they took poſſeſſion of part of the Cherſoneſus Taurica, the modern Crimæa, and rendered Caffa, its principal town, the chief ſeat of their trade with the Eaſt, and the port in which all its productions, conveyed to the Black Sea by the different routes I have formerly deſcribed, were landed [c].

In conſequence of this revolution, Genoa became the greateſt commercial power in Europe; and if the enterpriſing induſtry and intrepid courage of its citizens had been under the direction of wiſe domeſtic policy, it might have long held that rank. But never was there a contraſt more ſtriking, than between the internal adminiſtration of the two rival republics of Venice and Genoa. In the former, government was conducted with ſteady ſyſtematic prudence; in the latter, it was

[b] Niceph. Gregor. lib. xi. c. 1. §. 6. lib. xvii. c. 1. §. 2.

[c] Folieta Hiſt. Genuenſ. ap. Græv. Theſ. Antiq. Ital. i. 387. De Marinis de Genuenſ. Dignit. ib. 1486. Niceph. Greg. lib. xiii. c. 12. Murat. Annal. d' Ital. lib. vii. c. 351. See NOTE XLI.

Q consiſtent

SECT. III. consistent in nothing but a fondness for novelty, and a propensity to change. The one enjoyed a perpetual calm, the other was agitated with all the storms and vicissitudes of faction. The increase of wealth, which flowed into Genoa from the exertions of its merchants, did not counterbalance the defects in its political constitution; and even in its most prosperous state we may discern the appearance of symptoms which foreboded a diminution of its opulence and power.

As long, however, as the Genoese retained the ascendant which they had acquired in the Greek empire, the Venetians felt their commercial transactions with it to be carried on upon such unequal terms, that their merchants visited Constantinople seldom, and with reluctance; and in order to procure the commodities of the East in such quantities as were demanded in the various parts of Europe which they were accustomed to supply, they were obliged to resort to the ancient staples of that trade. Of these Alexandria was the chief, and the most abundantly supplied, as the conveyance of Indian goods by land through Asia, to any of the ports of the Mediterranean, was often rendered impracticable by the incursions of Turks, Tartars, and other hordes, which successively desolated that fertile country, or contended for the dominion of it. But under the military and vigorous government of the Soldans of the Mameluks, security and order were steadily maintained in Egypt, and trade, though loaded with heavy duties, was open to all. In proportion to the progress of the Genoese, in engrossing the commerce of Constantinople and the Black Sea,

Sea[d], the Venetians found it more and more neceſſary to enlarge their tranſactions with Alexandria. SECT. III.

But ſuch an avowed intercourſe with infidels being conſidered, in that age, as unbecoming the character of Chriſtians, the ſenate of Venice, in order to ſilence its own ſcruples, or thoſe of its ſubjects, had recourſe to the infallible authority of the Pope, who was ſuppoſed to be poſſeſſed of power to diſpenſe with the rigorous obſervation of the moſt ſacred laws, and obtained permiſſion from him to fit out annually a ſpecified number of ſhips for the ports of Egypt and of Syria[e]. Under this ſanction, the republic concluded a treaty of commerce with the Soldans of Egypt, on equitable terms; in conſequence of which the ſenate appointed one conſul to reſide in Alexandria, and another in Damaſcus, in a public character, and to exerciſe a mercantile juriſdiction, authoriſed by the Soldans. Under their protection, Venetian merchants and artiſans ſettled in each of theſe cities. Ancient prejudices and antipathies were forgotten, and their mutual intereſts eſtabliſhed, for the firſt time, a fair and open trade between Chriſtians and Mahomedans[f].

While the Venetians and Genoeſe were alternately making thoſe extraordinary efforts, in order to engroſs all the advantages of ſupplying Europe with the productions of the Eaſt, the republic of Florence, originally a commercial democracy,

[d] See NOTE XLII. [e] See NOTE XLIII.
[f] Sandi Storia Civile Veneziana, lib. v. c. 15. p. 248, &c.

SECT. III.

applied with ſuch perſevering vigour to trade, and the genius of the people, as well as the nature of their inſtitutions, were ſo favourable to its progreſs, that the ſtate advanced rapidly in power, and the people in opulence. But as the Florentines did not poſſeſs any commodious ſea-port, their active exertions were directed chiefly towards the improvement of their manufactures, and domeſtic induſtry. About the beginning of the fourteenth century, the Florentine manufactures of various kinds, particularly thoſe of ſilk and woollen cloth, appear from the enumeration of a well-informed Hiſtorian, to have been very conſiderable [g]. The connection which they formed in different parts of Europe, by furniſhing them with the productions of their own induſtry, led them to engage in another branch of trade, that of banking. In this they ſoon became ſo eminent, that the money-tranſactions of almoſt every kingdom in Europe paſſed through their hands, and in many of them they were entruſted with the collection and adminiſtration of the public revenues. In conſequence of the activity and ſucceſs with which they conducted their manufactures and money-tranſactions, the former always attended with certain though moderate profit, the latter lucrative in an high degree, at a period when neither the intereſt of money, nor the premium on bills of exchange, were ſettled with accuracy, Florence became one of the firſt cities in Chriſtendom, and many of its citizens extremely opulent. Coſmo di Medici, the head of a family which roſe from obſcurity by its ſucceſs in trade, was reckoned the moſt wealthy merchant ever known in Eu-

[g] Giov. Villani Hiſt. Fiorent. ap. Murat. Script. Rer. Ital. vol. xiii. p. 823.

rope;

SECT. III.

rope[h]; and in acts of public munificence, as well as of private generosity, in the patronage of learning, and in the encouragement of useful and elegant arts, no monarch of the age could vie with him. Whether the Medici, in their first mercantile transactions, carried on any commerce with the East, I have not been able to discover[i]. It is more probable, I should think, that their trade was confined to the same articles with that of their countrymen. But as soon as the commonwealth, by the conquest of Pisa, had acquired a communication with A.C. 1405.
the ocean, Cosmo di Medici, who had the chief direction of its affairs, endeavoured to procure for his country a share in that lucrative commerce, which had raised Venice and Genoa so far above all the other Italian states. With this view am- A.C. 1425.
bassadors were sent to Alexandria, in order to prevail with the Soldan to open that, and the other ports of his dominions, to the subjects of the republic, and to admit them to a participation of all the commercial privileges which were enjoyed by the Venetians. The negociation terminated with such success, that the Florentines seem to have obtained some share in the Indian trade[k]; and soon after this period, we find spices enumerated among the commodities imported by the Florentines into England[l].

[h] Fr. Mich. Brutus Hist. Flor. p. 37, 62. Chron. Eugubinum ap. Murat. Script. Rer. Ital. vol. xiv. p. 1007. Denina Revol. d' Italie, tom. vi. p. 263, &c.

[i] See NOTE XLIV. [k] See NOTE XLV.

[l] Hakluyt, vol. i. p. 193.

IN

SECT. III.

In ſome parts of this Diſquiſition, concerning the nature and courſe of trade with the Eaſt, I have been obliged to grope my way, and often under the guidance of very feeble lights. But as we are now approaching to the period when the modern ideas, with reſpect to the importance of commerce, began to unfold, and attention to its progreſs and effects became a more conſiderable object of policy, we may hope to carry on what reſearches yet remain to be made, with greater certainty and preciſion. To this growing attention we are indebted for the account which Marino Sanudo, a Venetian nobleman, gives of the Indian trade, as carried on by his countrymen, about the beginning of the fourteenth century. They were ſupplied, as he informs us, with the productions of the Eaſt in two different ways. Thoſe of ſmall bulk and high value, ſuch as cloves, nutmegs, mace, gems, pearls, &c. were conveyed from the Perſian Gulf up the Tigris to Baſſora, and thence to Bagdat, from which they were carried to ſome port on the Mediterranean. All more bulky goods, ſuch as pepper, ginger, cinnamon, &c. together with ſome portion of the more valuable articles, were conveyed by the ancient route to the Red Sea, and thence acroſs the deſart, and down the Nile to Alexandria. The goods received by the former route were, as Sanudo obſerves, of ſuperior quality but from the tedioufneſs and expence of a diſtant land-carriage, the ſupply was often ſcanty, nor can he conceal (though contrary to a favourite project which he had in view when he wrote the treatiſe to which I refer) that, from the ſtate of the countries through which the caravans paſſed, this

6 mode

mode of conveyance was frequently precarious, and attended with danger [m].

It was in Alexandria only, that the Venetians found always a certain and full ſupply of Indian goods; and as theſe were conveyed thither chiefly by water-carriage, they might have purchaſed them at a moderate price, if the Soldans had not impoſed upon them duties which amounted to a third part of their full value. Under this and every other diſadvantage, however, it was neceſſary to procure them, as from many concurring circumſtances, particularly a more extenſive intercourſe eſtabliſhed among the different nations of Europe, the demand for them continued to increaſe greatly during the fourteenth century. By the irruptions of the various hoſtile tribes of Barbarians, who took poſſeſſion of the greater part of Europe, that powerful bond by which the Romans had united together all the people of their vaſt empire was entirely diſſolved, and ſuch diſcouragement was given to the communication of one nation with another, as would appear altogether incredible, if the evidence of it reſted only upon the teſtimony of hiſtorians, and were not confirmed by what is ſtill more authentic, the expreſs enactment of laws. Several ſtatutes of this kind, which diſgrace the juriſprudence of almoſt every European nation, I have enumerated and explained in another work [n]. But when the wants and deſires of men multiplied, and they found that other countries could furniſh the means of ſupplying

[m] Mar. Sanuti Secreta Fidelium Crucis, p. 22, &c. ap. Bongarſium.

[n] Hiſt. of Charles V. vol. i. p. 92. 291. &c.

and

SECT. III.

and gratifying them, the hoſtile ſentiments which kept nations at a diſtance from each other abated, and mutual correſpondence gradually took place. From the time of the cruſades, which firſt brought people hardly known to one another, to aſſociate and to act in concert during two centuries, in purſuit of one common end, ſeveral circumſtances had co-operated towards accelerating this general intercourſe. The people around the Baltic, hitherto dreaded and abhorred by the reſt of Europe as pirates and invaders, aſſumed more pacific manners, and began now to viſit their neighbours as merchants. Occurrences foreign from the ſubject of the preſent inquiry, united them together in the powerful commercial confederacy ſo famous in the middle ages, under the name of the Hanſeatic League, and led them to eſtabliſh the ſtaple of their trade with the ſouthern parts of Europe in Bruges. Thither the merchants of Italy, particularly thoſe of Venice, reſorted; and in return for the productions of the Eaſt, and the manufactures of their own country, they received not only the naval ſtores and other commodities of the North, but a conſiderable ſupply of gold and ſilver from the mines in various provinces of Germany, the moſt valuable and productive of any known at that time in Europe[o]. Bruges continued to be the great mart or ſtorehouſe of European trade during the period to which my inquiries extend. A regular communication, formerly unknown, was kept up there among all the kingdoms into which our continent is divided, and we are enabled to account for the rapid progreſs of the Italian ſtates in wealth and power, by obſerving

[o] Zimmermann's Polit. Survey of Europe, p. 102.

2 how

how much their trade, the ſource from which both were derived, muſt have augmented upon the vaſt increaſe in the conſumption of Aſiatic goods, when all the extenſive countries towards the north-eaſt of Europe were opened for their reception.

DURING this proſperous and improving ſtate of Indian commerce, Venice received from one of its citizens, ſuch new information concerning the countries which produced the precious commodities that formed the moſt valuable article of its trade, as gave an idea of their opulence, their population, and their extent, which roſe far above all the former conceptions of Europeans. From the time that the Mahomedans became maſters of Egypt, as no chriſtian was permitted to paſs through their dominions to the Eaſt [p], the direct intercourſe of Europeans with India ceaſed entirely. The account of India by Coſmas Indico-pleuſtes in the ſixth century, is, as far as I know, the laſt which the nations of the Weſt received from any perſon who had viſited that country. But about the middle of the thirteenth century, the ſpirit of commerce, now become more enterprizing, and more eager to diſcover new routes which led to wealth, induced Marco Polo, a Venetian of a noble family, after trading for ſome time in many of the opulent cities of the leſſer Aſia, to penetrate into the more eaſtern parts of that continent, as far as to the court of the Great Khan on the frontier of China. During the courſe of twenty-ſix years, partly employed in mercantile tranſactions, and partly in conducting

[p] Sanuto, p. 23.

R negocia-

SECT. III. negociations with which the Great Khan entrufted him, he explored many regions of the Eaft which no European had ever vifited.

He defcribes the great kingdom of Cathay, the name by which China is ftill known in many parts of the Eaft [q], and travelled through it from Chambalu, or Peking, on its northern frontier, to fome of its moft fouthern provinces. He vifited different parts of Indoftan, and is the firft who mentions Bengal and Guzzerat, by their prefent names, as great and opulent kingdoms. Befides what he difcovered in his journies by land, he made more than one voyage in the Indian ocean, and acquired fome information concerning an ifland which he calls Zipangri or Cipango, probably Japan. He vifited in perfon Java, and feveral iflands contiguous to it, the ifland of Ceylon, and the coaft of Malabar as far as the Gulf of Cambay, to all which he gives the names that they now bear. This was the moft extenfive furvey hitherto made of the Eaft, and the moft complete defcription of it ever given by any European; and in an age which had hardly any knowledge of thofe regions but what was derived from the geography of Ptolemy, not only the Venetians, but all the people of Europe, were aftonifhed at the difcovery of immenfe countries opened to their view beyond what had hitherto been reputed the utmoft boundary of the earth in that quarter [r].

But while men of leifure and fpeculation occupied themfelves with examining the difcoveries of Marco Polo, which gave rife

[q] Herbelot Bib. Orient. artic. *Khathai.* Stewart, Account of Thibet, Phil. Tranf. lxvii. 474. Voyage of A. Jenkinfon, Hakluyt. i. 333.

[r] See NOTE XLVI.

2 10

to conjectures and theories, productive of most important consequences; an event happened, that drew the attention of all Europe, and had a most conspicuous effect upon the course of that trade, the progress of which I am endeavouring to trace. SECT. III.

The event to which I allude, is the final conquest of the Greek empire by Mahomet II. and the establishing the seat of the Turkish government in Constantinople. The immediate effect of this great revolution was, that the Genoese residing in Pera, involved in the general calamity, were obliged not only to abandon that settlement, but all those which they had made on the adjacent sea-coast, after they had been in their possession near two centuries. Not long after, the victorious arms of the Sultan expelled them from Caffa, and every other place which they held in the Crimea [a]. Constantinople was no longer a mart open to the nations of the West for Indian commodities, and no supply of them could now be obtained but in Egypt and the ports of Syria, subject to the Soldans of the Mameluks. The Venetians, in consequence of the protection and privileges which they had secured by their commercial treaty with those powerful princes, carried on trade in every part of their dominions with such advantage, as gave them a superiority over every competitor. Genoa, which had long been their most formidable rival, humbled by the loss of its possessions in the East, and weakened by domestic dissensions, declined so fast, that it was obliged to court foreign protection, and submitted alternately to the dominion of the Dukes of Milan and the Kings of France. In consequence of this diminution of their political

A. D. 1453.

A. D. 1474.

[a] Folieta Hist. Genu. 602, 626. Murat. Annali d'Ital. ix. 451.

R 2 power,

SECT. III. power, the commercial exertions of the Genoese became less vigorous. A feeble attempt which they made to recover that share of the Indian trade which they had formerly enjoyed, by offering to enter into treaty with the Soldans of Egypt upon terms similar to those which had been granted to the Venetians, proved unsuccessful; and during the remainder of the fifteenth century, Venice supplied the greater part of Europe with the productions of the East, and carried on trade to an extent far beyond what had been known in those times.

The state of the other European nations was extremely favourable to the commercial progress of the Venetians. England, desolated by the civil wars which the unhappy contest between the houses of York and Lancaster excited, had hardly begun to turn its attention towards those objects and pursuits to which it is indebted for its present opulence and power. In France, the fatal effects of the English arms and conquests were still felt, and the king had neither acquired power, nor the people inclination, to direct the national genius and activity to the arts of peace. The union of the different kingdoms of Spain was not yet completed; some of its most fertile provinces were still under the dominion of the Moors, with whom the Spanish monarchs waged perpetual war; and, except by the Catalans, little attention was paid to foreign trade. Portugal, though it had already entered upon that career of discovery which terminated with most splendid success, had not yet made such progress in it as to be entitled to any high rank among the commercial states of Europe. Thus the Venetians, almost without rival or competitor, except from some of the inferior

inferior Italian ſtates, were left at liberty to concert and to execute their mercantile plans; and the trade with the cities of the Hanſeatic League, which united the North and South of Europe, and which hitherto had been common to all the Italians, was now engroſſed, in a great meaſure, by them alone.

WHILE the increaſing demand for the productions of Aſia induced all the people of Europe to court intercourſe with the Venetians ſo eagerly, as to allure them, by various immunities, to frequent their ſea-ports, we may obſerve a peculiarity in their mode of carrying on trade with the Eaſt, which diſtinguiſhes it from what has taken place in other countries in any period of hiſtory. In the ancient world, the Tyrians, the Greeks who were maſters of Egypt, and the Romans, ſailed to India in queſt of thoſe commodities with which they ſupplied the people of the Weſt. In modern times, the ſame has been the practice of the Portugueſe, the Dutch, the Engliſh, and, after their example, of other European nations. In both periods loud complaints have been made, that in carrying on this trade every ſtate muſt be drained of the precious metals which, in the courſe of it, flow inceſſantly from the Weſt to the Eaſt, never to return. From whatever loſs might have been occaſioned by this gradual but unavoidable diminution of their gold and ſilver (whether a real or only an imaginary loſs, it is not incumbent upon me, in this place, to inquire or to determine), the Venetians were, in a great meaſure, exempted. They had no direct intercourſe with India. They found in Egypt, or in Syria, warehouſes filled with all the commodities of the Eaſt, imported by the Mahomedans;

SECT. III. homedans; and from the beſt accounts we have, with reſpect to the nature of their trade, they purchaſed them more frequently by barter, than with ready money. Egypt, the chief mart for Indian goods, though a moſt fertile country, is deſtitute of many things requiſite in an improved ſtate of ſociety, either for accommodation or for ornament. Too limited in extent, and too highly cultivated to afford ſpace for foreſts; too level to have mines of the uſeful metals; it muſt be ſupplied with timber for building, with iron, lead, tin, and braſs, by importation from other countries. The Egyptians, while under the dominion of the Mameluks, ſeem not themſelves to have traded in the ports of any Chriſtian ſtate, and it was principally from the Venetians that they received all the articles which I have enumerated. Beſides theſe, the ingenuity of the Venetian artiſts furniſhed a variety of manufactures of woollen cloths, ſilk ſtuffs of various fabric, camblets, mirrors, arms, ornaments of gold and ſilver, glaſs, and many other articles, for all which they found a ready market in Egypt and Syria. In return they received from the merchants of Alexandria, ſpices of every kind, drugs, gems, pearls, ivory, cotton and ſilk, unwrought as well as manufactured, in many different forms, and other productions of the Eaſt, together with ſeveral valuable articles of Egyptian growth or fabric. In Aleppo, Baruth, and other cities, beſides the proper commodities of India brought thither by land, they added to their cargoes the carpets of Perſia, the rich wrought ſilks of Damaſcus, ſtill known by a name taken from that city, and various productions of art and nature peculiar to Syria, Paleſtine, and Arabia. If, at any time, their demand for the productions of the Eaſt went

went beyond what they could procure in exchange for their own manufactures, that trade with the cities of the Hanseatic League, which I have mentioned, furnished them from the mines of Germany, with a regular supply of gold and silver, which they could carry, with advantage, to the markets of Egypt and Syria.

From a propensity, remarkable in all commercial states, to subject the operations of trade to political regulation and restraint, the authority of the Venetian government seems to have been interposed, both in directing the importation of Asiatic goods, and in the mode of circulating them among the different nations of Europe. To every considerable staple in the Mediterranean a certain number of large vessels, known by the name of *Galeons* or *Caracks*, was fitted out on the public account, and returned loaded with the richest merchandise [t], the profit arising from the sale of which must have been no slender addition to the revenue of the republic. Citizens, however, of every class, particularly persons of noble families, were encouraged to engage in foreign trade, and whoever employed a vessel of a certain burden for this purpose, received a considerable bounty from the state [u]. It was in the same manner, partly in ships belonging to the public, and partly in those of private traders, that the Venetians circulated through Europe the goods imported from

[t] Sabellicus, Hist. Rer. Venet. Dec. iv. lib. iii. p. 868. Denina Revol. d'Italie, tom. vi. 340.

[u] Sandi Stor. Civ. Venez. lib. viii. 891.

the

SECT. III. the Eaſt, as well as the produce of their own dominions and manufactures.

THERE are two different ways by which we may come at ſome knowledge of the magnitude of thoſe branches of commerce carried on by the Venetians. The one, by attending to the great variety and high value of the commodities which they imported into Bruges, the ſtore-houſe from which the other nations of Europe were ſupplied. A full enumeration of theſe is given by a well-informed author, in which is contained almoſt every article deemed, in that age, eſſential to accommodation or to elegance [x]. The other, by conſidering the effects of the Venetian trade upon the cities admitted to a participation of its advantages. Never did wealth appear more conſpicuouſly in the train of commerce. The citizens of Bruges, enriched by it, diſplayed in their dreſs, their buildings, and mode of living, ſuch magnificence as even to mortify the pride and excite the envy of royalty [y]. Antwerp, when the ſtaple was removed thither, ſoon rivalled Bruges in opulence and ſplendour. In ſome cities of Germany, particularly in Augſburg, the great mart for Indian commodities in the interior parts of that extenſive country, we meet with early examples of ſuch large fortunes accumulated by mercantile induſtry, as raiſed the proprietors of them to high rank and conſideration in the empire.

[x] Lud. Guicciardini Deſcript. de Paeſi Baſſi, p. 173.

[y] See NOTE XLVII.

SECT. III.

FROM obſerving this remarkable increaſe of opulence in all the places where the Venetians had an eſtabliſhed trade, we are led to conclude, that the profit accruing to themſelves from the different branches of it, eſpecially that with the Eaſt, muſt have been ſtill more conſiderable. It is impoſſible, however, without information much more minute than that to which we have acceſs, to form an eſtimate of this with accuracy; but various circumſtances may be produced to eſtabliſh, in general, the juſtneſs of this concluſion. From the firſt revival of a commercial ſpirit in Europe, the Venetians poſſeſſed a large ſhare of the trade with the Eaſt. It continued gradually to increaſe, and during a great part of the fifteenth century, they had nearly a monopoly of it. This was productive of conſequences attending all monopolies. Wherever there is no competition, and the merchant has it in his power to regulate the market, and to fix the price of the commodities which he vends, his gains will be exorbitant. Some idea of their magnitude, during ſeveral centuries, may be formed, by attending to the rate of the premium or intereſt then paid for the uſe of money. This is undoubtedly the moſt exact ſtandard by which to meaſure the profit ariſing from the capital ſtock employed in commerce; for, according as the intereſt of money is high or low, the gain acquired by the uſe of it muſt vary, and become exceſſive or moderate. From the cloſe of the eleventh century to the commencement of the ſixteenth, the period during which the Italians made their chief commercial exertions, the rate of intereſt was extremely high. It was uſually twenty per cent. ſometimes above that; and ſo late as the year one thouſand five hundred, it had not ſunk below

S ten

SECT. III.

ten or twelve per cent. in any part of Europe [z]. If the profits of a trade ſo extenſive as that of the Venetians correſponded to this high value of money, it could not fail of proving a ſource of great wealth, both public and private [a]. The condition of Venice, accordingly, during the period under review, is deſcribed by writers of that age, in terms which are not applicable to that of any other country in Europe. The revenues of the republic, as well as the wealth amaſſed by individuals, exceeded whatever was elſewhere known. In the magnificence of their houſes, in richneſs of furniture, in profuſion of plate, and in every thing which contributed either towards elegance or parade in their mode of living, the nobles of Venice ſurpaſſed the ſtate of the greateſt monarch beyond the Alps. Nor was all this diſplay the effect of an oſtentatious and inconſiderate diſſipation, it was the natural conſequence of ſucceſsful induſtry, which, having accumulated wealth with eaſe, is entitled to enjoy it in ſplendour [b].

NEVER did the Venetians believe the power of their country to be more firmly eſtabliſhed, or rely with greater confidence on the continuance and increaſe of its opulence, than towards the cloſe of the fifteenth century, when two events (which they could neither foreſee nor prevent) happened, that proved fatal to both. The one was the diſcovery of America. The other was the opening a direct courſe of navigation to the Eaſt Indies, by the Cape of Good Hope. Of all occurrences in

[z] Hiſt. of Charles V. vol. i. p. 401, &c.

[a] See NOTE XLVIII. [b] See NOTE XLIX.

5 the

SECT. III.

the hiſtory of the human race, theſe are undoubtedly among the moſt intereſting; and as they occaſioned a remarkable change of intercourſe among the different quarters of the globe, and finally eſtabliſhed thoſe commercial ideas and arrangements which conſtitute the chief diſtinction between the manners and policy of ancient and of modern times, an account of them is intimately connected with the ſubject of this Diſquiſition, and will bring it to that period which I have fixed upon for its boundary. But as I have related the riſe and progreſs of theſe diſcoveries at great length in another work [c], a rapid view of them is all that is requiſite in this place.

THE admiration or envy with which the other nations of Europe beheld the power and wealth of Venice, led them naturally to enquire into the cauſes of this pre-eminence; and among theſe, its lucrative commerce with the Eaſt appeared to be by far the moſt conſiderable. Mortified with being excluded from a ſource of opulence, which to the Venetians had proved ſo abundant, different countries had attempted to acquire a ſhare of the Indian trade. Some of the Italian ſtates (as I have formerly hinted) endeavoured to obtain admiſſion into the ports of Egypt and Syria, upon the ſame terms with the Venetians; but either by the ſuperior intereſt of the Venetians in the court of the Soldans, their negociations for that purpoſe were rendered unſucceſsful; or from the manifold advantages which merchants, long in poſſeſſion of any branch of trade, have in a competition with new adventurers,

[c] Hiſt. of America, Books I. and II.

SECT. III. all their exertions did not produce effects of any consequence[d]. In other countries, various schemes were formed with the same view. As early as the year one thousand four hundred and eighty, the inventive and enterprising genius of Columbus conceived the idea of opening a shorter and more certain communication with India, by holding a direct westerly course towards those regions, which, according to Marco Polo and other travellers, extended eastward far beyond the utmost limits of Asia known to the Greeks or Romans. This scheme, supported by arguments deduced from a scientific acquaintance with cosmography, from his own practical knowledge of navigation, from the reports of skilful pilots, and from the theories and conjectures of the ancients, he proposed first to the Genoese his countrymen, and next to the king of Portugal, into whose service he had entered. It was rejected by the former from ignorance, and by the latter with circumstances most humiliating to a generous mind. By perseverance, however, and address, he at length induced the most wary and least adventurous court in Europe to undertake the execution of his plan; and Spain, as the reward of this deviation from its usual cautious maxims, had the glory of discovering a new world, hardly inferior in magnitude to a third part of the habitable globe. Astonishing as the success of Columbus was, it did not fully accomplish his own wishes, or conduct him to those regions of the East, the expectation of reaching which was the original object of his voyage. The effects, however, of his discoveries were great and extensive. By giving Spain

[d] See NOTE L.

the

the poſſeſſion of immenſe territories, abounding in rich mines, and many valuable productions of nature, ſeveral of which had hitherto been deemed peculiar to India, wealth began to flow ſo copiouſly into that kingdom, and thence was ſo diffuſed over Europe, as gradually awakened a general ſpirit of induſtry, and called forth exertions, which alone muſt have ſoon turned the courſe of commerce into new channels.

But this was accompliſhed more ſpeedily, as well as more completely, by the other great event which I mentioned, the diſcovery of a new route of navigation to the Eaſt by the Cape of Good Hope. When the Portugueſe, to whom mankind are indebted for opening this communication between the moſt remote parts of the habitable globe, undertook their firſt voyage of diſcovery, it is probable that they had nothing farther in view than to explore thoſe parts of the coaſt of Africa which lay neareſt to their own country. But a ſpirit of enterpriſe, when rouſed and put in motion, is always progreſſive; and that of the Portugueſe, though ſlow and timid in its firſt operations, gradually acquired vigour, and prompted them to advance along the weſtern ſhore of the African continent, far beyond the utmoſt boundary of ancient navigation in that direction. Encouraged by ſucceſs, it became more adventurous, deſpiſed dangers which formerly appalled it, and ſurmounted difficulties which it once deemed inſuperable. When the Portugueſe found in the torrid zone, which the ancients had pronounced to be uninhabitable, fertile countries, occupied by numerous nations; and perceived that the continent of Africa, inſtead of extending in breadth towards the Weſt, according to the

SECT. III. the opinion of Ptolemy, appeared to contract itſelf, and to bend Eaſtwards, more extenſive proſpects opened to their view, and inſpired them with hopes of reaching India, by continuing to hold the ſame courſe which they had ſo long purſued.

After ſeveral unſucceſsful attempts to accompliſh what they had in view, a ſmall ſquadron ſailed from the Tagus, under the command of Vaſco de Gama, an officer of rank, whoſe abilities and courage fitted him to conduct the moſt difficult and arduous enterpriſes. From unacquaintance, however, with the proper ſeaſon and route of navigation in that vaſt ocean through which he had to ſteer his courſe, his voyage was long and dangerous. At length he doubled that promontory, which, for ſeveral years, had been the object of terror and of hope to his countrymen. From that, after a proſperous navigation along the ſouth-eaſt of Africa, he arrived at the city of Melinda, and had the ſatisfaction of diſcovering there, as well as at other places where he touched, people of a race very different from the rude inhabitants of the Weſtern ſhore of that continent, which alone the Portugueſe had hitherto viſited. Theſe he found to be ſo far advanced in civilization, and acquaintance with the various arts of life, that they carried on an active commerce, not only with the nations on their own coaſt, but with remote countries of Aſia. Conducted by their pilots, who held a courſe (with which experience had rendered them well acquainted) he ſailed acroſs the Indian ocean, and landed at Calecut, on the coaſt of Malabar, on the twenty-ſecond of May, one thouſand four hundred and ninety-eight, ten months and two days after his departure from the port of Liſbon.

The

SECT. III.

The Samorin, or Monarch of the country, aſtoniſhed at this unexpected viſit of an unknown people, whoſe aſpect, and arms, and manners, bore no reſemblance to any of the nations accuſtomed to frequent his harbours, and who arrived in his dominions by a route hitherto deemed impracticable, received them, at firſt, with that fond admiration which is often excited by novelty. But in a ſhort time, as if he had been inſpired with foreſight of all the calamities now approaching India by this fatal communication opened with the inhabitants of Europe, he formed various ſchemes to cut off Gama and his followers. But from every danger to which he was expoſed, either by the open attacks or ſecret machination of the Indians, the Portuguese Admiral extricated himſelf with ſingular prudence and intrepidity, and at laſt ſailed from Calecut with his ſhips loaded, not only with the commodities peculiar to that coaſt, but with many of the rich productions of the Eaſtern parts of India.

On his return to Liſbon, he was received with the admiration and gratitude due to a man, who, by his ſuperior abilities and reſolution, had conducted to ſuch an happy iſſue an undertaking of the greateſt importance, which had long occupied the thoughts of his Sovereign, and excited the hopes of his fellow-ſubjects [e]. Nor did this event intereſt the Portugueſe alone. No nation in Europe beheld it with unconcern. For although the diſcovery of a new world, whether we view it as a diſplay of genius in the perſon who firſt conceived an idea of that undertaking which led mankind to the knowledge of it, whether

[e] Aſia de João de Barros, dec. i. lib. iv. c. 11. Caſtagneda, Hiſt. de l'Inde trad. en Francois, liv. i. c. 2—28.

we

SECT. III. we contemplate its influence upon ſcience by giving a more complete knowledge of the globe which we inhabit, or whether we conſider its effects upon the commercial intercourſe of mankind, be an event far more ſplendid than the voyage of Gama, yet the latter ſeems originally to have excited more general attention. The former, indeed, filled the minds of men with aſtoniſhment; it was ſome time, however, before they attained ſuch a ſufficient knowledge of that portion of the earth now laid open to their view, as to form any juſt idea, or even probable conjecture, with reſpect to what might be the conſequences of communication with it. But the immenſe value of the Indian trade, which both in ancient and in modern times had enriched every nation by which it was carried on, was a ſubject familiar to the thoughts of all intelligent men, and they at once perceived that the diſcovery of this new route of navigation to the Eaſt, muſt occaſion great revolutions, not only in the courſe of commerce, but in the political ſtate of Europe.

WHAT theſe revolutions were moſt likely to be, and how they would operate, were points examined with particular attention in the cities of Liſbon and of Venice, but with feelings very different. The Portugueſe, founding upon the rights to which, in that age, priority of diſcovery, confirmed by a papal grant, were ſuppoſed to confer, deeming themſelves intitled to an excluſive commerce with the countries which they had firſt viſited, began to enjoy, by anticipation, all the benefits of it, and to fancy that their capital would ſoon be what Venice then was, the great ſtore-houſe of Eaſtern commodities to all Europe, and the ſeat of opulence and power. On the firſt

6 intelligence

intelligence of Gama's ſucceſsful voyage, the Venetians, with the quick-ſighted diſcernment of merchants, foreſaw the immediate conſequence of it to be the ruin of that lucrative branch of commerce which had contributed ſo greatly to enrich and aggrandize their country; and they obſerved this with more poignant concern, as they were apprehenſive that they did not poſſeſs any effectual means of preventing, or even retarding, its operation.

THE hopes and fears of both were well founded. The Portugueſe entered upon the new career opened to them with activity and ardour, and made exertions, both commercial and military, far beyond what could have been expected from a kingdom of ſuch inconſiderable extent. All theſe were directed by an intelligent monarch, capable of forming plans of the greateſt magnitude with calm ſyſtematic wiſdom, and of proſecuting them with unremitting perſeverance. The prudence and vigour of his meaſures, however, would have availed little without proper inſtruments to carry them into execution. Happily for Portugal, the diſcerning eye of Emanuel ſelected a ſucceſſion of officers to take the ſupreme command in India, who, by their enterprizing valour, military ſkill, and political ſagacity, accompanied with diſintereſted integrity, public ſpirit, and love of their country, have a title to be ranked with the perſons moſt eminent for virtue and abilities in any age or nation. Greater things perhaps were atchieved by them, than were ever accompliſhed in ſo ſhort a time. Before the cloſe of Emanuel's reign, twenty-four years only after the voyage of Gama, the Portugueſe had rendered themſelves maſters of the city of Malacca, in which the great ſtaple of trade carried on

T among

SECT. III. among the inhabitants of all those regions in Asia, which Europeans have distinguished by the general name of the East-Indies, was then established. To this port, situated nearly at an equal distance from the Eastern and Western extremities of these countries, and possessing the command of that strait, by which they keep communication with each other, the merchants of China, of Japan, of every kingdom on the continent, of the Moluccas and all the islands in the Archipelago, resorted from the East; and those of Malabar, of Ceylon, of Coromandel, and of Bengal, from the West[f]. This conquest secured to the Portuguese great influence over the interior commerce of India, while, at the same time, by their settlements at Goa and Diu, they were enabled to engross the trade of the Malabar coast, and to obstruct greatly the long established intercourse of Egypt with India by the Red Sea. Their ships frequented every port in the East where valuable commodities were to be found, from the Cape of Good Hope to the river of Canton; and along this immense stretch of coast, extending upwards of four thousand leagues[g], they had established, for the conveniency or protection of trade, a chain of forts or factories. They had likewise taken possession of stations most favourable to commerce along the Southern coast of Africa, and in many of the islands which lie between Madagascar and the Moluccas. In every part of the East they were received with respect, in many they had acquired the absolute command. They carried on trade there without

[f] Decad. de Barros, dec. i. liv. viii. c. i. Osor. de reb. Eman. lib. vii. 213, &c.

[g] Hist. Gener. des Voyages, tom. i. p. 140.

5 rival

rival or controul; they prescribed to the natives the terms of their mutual intercourse; they often set what price they pleased on the goods which they purchased; and were thus enabled to import from Indostan and the regions beyond it, whatever is useful, rare, or agreeable, in greater abundance, and of more various kinds, than had been known formerly in Europe.

Not satisfied with this ascendant which they had acquired in India, the Portuguese early formed a scheme, no less bold than interested, of excluding all other nations from participating of the advantages of commerce with the East. In order to effect this, it was necessary to obtain possession of such stations in the Arabian and Persian Gulfs, as might render them masters of the navigation of these two inland seas, and enable them both to obstruct the ancient commercial intercourse between Egypt and India, and to command the entrance of the great rivers, which facilitated the conveyance of Indian goods, not only through the interior provinces of Asia, but as far as Constantinople. The conduct of the measures for this purpose was committed to Alphonso Albuquerque, the most eminent of all the Portuguese generals who distinguished themselves in India. After the utmost efforts of genius and valour, he was able to accomplish one-half only of what the ambition of his countrymen had planned. By wresting the island of Ormus, which commanded the mouth of the Persian Gulf, from the petty princes, who, as tributaries to the monarchs of Persia, had established their dominion there, he secured to Portugal that extensive trade with the East, which (as I have formerly described) the Persians had carried on for

T 2 several

SECT. III. ſeveral centuries. In the hands of the Portugueſe, Ormuz ſoon became the great mart from which the Perſian empire, and all the provinces of Aſia to the weſt of it, were ſupplied with the productions of India; and a city which they built on that barren iſland, deſtitute of water, was rendered one of the chief ſeats of opulence, ſplendour, and luxury in the Eaſtern world [h].

THE operations of Albuquerque in the Red Sea were far from being attended with equal ſucceſs. Partly by the vigorous reſiſtance of the Arabian princes, whoſe ports he attacked, and partly by the damage his fleet ſuſtained in a ſea of which the navigation is remarkably difficult and dangerous, he was conſtrained to retire, without effecting any ſettlement of importance [i]. The ancient channel of intercourſe with India by the Red Sea ſtill continued open to the Egyptians; but their commercial tranſactions in that country were greatly circumſcribed and obſtructed, by the influence which the Portugueſe had acquired in every port to which they were accuſtomed to reſort.

IN conſequence of this, the Venetians ſoon began to feel that decreaſe of their own Indian trade which they had foreſeen and dreaded. In order to prevent the farther progreſs of this evil, they perſuaded the Soldan of the Mameluks, equally

[h] Oſorius de reb. geſtis Eman. lib. x. p. 274, &c. Tavernier's Travels, Book v. c. 23.

[i] Oſorius, lib. ix. p. 248, &c.

alarmed

SECT. III.

alarmed with themselves at the rapid success of the Portuguese in the East, and no less interested to hinder them from engrossing that commerce, which had so long been the chief source of opulence both to the monarchs and to the people of Egypt, to enter into a negociation with the Pope and the King of Portugal. The tone which the Soldan assumed in this negociation was such as became the fierce chief of a military government. After stating his exclusive right to the trade with India, he forewarned Julius II. and Emanuel, that, if the Portuguese did not relinquish that new course of navigation by which they had penetrated into the Indian ocean, and cease from encroaching on that commerce, which from time immemorial had been carried on between the East of Asia and his dominions, he would put to death all the christians in Egypt, Syria, and Palestine, burn their churches, and demolish the holy sepulchre itself [k]. This formidable threat, which, a few centuries before this period, would have made all Christendom tremble, seems to have made so little impression, that the Venetians, as the last expedient, had recourse to a measure, which, in that age, was deemed not only reprehensible, but impious. They incited the Soldan to fit out a fleet in the Red Sea, and to attack those unexpected invaders of a gainful monopoly, of which he and his predecessors had long enjoyed undisturbed possession. As Egypt did not produce timber proper for building ships of force, the Venetians permitted the Soldan to cut it in their forests of Dalmatia, whence it was conveyed to Alexandria, and

[k] Osorius de rebus Eman. lib. iv. p. 110. edit. 1580. Asia de Barros, decad. i. lib. viii. c. 2.

then

SECT. III. then carried, partly by water and partly by land, to Suez. There twelve ſhips of war were built, on board of which a body of Mameluks was ordered to ſerve, under the command of an officer of merit. Theſe new enemies, far more formidable than the natives of India with whom the Portugueſe had hitherto contended, they encountered, with undaunted courage, and after ſome ſevere conflicts, they entirely ruined the ſquadron, and remained maſters of the Indian ocean [l].

Soon after this diſaſter, the dominion of the Mameluks was overturned, and Egypt, Syria, and Paleſtine were ſubjected to the Turkiſh empire by the victorious arms of Selim I. Their mutual intereſt quickly induced the Turks and Venetians to forget ancient animoſities, and to co-operate towards the ruin of the Portugueſe trade in India. With this view Selim confirmed to the Venetians the extenſive commercial privileges which they had enjoyed under the government of the Mameluks, and publiſhed an edict permitting the free entry of all the productions of the Eaſt, imported directly from Alexandria, into every part of his dominions, and impoſing heavy duties upon ſuch as were brought from Liſbon [m].

But all theſe were unavailing efforts againſt the ſuperior advantages which the Portugueſe poſſeſſed, in ſupplying Europe with the commodities of the Eaſt, in conſequence

[l] Aſia de Barros, dec. ii. lib. ii. c. 6. Lafitau, Hiſt. de Decouvertes des Portugais, i. 292, &c. Oſor. lib. iv. p. 120.

[m] Sandi Stor. Civ. Venez. part ii. 901. part iii. 432.

of

of having opened a new mode of communication with it. At the ſame time, the Venetians, brought to the brink of ruin by the fatal league of Cambray, which broke the power and humbled the pride of the republic, were incapable of ſuch efforts for the preſervation of their commerce, as they might have made in the more vigorous age of their government, and were reduced to the feeble expedients of a declining ſtate. Of this there is a remarkable inſtance in an offer made by them to the King of Portugal in the year one thouſand five hundred and twenty-one, to purchaſe, at a ſtipulated price, all the ſpices imported into Liſbon, over and above what might be requiſite for the conſumption of his own ſubjects. If Emanuel had been ſo inconſiderate as to cloſe with this propoſal, Venice would have recovered all the benefit of the gainful monopoly which ſhe had loſt. But the offer met with the reception that it merited, and was rejected without heſitation [n].

THE Portugueſe, almoſt without obſtruction, continued their progreſs in the Eaſt, until they eſtabliſhed there a commercial empire; to which, whether we conſider its extent, its opulence, the ſlender power by which it was formed, or the ſplendour with which the government of it was conducted, there had hitherto been nothing comparable in the hiſtory of nations. Emanuel, who laid the foundation of this ſtupendous fabric, had the ſatisfaction to ſee it almoſt completed. Every part of Europe was ſupplied by the Portugueſe with the productions of the Eaſt; and if we except ſome inconſiderable

[n] Oſor. de reb. Eman. lib. xii. 265.

quantity

SECT. III. quantity of them, which the Venetians ſtill continued to receive by the ancient channels of conveyance, our quarter of the globe had no longer any commercial intercourſe with India, and the regions of Aſia beyond it, but by the Cape of Good Hope.

THOUGH from this period the people of Europe have continued to carry on their trade with India by ſea, yet a conſiderable portion of the valuable productions of the Eaſt is ſtill conveyed to other regions of the earth by land-carriage. In tracing the progreſs of trade with India, this branch of it is an object of conſiderable magnitude, which has not been examined with ſufficient attention. That the ancients ſhould have had recourſe frequently to the tedious and expenſive mode of tranſporting goods by land, will not appear ſurpriſing, when we recollect the imperfect ſtate of navigation among them: The reaſon of this mode of conveyance being not only continued, but increaſed, in modern times, demands ſome explanation.

IF we inſpect a map of Aſia, we cannot fail to obſerve, that the communication throughout all the countries of that great continent to the weſt of Indoſtan and China, though opened in ſome degree towards the ſouth by the navigable rivers Euphrates and Tigris, and towards the north by two inland ſeas, the Euxine and Caſpian, muſt be carried on in many extenſive provinces wholly by land. This, as I have obſerved, was the firſt mode of intercourſe between different countries, and during the infancy of navigation it was the

2 only

only one. Even after that art had attained ſome degree of improvement, the conveyance of goods by the two rivers which I have mentioned, extended ſo little way into the interior country, and the trade of the Euxine and Caſpian ſeas was ſo often obſtructed by the barbarous nations ſcattered along their ſhores, that, partly on that account, and partly from the adherence of mankind to ancient habits, the commerce of the various provinces of Aſia, particularly that with India and the regions beyond it, continued to be conducted by land. SECT. III.

THE ſame circumſtances which induced the inhabitants of Aſia to carry on ſuch a conſiderable part of their commerce with each other in this manner, operated with ſtill more powerful effect in Africa. That vaſt continent, which little reſembles the other diviſions of the earth, is not penetrated by inland ſeas, like Europe and Aſia, or by a chain of lakes, like North America, or opened by rivers (the Nile alone excepted) of extended navigation. It forms one uniform, continuous ſurface, between the various parts of which there could be no intercourſe, from the earlieſt times, but by land. Rude as all the people of Africa are, and ſlender as the progreſs is which they have made in the arts of life, ſuch a communication appears to have been always kept up. How far it extended in the more early periods to which I have directed my reſearches, and by what different routes it was carried on, I have not ſufficient information to determine with accuracy. It is highly probable that, from time immemorial, the gold, the ivory, the perfumes, both of the ſouthern parts of Africa, and of its more northern

U diſtricts,

SECT. III. diſtricts, were conveyed either to the Arabian Gulf, or to Egypt, and exchanged for the ſpices and other productions of the Eaſt.

The Mahomedan religion, which ſpread with amazing rapidity over all Aſia and a conſiderable part of Africa, contributed greatly towards the increaſe of commercial intercourſe by land in both theſe quarters of the globe, and has given it additional vigour, by mingling with it a new principle of activity, and by directing it to a common centre. Mahomet enjoined all his followers to viſit once in their life-time, the Caaba or ſquare building in the temple of Mecca, the immemorial object of veneration among his countrymen; and, according to their tradition, the firſt ſpot on this earth which was conſecrated to the worſhip of God: In order to preſerve continually upon their minds a ſenſe of their obligation to perform this duty, he directed that, in all the multiplied acts of devotion which his religion preſcribes, true believers ſhould always turn their faces towards that holy place [o]. In obedience to a precept ſolemnly enjoined and ſedulouſly inculcated, numerous caravans of pilgrims aſſemble annually in every country where the Mahomedan faith is eſtabliſhed. From the ſhores of the Atlantic on one hand, and from the moſt remote regions of the Eaſt on the other, the votaries of the Prophet advance to Mecca. Commercial ideas and objects mingle with thoſe of devotion. The numerous camels [p] of each caravan are loaded with thoſe

[o] Herbelot Biblioth. Orient. artic. *Caaba* & *Keblah*.

[p] See NOTE LI.

9 com-

commodities of every country which are of eaſieſt carriage and moſt ready ſale. The holy city is crowded, not only with zealous devotees, but with opulent merchants. During the few days they remain there, the fair of Mecca is the greateſt, perhaps, on the face of the earth. Mercantile tranſactions are carried on in it to an immenſe value, of which the diſpatch, the ſilence, the mutual confidence and good faith in conducting them, are the moſt unequivocal proof. The productions and manufactures of India form a capital article in this great traffic, and the caravans, on their return, diſſeminate them through every part of Aſia and Africa. Some of theſe are deemed neceſſary, not only to the comfort, but to the preſervation of life, and others contribute to its elegance and pleaſure. They are ſo various as to ſuit the taſte of mankind in every climate, and in different ſtages of improvement; and are in high requeſt among the rude natives of Africa, as well as the more luxurious inhabitants of Aſia. In order to ſupply their ſeveral demands, the caravans return loaded with the muſlins and chintzes of Bengal and the Deccan, the ſhawls of Cachemire, the pepper of Malabar, the diamonds of Golconda, the pearls of Kilkare, the cinnamon of Ceylon, the nutmeg cloves and mace of the Moluccas, and an immenſe number of other Indian commodities.

Beside theſe great caravans, formed partly by reſpect for a religious precept, and partly with a view to extend a lucrative branch of commerce, there are other caravans, and theſe not inconſiderable, compoſed entirely of merchants, who have no object but trade. Theſe, at ſtated ſeaſons, ſet out from different parts

SECT. III. of the Turkish and Persian dominions, and proceeding to Indostan, and even to China, by routes which were anciently known, they convey by land-carriage the most valuable commodities of these countries to the remote provinces of both empires. It is only by considering the distance to which large quantities of these commodities are carried, and frequently across extensive deserts, which, without the aid of camels, would have been impassable, that we can form any idea of the magnitude of the trade with India by land, and are led to perceive, that in a Disquisition concerning the various modes of conducting this commerce, it is well entitled to the attention which I have bestowed in endeavouring to trace it [q].

[q] See NOTE LII.

AN

HISTORICAL DISQUISITION

CONCERNING

ANCIENT INDIA.

SECTION IV.

General Obſervations.

THUS I have endeavoured to deſcribe the progreſs of trade with India, both by ſea and by land, from the earlieſt times in which hiſtory affords any authentic information concerning it, until an entire revolution was made in its nature, and the mode of carrying it on, by that great diſcovery which I originally fixed as the utmoſt boundary of my inquiries. Here, then, this Diſquiſition might have been terminated. But as I have conducted my readers to that period when a new order of ideas, and SECT. IV.

7 new

SECT. IV. new arrangements of policy began to be introduced into Europe, in consequence of the value and importance of commerce being so thoroughly understood, that in almost every country the encouragement of it became a chief object of public attention; as we have now reached that point whence a line may be drawn which marks the chief distinction between the manners and political institutions of ancient and modern times, it will render the work more instructive and useful, to conclude it with some general observations, which naturally arise from a survey of both, and a comparison of the one with the other. These observations, I trust, will be found, not only to have an intimate connection with the subject of my researches, and to throw additional light upon it; but will serve to illustrate many particulars in the general history of commerce, and to point out effects or consequences of various events, which have not been generally observed, or considered with that attention which they merited.

I. After viewing the great and extensive effects of finding a new course of navigation to India by the Cape of Good Hope, it may appear surprising to a modern observer, that a discovery of such importance was not made, or even attempted, by any of the commercial states of the ancient world. But in judging with respect to the conduct of nations in remote times, we never err more widely, than when we decide with regard to it, not according to the ideas and views of their age, but of our own. This is not, perhaps, more conspicuous in any instance, than in that under consideration. It was by the Tyrians, and by the Greeks, who were masters of Egypt, that the

the different people of Europe were firſt ſupplied with the productions of the Eaſt. From the account that has been given of the manner in which they procured theſe, it is manifeſt that they had neither the ſame inducements with modern nations to wiſh for any new communication with India, nor the ſame means of accompliſhing it. All the commercial tranſactions of the ancients with the Eaſt were confined to the ports on the Malabar coaſt, or extended at fartheſt to the iſland of Ceylon. To theſe ſtaples, the natives of all the different regions in the eaſtern parts of Aſia brought the commodities which were the growth of their ſeveral countries, or the product of their ingenuity, in their own veſſels, and with them the ſhips from Tyre and from Egypt completed their inveſtments. While the operations of their Indian trade were carried on within a ſphere ſo circumſcribed, the conveyance of a cargo by the Arabian Gulf, notwithſtanding the expence of land-carriage, either from Elath to Rhinocclura, or acroſs the deſart to the Nile, was ſo ſafe and commodious, that the merchants of Tyre and Alexandria had little reaſon to be ſolicitous for the diſcovery of any other. The ſituation of both theſe cities, as well as that of the other conſiderable commercial ſtates of antiquity, was very different from that of the countries to which, in later times, mankind have been indebted for keeping up intercourſe with the remote parts of the globe. Portugal, Spain, England, Holland, which have been moſt active and ſucceſsful in this line of enterpriſe, all lie on the Atlantic ocean, (in which every European voyage of diſcovery muſt commence,) or have immediate acceſs to it. But Tyre was ſituated at the eaſtern extremity of the Mediterranean, Alexandria

SECT. IV. Alexandria not far from it; Rhodes, Athens, Corinth, which came afterwards to be ranked among the most active trading cities of antiquity, lay considerably advanced towards the same quarter in that sea. The commerce of all these states was long confined within the precincts of the Mediterranean; and in some of them never extended beyond it. The pillars of Hercules, or the Straits of Gibraltar, were long considered as the utmost boundary of navigation. To reach this was deemed a signal proof of naval skill; and before any of these states could give a beginning to an attempt towards exploring the vast unknown ocean which lay beyond it, they had to accomplish a voyage (according to their ideas) of great extent and much danger. This was sufficient to deter them from engaging in an arduous undertaking, from which, even if attended with success, their situation prevented their entertaining hopes of deriving great advantage [a].

BUT could we suppose the discovery of a new passage to India to have become an object of desire or pursuit to any of these states, their science as well as practice of navigation was so defective, that it would have been hardly possible for them to attain it. The vessels which the ancients employed in trade were so small, as not to afford stowage for provisions sufficient to subsist a crew during a long voyage. Their construction was such that they could seldom venture to depart far from land, and their mode of steering along the coast (which I have been obliged to mention often) so circuitous and slow, that from these as well as from other

[a] See NOTE LIII.

circum-

circumſtances which I might have ſpecified [b], we may pronounce a voyage from the Mediterranean to India by the Cape of Good Hope, to have been an undertaking beyond their power to accompliſh, in ſuch a manner as to render it, in any degree, ſubſervient to commerce. To this deciſion, the account preſerved by Herodotus, of a voyage performed by ſome Phenician ſhips employed by a king of Egypt, which, taking their departure from the Arabian Gulf, doubled the Southern promontory of Africa, and arrived, at the end of three years, by the Straits of Gades, or Gibraltar, at the mouth of the Nile [c], can hardly be conſidered as repugnant; for ſeveral writers of the greateſt eminence among the ancients, and moſt diſtinguiſhed for their proficiency in the knowlege of geography, regarded this account rather as an amuſing tale, than the hiſtory of a real tranſaction; and either entertained doubts concerning the poſſibility of ſailing round Africa, or abſolutely denied it [d]. But if what Herodotus relates concerning the courſe held by theſe Phenician ſhips had ever been received by the ancients with general aſſent, we can hardly ſuppoſe, that any ſtate could have been ſo wildly adventurous, as to imagine that a voyage, which it required three years to complete, could be undertaken with a proſpect of commercial benefit.

II. THE rapid progreſs of the moderns in exploring India, as well as the extenſive power and valuable ſettlements which

[b] Goguet Orig. des Loix des Arts, &c. ii. 303, 329.

[c] Lib. iv. c. 42.

[d] Polyb. lib. iii. p. 193. edit. Caſaub. Plin. Nat. Hiſt. lib. ii. c. 6. Ptol. Geogr. lib. iv. c. 9. See NOTE LIV.

X they

SECT. IV.

they early acquired there, mark ſuch a diſtinction between their mode of conducting naval operations, and that of the ancients, as merits to be conſidered and explained with attention. From the reign of the firſt Ptolemy, to the conqueſt of Egypt by the Mahomedans, Europe had been ſupplied with the productions of the Eaſt by the Greeks of Alexandria, by the Romans while they were maſters of Egypt, and by the ſubjects of the Emperors of Conſtantinople, when that kingdom became a province of their dominions. During this long period, extending almoſt to a thouſand years, none of thoſe people, the moſt enlightened, undoubtedly, in the ancient world, ever advanced by ſea farther towards the Eaſt than the Gulf of Siam, and had no regular eſtabliſhed trade but with the ports on the coaſt of Malabar, or thoſe in the iſland of Ceylon. They attempted no conqueſts in any part of India, they made no ſettlements, they erected no forts. Satisfied with an intercourſe merely commercial, they did not aim at acquiring any degree of power or dominion in the countries where they traded, though it ſeems to be probable that they might have eſtabliſhed it without much oppoſition from the natives, a gentle effeminate people, with whom, at that time, no foreign and more warlike race was mingled. But the enterprizing activity of the Portugueſe was not long confined within the ſame limits; a few years after their arrival at Calecut, they advanced towards the Eaſt, into regions unknown to the ancients. The kingdoms of Cambodia, Cochin China, Tonquin, the vaſt empire of China, and all the fertile iſlands in the great Indian Archipelago, from Sumatra to the Philippines, were diſcovered, and

2 the

the Portugueſe, though oppoſed in every quarter by the Mahomedans of Tartar or Arabian origin ſettled in many parts of India, enemies much more formidable than the natives, eſtabliſhed there that extenſive influence and dominion which I have formerly deſcribed.

Of this remarkable difference between the progreſs and operations of the ancients and moderns in India, the imperfect knowlege of the former, with reſpect both to the theory and practice of navigation, ſeems to have been the principal cauſe. From the coaſt of Malabar to the Philippines, was a voyage of an extent far beyond any that the ancients were accuſtomed to undertake, and, according to their manner of ſailing, muſt have required a great length of time to perform it. The nature of their trade with India was ſuch, that they had not (as I have already obſerved) the ſame inducements with the moderns, to proſecute diſcovery with ardour; and, according to the deſcription given of the veſſels in which the merchants of Alexandria carried on their trade from the Arabian Gulf, they appear to have been very unfit for that purpoſe. On all theſe accounts, the ancients remained ſatisfied with a ſlender knowlege of India; and influenced by reaſons proceeding from the ſame cauſe, they attempted neither conqueſt nor ſettlement there. In order to accompliſh either of theſe, they muſt have tranſported a conſiderable number of men from India. But, from the defective ſtructure of their ſhips, as well as from the imperfection of their art in

 navigating

SECT. IV.

navigating them, the ancients seldom ventured to convey a body of troops to any distance by sea. From Berenice to Musiris, was to them, even after Hippalus had discovered the method of steering a direct course, and when their naval skill had attained to its highest state of improvement, a voyage of no less than seventy days. By the ancient route along the coast of Persia, a voyage from the Arabian Gulf to any part of India must have been of greater length, and accomplished more slowly. As no hostile attack was ever made upon India by sea, either by the Greek monarchs of Egypt, though the two first of them were able and ambitious Princes, or by the most enterprizing of the Roman Emperors, it is evident that they must have deemed it an attempt beyond their power to execute. Alexander the Great, and, in imitation of him, his successors, the monarchs of Syria, were the only persons in the ancient world who formed an idea of establishing their dominion in any part of India; but it was with armies led thither by land, that they hoped to atchieve this.

III. The sudden effect of opening a direct communication with the East, in lowering the price of Indian commodities, is a circumstance that merits observation. How compendious soever the ancient intercourse with India may appear to have been, it was attended with considerable expence. The productions of the remote parts of Asia, brought to Ceylon, or the ports on the Malabar coast, by the natives, were put on board the ships which arrived from the Arabian Gulf. At Berenice they were landed, and carried by camels two hundred

hundred and fifty-eight miles to the banks of the Nile. There they were again embarked, and conveyed down the river to Alexandria, whence they were dispatched to different markets. The addition to the price of goods by such a multiplicity of operations must have been considerable, especially when the rate chargeable on each operation was fixed by monopolists, subject to no controul. But after the passage to India by the Cape of Good Hope was discovered, its various commodities were purchased at first hand in the countries of which they were the growth or manufacture. In all these, particularly in Indostan and in China, the subsistence of man is more abundant than in any other part of the earth. The people live chiefly upon rice, the most prolific of all grains. Population, of consequence, is so great, and labour so extremely cheap, that every production of nature or of art is sold at a very low price. When these were shipped in different parts of India, they were conveyed directly to Lisbon, by a navigation, long indeed, but uninterrupted and safe, and thence circulated through Europe. The carriage of mercantile goods by water is so much less expensive than by any other mode of conveyance, that as soon as the Portuguese could import the productions of India in sufficient quantities to supply the demands of Europe, they were able to afford them at such a reduced price, that the competition of the Venetians ceased almost entirely, and the full stream of commerce flowed in its natural direction towards the cheapest market. In what proportion the Portuguese lowered the price of Indian commodities, I cannot ascertain with precision, as I have not found in contemporary writers sufficient information with respect

SECT. IV.

to that point. Some idea, however, of this, approaching perhaps near to accuracy, may be formed, from the computations of Mr. Munn, an intelligent English merchant. He has published a table of the prices paid for various articles of goods in India, compared with the prices for which they were sold in Aleppo, from which the difference appears to be nearly as three to one; and he calculates, that, after a reasonable allowance for the expence of the voyage from India, the same goods may be sold in England at half the price which they bear in Aleppo. The expence of conveying the productions of India up the Persian Gulf to Bassora, and thence either through the Great or Little Desert to Aleppo, could not, I should imagine, differ considerably from that by the Red Sea to Alexandria. We may therefore suppose, that the Venetians might purchase them from the merchants of that city, at nearly the same rate for which they were sold in Aleppo; and when we add to this, what they must have charged as their own profit in all the markets which they frequented, it is evident that the Portuguese might afford to reduce the commodities of the East to a price below that which I have mentioned, and might supply every part of Europe with them more than one-half cheaper than formerly. The enterprizing schemes of the Portuguese monarchs were accomplished sooner, as well as more completely, than in the hour of most sanguine hope they could have presumed to expect; and early in the sixteenth century, their subjects became possessed of a monopoly of the trade with India, founded upon the only equitable title, that of furnishing its productions in greater abundance, and at a more moderate price.

IV. We

IV. We may obſerve, that in conſequence of a more plentiful ſupply of Indian goods, and at a cheaper rate, the demand for them increaſed rapidly in every part of Europe. To trace the progreſs of this in detail, would lead me far beyond the period which I have fixed as the limit of this Diſquiſition, but ſome general remarks concerning it will be found intimately connected with the ſubject of my inquiries. What were the chief articles of importation from India, while the Romans had the direction of the trade with that country, I have formerly mentioned. But upon the ſubverſion of their empire, and the ſettlement of the fierce warriors of Scythia and Germany in the various countries of Europe, the ſtate of ſociety, as well as the condition of individuals, became ſo extremely different, that the wants and deſires of men were no longer the ſame. Barbarians, many of them not far advanced in their progreſs beyond the rudeſt ſtate of ſocial life, had little reliſh for thoſe accommodations, and that elegance, which are ſo alluring to poliſhed nations. The curious manufactures of ſilk, the precious ſtones and pearls of the Eaſt, which had been the ornament and pride of the wealthy and luxurious citizens of Rome, were not objects of deſire to men, who, for a conſiderable time after they took poſſeſſion of their new conqueſts, retained the original ſimplicity of their paſtoral manners. They advanced, however, from rudeneſs to refinement in the uſual courſe of progreſſion which nations are deſtined to hold, and an increaſe of wants and deſires requiring new objects to gratify them, they began to acquire a reliſh for ſome of the luxuries of India. Among theſe they had a ſingular predilection for the ſpiceries and aromatics which

SECT. IV.

which that country yields in ſuch variety and abundance. Whence their peculiar fondneſs for theſe aroſe, it is not of importance to inquire. Whoever peruſes the writers of the middle ages, will find many particulars which confirm this obſervation. In every enumeration of Indian commodities which they give, ſpices are always mentioned as the moſt conſiderable and precious article [e]. In their cookery, all diſhes were highly ſeaſoned with them. In every entertainment of parade, a profuſion of them was deemed eſſential to magnificence. In every medical preſcription they were principal ingredients [f]. But conſiderable as the demand for ſpices had become, the mode in which the nations of Europe had hitherto been ſupplied with them was extremely diſadvantageous. The ſhips employed by the merchants of Alexandria never ventured to viſit thoſe remote regions which produce the moſt valuable ſpices, and before they could be circulated through Europe, they were loaded with the accumulated profits received by four or five different hands through which they had paſſed. But the Portugueſe, with a bolder ſpirit of navigation, having penetrated into every part of Aſia, took in their cargo of ſpices in the places where they grew, and could afford to diſpoſe of them at ſuch a price, that, from being an expenſive luxury, they became an article of ſuch general uſe, as greatly augmented the demand for them. An effect ſimilar to this may

[e] Jac. de Vitriac. Hiſt. Hieroſ. ap. Bongars, i. p. 1099. Wilh. Tyr. lib. xii. c. 23.

[f] Du Cange, Gloſſar. Verb. *Aromata, Species.* Henry's Hiſt. of G. Brit. vol. iv. p. 597, 598.

be

SECT. IV.

be obſerved, with reſpect to the demand for other commodities imported from India, upon the reduction of their price by the Portugueſe. From that period a growing taſte for Aſiatic luxuries may be traced in every country of Europe, and the number of ſhips fitted out for that trade at Liſbon, continued to increaſe every year[g].

V. Lucrative as the trade with India was, and had long been deemed, it is remarkable that the Portugueſe were ſuffered to remain in the undiſturbed and excluſive poſſeſſion of it, during the courſe of almoſt a century. In the ancient world, though Alexandria, from the peculiar felicity of its ſituation, could carry on an intercourſe with the Eaſt by ſea, and circulate its productions through Europe with ſuch advantage, as gave it a decided ſuperiority over every rival; yet various attempts (which I have deſcribed in their proper places) were made, from time to time, to obtain ſome ſhare in a commerce ſo apparently beneficial. From the growing activity of the commercial ſpirit in the ſixteenth century, as well as from the example of the eager ſolicitude with which the Venetians and Genoeſe exerted themſelves alternately to ſhut out each other from any ſhare in the Indian trade, it might have been expected that ſome competitor would have ariſen to call in queſtion the claim of the Portugueſe to an excluſive right of traffic with the Eaſt, and to wreſt from them ſome portion of it. There were, however, at that time, ſome peculiar circumſtances in the political ſtate of all thoſe nations in Europe,

[g] See NOTE LV.

Y whoſe

SECT. IV.

whofe intrufion, as rivals, the Portuguefe had any reafon to dread, which fecured to them the quiet enjoyment of their monopoly of Indian commerce, during fuch a long period. From the acceffion of Charles V. to the throne, Spain was either fo much occupied in a multiplicity of operations in which it was engaged by the ambition of that monarch, and of his fon Philip II. or fo intent on profecuting its own difcoveries and conquefts in the New World, that, although, by
A.D. 1521. the fuccefsful enterprize of Magellan, its fleets were unexpectedly conducted by a new courfe to that remote region of Afia which was the feat of the moft gainful and alluring branch of trade carried on by the Portuguefe, it could make no confiderable effort to avail itfelf of the commercial advantages which it might have derived from that event. By the acquifition of the crown of Portugal, in the year one thoufand five hundred and eighty, the kings of Spain, inftead of the rivals, became the protectors of the Portuguefe trade, and the guardians of all its extenfive rights. Throughout the fixteenth century, the ftrength and refources of France were fo much wafted by the fruitlefs expeditions of their monarchs into Italy, by their unequal conteft with the power and policy of Charles V. and by the calamities of the civil wars which defolated the kingdom upwards of forty years, that it could neither beftow much attention upon objects of commerce, nor engage in any fcheme of diftant enterprize. The Venetians, how fenfibly foever they might feel the mortifying reverfe of being excluded, almoft entirely, from the Indian trade, of which their capital had been formerly the chief feat, were fo debilitated and humbled by the League of Cambray, that they were no longer

capable

capable of engaging in any undertaking of magnitude. England, weakened (as I formerly obſerved) by the long conteſt between the houſes of York and Lancaſter, and juſt beginning to recover its proper vigour, was reſtrained from active exertion, during one part of the ſixteenth century, by the cautious maxims of Henry VII. and waſted its ſtrength, during another part of it, by engaging inconſiderately in the wars between the princes on the continent. The nation, though deſtined to acquire territories in India more extenſive and valuable than were ever poſſeſſed by any European power, had no ſuch preſentiment of its future eminence there, as to take an early part in the commerce or tranſactions of that country, and a great part of the century elapſed before it began to turn its attention towards the Eaſt.

While the moſt conſiderable nations in Europe found it neceſſary, from the circumſtances which I have mentioned, to remain inactive ſpectators of what paſſed in the Eaſt, the Seven United Provinces of the Low Countries, recently formed into a ſmall ſtate, ſtill ſtruggling for political exiſtence, and yet in the infancy of its power, ventured to appear in the Indian ocean as the rivals of the Portugueſe; and, deſpiſing their pretenſions to an excluſive right of commerce with the extenſive countries to the eaſtward of the Cape of Good Hope, invaded that monopoly which they had hitherto guarded with ſuch jealous attention. The Engliſh ſoon followed the example of the Dutch, and both nations, at firſt by the enterprizing induſtry of private adventurers, and afterwards by the more powerful efforts of trading companies, under the protection of

 public

SECT. IV. public authority, advanced with aſtoniſhing ardour and ſucceſs in this new career opened to them. The vaſt fabric of power which the Portugueſe had erected in the Eaſt (a ſuperſtructure much too large for the baſis on which it had to reſt) was almoſt entirely overturned, in as ſhort time, and with as much facility, as it had been raiſed. England and Holland, by driving them from their moſt valuable ſettlements, and ſeizing the moſt lucrative branches of their trade, have attained to that pre-eminence in naval power and commercial opulence, by which they are diſtinguiſhed among the nations of Europe.

VI. The co-incidence, in point of time, of the diſcoveries made by Columbus in the Weſt, and thoſe of Gama in the Eaſt, is a ſingular circumſtance, which merits obſervation, on account of the remarkable influence of thoſe events in forming or ſtrengthening the commercial connection of the different quarters of the globe with each other. In all ages, gold and ſilver, particularly the latter, have been the commodities exported with the greateſt profit to India. In no part of the earth do the natives depend ſo little upon foreign countries, either for the neceſſaries or luxuries of life. The bleſſings of a favourable climate and fertile ſoil, augmented by their own ingenuity, afford them whatever they deſire. In conſequence of this, trade with them has always been carried on in one uniform manner, and the precious metals have been given in exchange for their peculiar productions, whether of nature or art. But when the communication with India was rendered ſo much more eaſy, that the demand for its commodities began to increaſe far beyond what had been formerly known, if

Europe

Europe had not been ſupplied with the gold and ſilver which it was neceſſary to carry to the markets of the Eaſt from ſources richer and more abundant than her own barren and impoveriſhed mines, ſhe muſt either have abandoned the trade with India altogether, or have continued it with manifeſt diſadvantage. By ſuch a continual drain of gold and ſilver, as well as by the unavoidable waſte of both in circulation and in manufactures, the quantity of thoſe metals muſt have gone on diminiſhing, and their value would have been ſo much enhanced, that they could not have continued long to be of the ſame utility in the commercial tranſactions between the two countries. But before the effects of this diminution could be very ſenſibly felt, America opened her mines, and poured in treaſures upon Europe in the moſt copious ſtream to which mankind ever had acceſs. This treaſure, in ſpite of innumerable anxious precautions to prevent it, flowed to the markets where the commodities neceſſary for ſupplying the wants, or gratifying the luxury of the Spaniards, were to be found; and from that time to the preſent, the Engliſh and Dutch have purchaſed the productions of China and Indoſtan, with ſilver brought from the mines of Mexico and Peru. The immenſe exportation of ſilver to the Eaſt, during the courſe of two centuries, has not only been replaced by the continual influx from America, but the quantity of it has been conſiderably augmented, and at the ſame time the proportional rate of its value in Europe and in India has varied ſo little, that it is chiefly with ſilver that many of the capital articles imported from the Eaſt are ſtill purchaſed.

WHILE America contributed in this manner to facilitate and extend the intercourſe of Europe with Aſia, it gave riſe to a traffic

SECT. IV.

traffic with Africa, which, from ſlender beginnings, has become ſo conſiderable, as to form the chief bond of commercial connection with that continent. Soon after the Portugueſe had extended their diſcoveries on the coaſt of Africa beyond the river Senegal, they endeavoured to derive ſome benefit from their new ſettlements there, by the ſale of ſlaves. Various circumſtances combined in favouring the revival of this odious traffic. In every part of America, of which the Spaniards took poſſeſſion, they found that the natives, from the feebleneſs of their frame, from their indolence, or from the injudicious manner of treating them, were incapable of the exertions requiſite either for working mines, or for cultivating the earth. Eager to find hands more induſtrious and efficient, the Spaniards had recourſe to their neighbours the Portugueſe, and purchaſed from them negroe ſlaves. Experience ſoon diſcovered, that they were men of a more hardy race, and ſo much better fitted for enduring fatigue, that the labour of one negroe was computed to be equal to that of four Americans [h]; and from that time the number employed in the New World has gone on increaſing with rapid progreſs. In this practice, no leſs repugnant to the feelings of humanity than to the principles of religion, the Spaniards have unhappily been imitated by all the nations of Europe, who have acquired territories in the warmer climates of the New World. At preſent the number of negroe ſlaves in the ſettlements of Great Britain and France in the Weſt Indies, exceeds a million; and as the eſtabliſhment of ſervitude has been found, both in ancient and in modern times, extremely unfavourable to population, it re-

[h] Hiſt. of America, vol. i. p. 320.

quires

quires an annual importation from Africa of at leaſt fifty-eight thouſand, to keep up the ſtock[1]. If it were poſſible to aſcertain, with equal exactneſs, the number of ſlaves in the Spaniſh dominions, and in North America, the total number of negroe ſlaves might be well reckoned at as many more.

THUS the commercial genius of Europe, which has given it a viſible aſcendent over the three other diviſions of the earth, by diſcerning their reſpective wants and reſources, and by rendering them reciprocally ſubſervient to one another, has eſtabliſhed an union among them, from which it has derived an immenſe increaſe of opulence, of power, and of enjoyments.

VII. THOUGH the diſcovery of a New World in the Weſt, and the opening of a more eaſy and direct communication with the remote regions of the Eaſt, co-operated towards extending the commerce, and adding to the enjoyments, of Europe, a remarkable difference may be obſerved, with reſpect both to the time and the manner in which they produced theſe effects. When the Portugueſe firſt viſited the different countries of Aſia, ſtretching from the coaſt of Malabar to China, they found them poſſeſſed by nations highly civilized, which had made conſiderable progreſs in elegant as well as uſeful arts, which were accuſtomed to intercourſe with ſtrangers, and well acquainted with all the advantages of commerce. But when the Spaniards began to explore the New World which they

[1] Report of Lords of the Privy Council, A. D. 1788.

2 diſcovered,

SECT. IV. discovered, the aspect which it presented to them was very different. The islands were inhabited by naked savages, so unacquainted with the simplest and most necessary arts of life, that they subsisted chiefly on the spontaneous productions of a fertile soil and genial climate. The continent appeared to be a forest of immense extent, along the coast of which were scattered some feeble tribes, not greatly superior to the islanders in industry or improvement. Even its two large monarchies, which have been dignified with the appellation of civilized states, had not advanced so far beyond their countrymen, as to be entitled to that name. The inhabitants, both of Mexico and Peru, unacquainted with the useful metals, and destitute of the address requisite for acquiring such command of the inferior animals as to derive any aid from their labour, had made so little progress in agriculture, the first of all arts, that one of the greatest difficulties with which the small number of Spaniards, who overturned those empires which have been so highly extolled, had to struggle, was how to procure in them what was sufficient for their subsistence.

It was of consequence, with a very different spirit, that the intercourse with two countries, resembling each other so little in their degree of improvement, was begun and carried on. The Portuguese, certain of finding in the East, not only the productions with which the bountiful hand of Nature has enriched that part of the globe, but various manufactures which had long been known and admired in Europe, engaged in this alluring trade with the greatest eagerness. The encouragement of it their monarchs considered as a chief object of government, towards which they directed all the power of the

 kingdom,

SECT. IV.

kingdom, and rouzed their ſubjects to ſuch vigorous exertions in the proſecution of it, as occaſioned that aſtoniſhing rapidity of progreſs which I have deſcribed. The ſanguine hopes with which the Spaniards entered upon their career of diſcovery, met not with the ſame ſpeedy gratification. From the induſtry of the rude inhabitants of the New World, they did not receive a ſingle article of commerce. Even the natural productions of the ſoil and climate, when not cheriſhed and multiplied by the foſtering and active hand of man, were of little account. Hope, rather than ſucceſs, incited them to perſiſt in extending their reſearches and conqueſts; and as government derived little immediate benefit from theſe, it left the proſecution of them chiefly to private adventurers, by whoſe enterprizing activity, more than by any effort of the ſtate, the moſt valuable poſſeſſions of Spain in America were acquired. Inſtead of the inſtantaneous and great advantages which the Portugueſe derived from their diſcoveries, above half a century elapſed before the Spaniards reaped any benefit of conſequence from their conqueſts, except the ſmall quantities of gold which the iſlanders were compelled to collect, and the plunder of the gold and ſilver employed by the Mexicans and Peruvians as ornaments of their perſons and temples, or as utenſils of ſacred or domeſtic uſe. It was not until the diſcovery of the mines of Potoſi in Peru, in the year one thouſand five hundred and forty-five, and of thoſe of Sacotecas in Mexico, ſoon after, that the Spaniſh territories in the New World brought a permanent and valuable addition of wealth and revenue to the mother country.

Z NOR

SECT. IV.

Nor did the trade with India differ more from that with America, in reſpect of the particular circumſtance which I have explained, than in reſpect to the manner of carrying it on, after it grew to be a conſiderable object of political attention. Trade with the Eaſt was a ſimple mercantile tranſaction, confined to the purchaſe either of the natural productions of the country, ſuch as ſpices, precious ſtones, pearls, &c. or of the manufactures which abounded among an induſtrious race of men, ſuch as ſilk and cotton ſtuffs, porcelane, &c. Nothing more was requiſite in conducting this trade, than to ſettle a few ſkilful agents in proper places, to prepare a proper aſſortment of goods for completing the cargoes of ſhips as ſoon as they arrived from Europe, or at the utmoſt to acquire the command of a few fortified ſtations, which might ſecure them admiſſion into ports where they might careen in ſafety, and find protection from the inſults of any hoſtile power. There was no neceſſity of making any attempt to eſtabliſh colonies, either for the cultivation of the ſoil, or the conduct of manufactures. Both theſe remained, as formerly, in the hands of the natives.

But as ſoon as that wild ſpirit of enterprize, which animated the Spaniards who firſt explored and ſubdued the New World, began to ſubſide, and when, inſtead of roving as adventurers from province to province in queſt of gold and ſilver, they ſeriouſly turned their thoughts towards rendering their conqueſts beneficial by cultivation and induſtry, they found it neceſſary to eſtabliſh colonies in every country which they wiſhed to improve. Other nations imitated their example in in the ſettlements which they afterwards made in ſome of the iſlands, and on the continent of North America. Europe, after having deſolated the New World, began to repeople it, and under a ſyſtem of colonization (the ſpirit and regulations of which it is not the object of this Diſquiſition to explain) the European race has multiplied there amazingly. Every article of commerce imported from the New World, if we except the furs and ſkins purchaſed from the independent tribes of hunters in North America, and from a few tribes in a ſimilar ſtate on the Southern continent, is the produce of the induſtry of Europeans ſettled there. To their exertions, or to thoſe of hands which they have taught or compelled to labour, we are indebted for ſugar, rum, cotton, tobacco, indigo, rice, and even the gold and ſilver extracted from the bowels of the earth. Intent on thoſe lucrative branches of induſtry, the inhabitants of the New World pay little attention to thoſe kinds of labour which occupy a conſiderable part of the members of other ſocieties, and depend, in ſome meaſure, for their ſubſiſtence, and entirely for every article of elegance and luxury, upon the ancient continent. Thus the Europeans have become manufacturers for America, and their induſtry has been greatly augmented by the vaſt demands for ſupplying the wants of extenſive countries, the population of which is continually increaſing. Nor is the influence of this demand confined ſolely to the nations which have a more immediate connection with the American colonies; it is felt in every part of Europe that furniſhes any article exported to them, and gives activity and vigour to the hand of the artiſan in the inland provinces of Germany, as well as to thoſe in Great

SECT. IV. Britain and other countries, which carry on a direct trade with the New World.

But while the discovery and conquest of America is allowed to be one principal cause of that rapid increase of industry and wealth, which is conspicuous in Europe during the two last centuries, some timid theorists have maintained, that throughout the same period Europe has been gradually impoverished, by being drained of its treasure, in order to carry on its trade with India. But this apprehension has arisen from inattention to the nature and use of the precious metals. They are to be considered in two different lights; either as the signs which all civilized nations have agreed to employ, in order to estimate or represent the value both of labour and of all commodities, and thus to facilitate the purchase of the former, and the conveyance of the latter from one proprietor to another; or gold and silver may be viewed as being themselves commodities or articles of commerce, for which some equivalent must be given by such as wish to acquire them. In this light, the exportation of the precious metals to the East should be regarded; for, as the nation by which they are exported must purchase them with the produce of its own labour and ingenuity, this trade must contribute, though not in the same obvious and direct manner as that with America, towards augmenting the general industry and opulence of Europe. If England, as the price of Mexican and Peruvian dollars which are necessary for carrying on its trade with India, must give a certain quantity of its woollen or cotton cloth or hard-ware, then the hands of an additional number of manufacturers are

7 rendered

rendered active, and work to a certain amount must be executed, for which, without this trade, there would not have been any demand. The nation reaps all the benefit arising from a new creation of industry. With the gold and silver which her manufactures have purchased in the West, she is enabled to trade in the markets of the East, and the exportation of treasure to India, which has been so much dreaded, instead of impoverishing, enriches the kingdom.

VIII. It is to the discovery of the passage to India by the Cape of Good Hope, and to the vigour and success with which the Portuguese prosecuted their conquests and established their dominion there, that Europe has been indebted for its preservation from the most illiberal and humiliating servitude that ever oppressed polished nations. For this observation I am indebted to an Author, whose ingenuity has illustrated, and whose eloquence has adorned the History of the Settlements and Commerce of Modern Nations in the East and West Indies[i]; and it appears to me so well founded as to merit more ample investigation. A few years after the first appearance of the Portuguese in India, the dominion of the Mameluks was overturned by the irresistible power of the Turkish arms, and Egypt and Syria were annexed as provinces to their empire. If after this event the commercial intercourse with India had continued to be carried on in its ancient channels, the Turkish Sultans, by being masters of Egypt and Syria, must have possessed the absolute command of it, whether the

[i] M. L'Abbé Raynal.

produc-

SECT. IV. productions of the East were conveyed by the Red Sea to Alexandria, or were transported by land-carriage from the Persian Gulf to Constantinople, and the ports of the Mediterranean. The monarchs who were then at the head of this great empire, were neither destitute of abilities to perceive the pre-eminence to which this would have elevated them, nor of ambition to aspire to it. Selim, the conqueror of the Mameluks, by confirming the ancient privileges of the Venetians in Egypt and Syria, and by his regulations concerning the duties on Indian goods, which I have already mentioned, early discovered his solicitude to secure all the advantages of commerce with the East to his own dominions. The attention of Solyman the Magnificent, his successor, seems to have been equally directed towards the same object. More enlightened than any monarch of the Ottoman race, he attended to all the transactions of the European states, and had observed the power as well as opulence to which the republic of Venice had attained by engrossing the commerce with the East. He now beheld Portugal rising towards the same elevation, by the same means. Eager to imitate and to supplant them, he formed a scheme suitable to his character for political wisdom and the appellation of *Institutor of Rules*, by which the Turkish Historians have distinguished him, and established, early in his reign, a system of commercial laws in his dominions, by which he hoped to render Constantinople the great staple of Indian trade, as it had been in the prosperous ages of the Greek empire[k]. For

[k] Paruta Hist. Venet. lib. vii. p. 589. Sandi Stor. Civil. Venez. part ii. p. 901.

accom-

accomplishing this scheme, however, he did not rely on the operation of laws alone; he fitted out about the same time a formidable fleet in the Red Sea, under the conduct of a confidential officer, with such a body of janizaries on board of it, as he deemed sufficient not only to drive the Portuguese out of all their new settlements in India, but to take possession of some commodious station in that country, and to erect his standard there. The Portuguese, by efforts of valour and constancy, entitled to the splendid success with which they were crowned, repulsed this powerful armament in every enterprize it undertook, and compelled the shattered remains of the Turkish fleet and army to return with ignominy to the harbours from which they had taken their departure, with the most sanguine hopes of terminating the expedition in a very different manner [1]. Solyman, though he never relinquished the design of expelling the Portuguese from India, and of acquiring some establishment there, was so occupied during the remainder of his reign, by the multiplicity of arduous operations in which an insatiable ambition involved him, that he never had leisure to resume the prosecution of it with vigour.

SECT. IV.

A.C. 1538.

If either the measures of Selim had produced the effect which he expected, or if the more adventurous and extensive plan of Solyman had been carried into execution, the command of the wealth of India, together with such a marine as the monopoly of trade with that country has, in every age, enabled the power which possessed it to create and maintain, must have brought

[1] Asia de Barros, dec. iv. lib. x. c. 1, &c.

SECT. IV. an acceſſion of force to an empire already formidable to mankind, that would have rendered it altogether irreſiſtible. Europe, at that period, was not in a condition to have defended itſelf againſt the combined exertions of ſuch naval and military power, ſupported by commercial wealth, and under the direction of a monarch whoſe comprehenſive genius was able to derive from each its peculiar advantages, and to employ all with the greateſt effect. Happily for the human race, the deſpotic ſyſtem of Turkiſh government, founded on ſuch illiberal fanaticiſm as has extinguiſhed ſcience in Egypt, in Aſſyria, and in Greece, its three favourite manſions in ancient times, was prevented from extending its dominion over Europe, and from ſuppreſſing liberty, learning, and taſte, when beginning to make ſucceſsful efforts to revive there, and again to bleſs, to enlighten, and to poliſh mankind.

NOTES

NOTES

AND

ILLUSTRATIONS.

Aa

N O T E S

AND

ILLUSTRATIONS.

NOTE I. Sect. I. p. 6.

CREDULITY and ſcepticiſm are two oppoſite extremes into which men are apt to run, in examining the events which are ſaid to have happened in the early ages of antiquity. Without incurring any ſuſpicion of a propenſity to the latter of theſe, I may be allowed to entertain doubts concerning the expedition of Seſoſtris into India, and his conqueſt of that country.——1. Few facts in ancient hiſtory ſeem to be better eſtabliſhed, than that of the early averſion of the Egyptians to a ſea-faring life. Even the power of deſpotiſm cannot at once change the ideas and manners of a nation, eſpecially when they have been confirmed by long habit, and rendered ſacred by the ſanction of religion. That Seſoſtris, in the courſe of a few years, ſhould have ſo

Aa 2 entirely

entirely overcome the prejudices of a ſuperſtitious people, as to be able to fit out four hundred ſhips of force in the Arabian Gulf, beſides another fleet which he had in the Mediterranean, appears to be extremely improbable. Armaments of ſuch magnitude would require the utmoſt efforts of a great and long eſtabliſhed maritime power.——2. It is remarkable that Herodotus, who enquired with the moſt perſevering diligence into the ancient hiſtory of Egypt, and who received all the information concerning it which the prieſts of Memphis, Heliopolis, and Thebes, could communicate, Herodot. edit. Weſſelingij, lib. ii. c. 3. although he relates the hiſtory of Seſoſtris at ſome length, does not mention his conqueſt of India. Lib. ii. c. 102, &c. That tale, it is probable, was invented in the period between the age of Herodotus and that of Diodorus Siculus, from whom we receive a particular detail of the Indian expedition of Seſoſtris. His account reſts entirely upon the authority of the Egyptian prieſts; and Diodorus himſelf not only gives it as his general opinion, "that many things which "they related, flowed rather from a deſire to promote the "honour of their country, than from attention to truth," lib. i. p. 34. edit. Weſſelingij, Amſt. 1746; but takes particular notice that the Egyptian prieſts, as well as the Greek writers, differ widely from one another in the accounts which they give of the actions of Seſoſtris, lib. i. p. 62.——3. Though Diodorus aſſerts, that in relating the hiſtory of Seſoſtris he had ſtudied to ſelect what appeared to him moſt probable, and moſt agreeable to the monuments of that monarch ſtill remaining in Egypt, he has admitted into his narrative many marvellous circumſtances which render the whole extremely ſuſpicious.

ſuſpicious. The father of Seſoſtris, as he relates, collected all the male children who were born in Egypt on the ſame day with his ſon, in order that they might be educated, together with him, conformable to a mode which he preſcribed, with a view of preparing them as proper inſtruments to carry into execution the great undertakings for which he deſtined Seſoſtris. Accordingly, when Seſoſtris ſet out upon his Indian expedition, which, from circumſtances mentioned by Diodorus, muſt have been about the fortieth year of his age, one thouſand ſeven hundred of his youthful aſſociates are ſaid to have been ſtill alive, and were entruſted with high command in his army. But if we apply to the examination of this ſtory the certain principles of political arithmetic, it is evident, that if one thouſand ſeven hundred of the male children born on the ſame day with Seſoſtris were alive when his great expedition commenced, the number of children born in Egypt on each day of the year muſt have been at leaſt ten thouſand, and the population of the kingdom muſt have exceeded ſixty millions; Goguet l'Origine des Loix, des Arts, &c. tom. ii. p. 12, &c. A number far beyond the bounds of credibility, in a kingdom which, from the accurate calculations of M. D'Anville, Memoire ſur l'Egypte Anc. et Moderne, p. 23, &c. does not contain more than two thouſand one hundred ſquare leagues of habitable country. Another marvellous particular is the deſcription of a ſhip of cedar, four hundred and ninety feet in length, covered on the outſide with gold, and on the inſide with ſilver, which Seſoſtris conſecrated to the deity who was the chief object of worſhip at Thebes. Lib. i. p. 67. Such too is the account he gives of the Egyptian army, in in which, beside six hundred thousand infantry, and twenty-four thousand cavalry, there were twenty-seven thousand armed chariots. Ibid. p. 64.——4. These and other particulars appeared so far to exceed the bounds of probability, that the sound understanding of Strabo the geographer rejected, without hesitation, the accounts of the Indian expedition of Sesostris; and he not only asserts, in the most explicit terms, that this monarch never entered India, lib. xv. p. 1007. C. edit. Casaub. Amst. 1707; but he ranks what has been related concerning his operations in that country, with the fabulous exploits of Bacchus and Hercules, p. 1007. D. 1009. B. The philosophical Historian of Alexander the Great seems to have entertained the same sentiments with respect to the exploits of Sesostris in India. Hist. Ind. c. 5. Arrian, Exped. Alex. edit. Gronov. L. Bat. 1704.—What slender information concerning India, or its inhabitants, Herodotus had received, seems to have been derived, not from the Egyptians, but from the Persians, lib. iii. c. 105, which renders it probable, that in his time there was little intercourse between Egypt and India.

NOTE II. Sect. I. p. 8.

When we consider the extent and effects of the Phenician commerce, the scanty information concerning it which we receive from ancient writers must, on a first view, appear surprising. But when we recollect that all the Greek Historians, (Herodotus excepted,) who give any account of the Phenicians, published their works long after the destruction of

3 Tyre

Tyre by Alexander the Great, we ſhall ceaſe to wonder at their not having entered into minute details with reſpect to a trade which was then removed to new ſeats, and carried on in other channels. But the power and opulence of Tyre, in the proſperous age of its commerce, muſt have attracted general attention. In the prophecies of Ezekiel, who flouriſhed two hundred and ſixty years before the fall of Tyre, there is the moſt particular account of the nature and variety of its commercial tranſactions that is to be found in any ancient writer, and which conveys, at the ſame time, a magnificent idea of the extenſive power of that ſtate. Ch. xxvi, xxvii, xxviii.

NOTE III. SECT. I. p. 11.

THE account given of the revenue of the Perſian monarchy by Herodotus is curious, and ſeems to have been copied from ſome public record, which had been communicated to him. According to it, the Perſian empire was divided into twenty Satrapy's, or governments. The tribute levied from each is ſpecified, amounting in all to 14,560 Eubæan talents, which Dr. Arbuthnot reckons to be equal to 2,807,437 l. ſterling money; a ſum extremely ſmall for the revenue of the Great King, and which ill accords with many facts concerning the riches, magnificence, and luxury of the Eaſt, that occur in ancient authors.

NOTE

NOTE IV. Sect. I. p. 16.

It is ſurpriſing that Alexander did not receive, in the provinces contiguous to India, ſuch an account of the periodical rains in that country, as to ſhew him the impropriety of carrying on military operations there, while theſe continued. His expedition into India commenced towards the end of Spring, Arrian, lib. iv. c. 22., when the rains were already begun in the mountains from which all the rivers in the Panjab flow, and of courſe they muſt have been conſiderably ſwelled before he arrived on their banks. Rennell, p. 268.—He paſſed the Hydaſpes at Midſummer, about the height of the rainy ſeaſon. In a country through which ſo many large rivers run, an army on ſervice at this time of the year muſt have ſuffered greatly. An accurate deſcription of the nature of the rains and inundations in this part of India, is given by Arrian, lib. v. c. 9.; and one ſtill fuller may be found in Strabo, lib. xv. 1013.—It was of what they ſuffered by theſe that Alexander's ſoldiers complained, Strabo, lib. xv. 1021. D.; and not without reaſon, as it had rained inceſſantly during ſeventy days, Diod. Sicul. xvii. c. 94.—A circumſtance which marks the accuracy with which Alexander's officers had attended to every thing in that part of India, deſerves notice. Ariſtobulus, in his Journal, which I have mentioned, takes notice that, though heavy rains fell in the mountains, and in the country near to them, in the plains below

below not ſo much as a ſhower fell. Strabo, lib. xv. 1013. B. 1015. B. Major Rennell was informed by a perſon of character, who had reſided in this diſtrict of India, which is now ſeldom viſited by Europeans, that during great part of the S. W. monſoon, or at leaſt in the months of July, Auguſt, and part of September, which is the rainy ſeaſon in moſt other parts of India, the atmoſphere in the Delta of the Indus is generally clouded, but no rain falls, except very near the ſea. Indeed, very few ſhowers fall during the whole ſeaſon. Captain Hamilton relates, that when he viſited Tatta, no rain had fallen for three years before. Memoirs, p. 288.—Tamerlane, who, by the vicinity of the ſeat of his government to India, had the means of being well informed concerning the nature of the country, avoided the error of Alexander, and made his Indian campaign during the dry ſeaſon. As Nadir Shah, both when he invaded India, A. D. 1738, and in his return next year, marched through the ſame countries with Alexander, and nearly in the ſame line of direction, nothing can give a more ſtriking idea of the perſevering ardour of the Macedonian conqueror, than the deſcription of the difficulties which Nadir Shah had to ſurmount, and the hardſhips which his army endured. Though poſ-ſeſſed of abſolute power and immenſe wealth, and diſtinguiſhed no leſs by great talents than long experience in the conduct of war, he had the mortification to loſe a great part of his troops in croſſing the rivers of the Panjab, in penetrating through the mountains to the north of India, and in conflicts with the fierce natives inhabiting the countries which ſtretch from the banks of the Oxus to the frontiers of Perſia. An interesting account of his retreat and sufferings is given in the Memoirs of Khojeh Abdulkurreem, a Cashmerian of distinction, who served in his army.

NOTE V. Sect. I. p. 18.

That a fleet so numerous should have been collected in such a short time, is apt to appear, at first sight, incredible. Arrian, however, assures us, that in specifying this number, he followed Ptolemy, the son of Lagus, whose authority he considered to be of the greatest weight, lib. vi. c. 3. But as the Panjab country is full of navigable rivers, on which all the intercourse among the natives was carried on, it abounded with vessels ready constructed to the conqueror's hands, so that he might easily collect that number. If we could give credit to the account of the invasion of India by Semiramis, no fewer than four thousand vessels were assembled in the Indus to oppose her fleet. Diod. Sicul. lib. ii. c. 74.—It is remarkable that when Mahmoud of Gaznah invaded India, a fleet was collected on the Indus to oppose him, consisting of the same number of vessels. We learn from the Ayeen Akbery, that the inhabitants of this part of India still continue to carry on all their communication with each other by water; the inhabitants of the Circar of Tatta alone have not less than forty thousand vessels of various constructions. Vol. ii. p. 143.

NOTE

NOTE VI. Sect. I. p. 19.

All these particulars are taken from the Indian History of Arrian, a work different from that already mentioned, and one of the most curious treatises transmitted to us from antiquity. The first part of it consists of extracts from the account given by Nearchus of the climate and soil of India, and the manners of the natives. The second contains that officer's journal of his voyage from the mouth of the Indus to the bottom of the Persian Gulf. The perusal of it gives rise to several observations.——1. It is remarkable that neither Nearchus nor Ptolemy, nor Aristobulus, nor even Arrian, once mention the voyage of Scylax. This could not proceed from their being unacquainted with it, for Herodotus was a favourite author in the hands of every Greek who had any pretensions to literature. It was probably occasioned by the reasons which they had to distrust the veracity of Scylax, of which I have already taken notice. Accordingly, in a speech which Arrian puts into the mouth of Alexander, he asserts that, except Bacchus, he was the first who had passed the Indus; which implies, that he disbelieved what is related concerning Scylax, and was not acquainted with what Darius Hystaspes is said to have done in order to subject that part of India to the Persian crown. Arrian, vii. c. 10. This opinion is confirmed by Megasthenes, who resided a considerable time in India. He asserts that, except Bacchus and Hercules, (to whose fabulous expeditions Strabo is astonished that he should have given any credit, lib. xv. p. 1007. D.) Alexander was the firft who had invaded India; Arrian, Hift. Indic. c. 5. We are informed by Arrian, that the Affacani, and other people who poffeffed that country, which is now called the kingdom of Candahar, paid tribute, firft to the Affyrians, and afterwards to the Medes and Perfians; Hift. Indic. c. 1. As all the fertile provinces on the north-weft of the Indus were anciently reckoned to be part of India, it is probable that what was levied from them is the fum mentioned in the tribute-roll, from which Herodotus drew his account of the annual revenue of the Perfian empire, and that none of the provinces to the fouth of the Indus were ever fubject to the kings of Perfia.——2. This voyage of Nearchus affords fome ftriking inftances of the imperfect knowledge which the ancients had of any navigation different from that to which they were accuftomed in the Mediterranean. Though the enterprifing genius and enlarged views of Alexander prompted him to attempt opening an intercourfe by fea between India and his Perfian dominions, yet both he and Nearchus knew fo little of the ocean which they wifhed to explore, as to be apprehenfive that it might be found impoffible to navigate it, on account of impervious ftraits, or other obftacles. Hift. Indic. c. 20. Q. Curt. lib. ix. c. 9. When the fleet arrived near the mouth of the Indus, the aftonifhment excited by the extraordinary flow and ebb of tide in the Indian ocean, a phenomenon (according to Arrian) with which Alexander and his foldiers were unacquainted, lib. vi. c. 19. is another proof of their ignorance in maritime fcience. Nor is there any reafon to be furprifed at their aftonifhment, as the tides are hardly perceptible in the Mediterranean, beyond which the knowledge

knowledge of the Greeks and Macedonians did not extend. For the ſame reaſon, when the Romans carried their victorious arms into the countries ſituated on the Atlantic Ocean, or on the ſeas that communicate with it, this new phenomenon of the tides was an object of wonder and terror to them. Cæſar deſcribes the amazement of his ſoldiers at a ſpring-tide, which greatly damaged the fleet with which he invaded Britain, and acknowledges that it was an appearance with which they were unacquainted; Bell. Gallic. lib. iv. c. 29. The tides on the coaſt near the mouth of the Indus are remarkably high, and the effects of them very great, eſpecially that ſudden and abrupt influx of the tide into the mouths of rivers or narrow ſtraits which is known in India by the name of *The Bore*, and is accurately deſcribed by Major Rennell, Introd. xxiv. Mem. 278. In the Periplus Maris Erythræi, p. 26., theſe high tides are mentioned, and the deſcription of them nearly reſembles that of the Bore. A very exaggerated account of the tides in the Indian ocean is given by Pliny, Nat. Hiſt. lib. xiii. c. 25. Major Rennell ſeems to think, that Alexander and his followers could not be ſo entirely unacquainted with the phenomenon of the tides, as Herodotus had informed the Greeks, "that in the "Red Sea there was a regular ebb and flow of the tide every "day;" lib. ii. c. 11. This is all the explanation of that phenomenon given by Herodotus. But among the ancients there occur inſtances of inattention to facts, related by reſpectable authors, which appear ſurpriſing in modern times. Though Herodotus, as I have juſt now obſerved, gave an account of the voyage performed by Scylax at conſiderable length, neither Alexander, nor his Hiſtorians, take any notice of that event.

I ſhall

I ſhall afterwards have occaſion to mention a more remarkable inſtance of the inattention of later writers to an accurate deſcription which Herodotus had given of the Caſpian Sea. From theſe, and other ſimilar inſtances which might have been produced, we may conclude, that the ſlight mention of the regular flow and ebb of tide in the Red Sea, is not a ſufficient reaſon for rejecting, as incredible, Arrian's account of the ſurpriſe of Alexander's ſoldiers when they firſt beheld the extraordinary effects of the tide at the mouth of the Indus.—— 3. The courſe of Nearchus's voyage, the promontories, the creeks, the rivers, the cities, the mountains, which came ſucceſſively in his view, are ſo clearly deſcribed, and the diſtances of ſuch as were moſt worthy of notice are ſo diſtinctly marked, that M. D'Anville, by comparing theſe with the actual poſition of the country, according to the beſt accounts of it, ancient as well as modern, has been able to point out moſt of the places which Nearchus mentions, with a degree of certainty which does as much honour to the veracity of the Grecian navigator, as to the induſtry, learning, and penetration of the French geographer. Mem. de Literat. tom. xxx. p. 132, &c.

In modern times, the Red Sea is a name appropriated to the Arabian Gulf, but the ancients denominated the ocean which ſtretches from that Gulf to India, the Erythræan Sea, from king Erythras, of whom nothing more is known than the name, which in the Greek language ſignifies red. From this caſual meaning of the word, it came to be believed, that it was of a different colour from other ſeas, and conſequently of more dangerous navigation.

NOTE

NOTE VII. SECT. I. p. 24.

ALEXANDER was ſo intent on rendering this union of his ſubjects complete, that after his death there was found in his tablets or commentaries, (among other magnificent ſchemes which he meditated) a reſolution to build ſeveral new cities, ſome in Aſia, and ſome in Europe, and to people thoſe in Aſia with Europeans, and thoſe in Europe with Aſiatics, "that, " (ſays the Hiſtorian) by intermarriages, and exchange of " good offices, the inhabitants of theſe two great continents " might be gradually moulded into a ſimilarity of ſentiments, " and become attached to each other with mutual affection." Diod. Sicul. lib. xviii. c. 4.

NOTE VIII. SECT. I. p. 26.

IT ſeems to be an opinion generally received, that Alexander built only two cities in India, Nicæa and Bucephalia, ſituated on the Hydaſpes, the modern Chelum, and that Craterus ſuperintended the building of both. But it is evident, from Arrian, lib. v. c. ult., that he built a third city on the Aceſines, now the Jenaub, under the direction of Hephæſtion; and if it was his object to retain the command of the country, a place of ſtrength on ſome of the rivers to the ſouth of the Hydaſpes ſeems to have been neceſſary for that purpoſe. This part of India has been ſo little viſited in modern times, that it is impoſſible

5 to

to point out with precision the situation of these cities. If P. Tieffenthaler were well founded in his conjecture, that the river now called Rauvee is the Acesines of Arrian, Bernouilli, vol. i. p. 39., it is probable that this city was built somewhere near Lahore, one of the most important stations in that part of India, and reckoned in the Ayeen Akbery to be a city of very high antiquity. But Major Rennell, in my opinion, gives good reasons for supposing the Jenaub to be the Acesines of the ancients.

NOTE IX. SECT. I. p. 26.

THE religious scruples which prevented the Persians from making any voyage by sea, were known to the ancients. Pliny relates of one of the Magi, who was sent on an embassy from Tiridates to the emperor Nero, "Navigare noluerat, "quoniam exspuere in Maria, alijsque mortalium necessitati-"bus violare naturam eam, fas non putant;" Nat. Hist. lib. xxx. c. 2. This aversion to the sea they carried so far, that, according to the observation of a well-informed Historian, there was not a city of any note in their empire built upon the sea-coast; Ammian. Marcel. lib. xxiii. c. 6. We learn from Dr. Hyde, how intimately these ideas were connected with the doctrines of Zoroaster; Rel. Vet. Pers. cap. vi. In all the wars of the Persians with Greece, the fleets of the Great King consisted entirely of ships furnished by the Phenicians, Syrians, the conquered provinces of the Lesser Asia, and the islands adjacent. Herodotus and Diodorus Siculus mention the

the quota furniſhed by each country, in order to compoſe the fleet of twelve hundred ſhips with which Xerxes invaded Greece, and among theſe there is not one belonging to Perſia. At the ſame time it is proper to obſerve, that according to Herodotus, whoſe authority is unexceptionable with regard to this point, the fleet was under the command of Ariabigines, a ſon of Darius, who had ſeveral ſatraps of high rank under his command, and both Perſians and Medes ſerved as ſoldiers on board of it; Herod. lib. vii. c. 96, 97. By what motives, or what authority, they were induced to act in this manner, I cannot explain. From ſome religious ſcruples, ſimilar to thoſe of the Perſians, many of the natives of Indoſtan, in our own time, refuſe to embark on board a ſhip, and to ſerve at ſea; and yet, on ſome occaſions, the ſepoys in the ſervice of the European powers have got the better of theſe ſcruples.

NOTE X. SECT. I. p. 27.

M. LE BARON DE SAINTE-CROIX, in his ingenious and learned Critique des Hiſtoriens d'Alexandre le Grand, p. 96, ſeems to entertain ſome doubt with reſpect to the number of the cities which Alexander is ſaid to have built. Plutarch de Fort. Alex. affirms, that he founded no fewer than ſeventy. It appears from many paſſages in ancient authors, that the building of cities, or, what may be conſidered as the ſame, the eſtabliſhment of fortified ſtations, was the mode of maintaining their authority in the conquered nations, adopted not only by Alexander, but by his ſucceſſors. Seleucus and Antiochus,

Cc to

to whom the greater part of the Perfian empire became fubject, were no lefs remarkable for founding new cities than Alexander, and thefe cities feem fully to have anfwered the purpofes of the founders, as they effectually prevented (as I fhall afterwards have occafion to obferve) the revolt of the conquered provinces. Though the Greeks, animated with the love of liberty and of their native country, refufed to fettle in the Perfian empire while under the dominion of its native monarchs, even when allured by the profpect of great advantage, as M. de Sainte-Croix remarks, the cafe became perfectly different, when that empire was fubjected to their own dominion, and they fettled there, not as fubjects, but as mafters. Both Alexander and his fucceffors difcovered much difcernment in chufing the fituation of the cities which they built. Seleucia, which Seleucus founded, was inferior only to Alexandria in number of inhabitants, in wealth, and in importance; Mr. Gibbon, vol. i. p. 250. M. D'Anville, Mem. de Literat. xxx.

NOTE XI. Sect. I. p. 29.

It is from Juftin we receive the flender knowledge we have of the progrefs which Seleucus made in India; lib. xv. c. 4. But we cannot rely on his evidence, unlefs when it is confirmed by the teftimony of other authors. Plutarch feems to affert, that Seleucus had penetrated far into India; but that refpectable writer is more eminent for his difcernment of characters, and his happy felection of thofe circumftances which mark and difcriminate them, than for the accuracy of his hiftorical refearches.

ſearches. Pliny, whoſe authority is of greater weight, ſeems to conſider it as certain, that Seleucus had carried his arms into diſtricts of India which Alexander never viſited; Plin. Nat. Hiſt. lib. vi. c. 17. The paſſage in which this is mentioned, is ſomewhat obſcure, but it ſeems to imply, that Seleucus had marched from the Hyphaſis to the Hyſudrus, from thence to Palibothra, and from that to the mouth of the Ganges. The diſtances of the principal ſtations in this march are marked, amounting to 2244 Roman miles. In this ſenſe, M. Bayer underſtands the words of Pliny; Hiſtor. Regni Græcorum Bactriani, p. 37. But to me it appears highly improbable, that the Indian expedition of Seleucus could have continued ſo long as to allow time for operations of ſuch extent. If Seleucus had advanced as far into India as the mouth of the Ganges, the ancients would have had a more accurate knowledge of that part of the country than they ſeem ever to have poſſeſſed.

NOTE XII. Sect. I. p. 30.

Major Rennell gives a magnificent idea of this, by informing us, that the Ganges, after it has "eſcaped from the "mountainous tract in which it had wandered above eight "hundred miles;" Mem. p. 233. "receives in its courſe "through the plains eleven rivers, ſome of them as large as "the Rhine, and none ſmaller than the Thames, beſides as "many more of leſſer note;" p. 257.

NOTE XIII. Sect. I. p. 31.

In fixing the poſition of Palibothra, I have ventured to differ from Major Rennell, and I venture to do ſo with diffidence. According to Strabo, Palibothra was ſituated at the junction of the Ganges and another river; lib. xv. p. 1028. A. Arrian is ſtill more explicit. He places Palibothra at the confluence of the Ganges and Erranaboas, the laſt of which he deſcribes as leſs than the Ganges or Indus, but greater than any other known river; Hiſt. Ind. c. 10. This deſcription of its ſituation correſponds exactly with that of Allahabad. P. Boudier, to whoſe obſervations the geography of India is much indebted, ſays, that the Jumna, at its junction with the Ganges, appeared to him not inferior in magnitude to that river; D'Anville, Antiq. de l' Inde, p. 53. Allahabad is the name which was given to that city by the emperor Akbar, who erected a ſtrong fortreſs there; an elegant delineation of which is publiſhed by Mr. Hodges, No. IV. of his Select Views in India. Its ancient name, by which it is ſtill known among the Hindoos, is *Praeg*, or *Piyag*, and the people of the diſtrict are called *Praegi*, which bears a near reſemblance to Praſij, the ancient appellation of the kingdom of which Palibothra was the capital; P. Tieſſenthaler chez Bernouilli, tom. i. 223. D'Anville, p. 56. Allahabad is ſuch a noted ſeat of Hindoo devotion, that it is denominated *The King of Worſhipped Places*; Ayeen Akbery, vol. ii. p. 35. "The territory around

2 "it

" it, to the extent of forty miles, is deemed holy ground. " The Hindoos believe, that when a man dies in this place, " whatever he wiſhes for he will obtain in his next regenera- " tion. Although they teach that ſuicide in general will be " puniſhed with torments hereafter, yet they conſider it as " meritorious for a man to kill himſelf at Allahabad;" Ayeen Akbery, iii. 256. P. Tieſſenthaler deſcribes the various objects of veneration at Allahabad, which are ſtill viſited with great veneration by an immenſe number of pilgrims; Bernouilli, tom. i. 224. From all theſe circumſtances, we may conclude it to be a place of great antiquity, and in the ſame ſituation with the Palibothra of antiquity.

Major Rennell has been induced to place Palibothra on the ſame ſite with Patna, chiefly by two conſiderations.—— 1. From having learned that on or near the ſite of Patna ſtood anciently a very large city named *Patelpoot-her* or *Patalipputra*, which nearly reſembles the ancient name of Palibothra. Although there is not now a confluence of two rivers at Patna, he was informed that the junction of the Soane with the Ganges, now twenty-two miles above Patna, was formerly under the walls of that city. The rivers of India ſometimes change their courſe in a ſingular manner, and he produces ſome remarkable inſtances of it. But even ſhould it be allowed, that the accounts which the natives give of this variation in the courſe of the Soane were perfectly accurate, I queſtion whether Arrian's account of the magnitude of the Erranaboas be applicable to that river, certainly not ſo juſtly as to the Jumna.

Jumna.——2. He ſeems to have been influenced, in ſome degree, by Pliny's Itinerary, or Table of Diſtances from Taxila (the modern Attock) to the mouth of the Ganges; Nat. Hiſt. lib. vi. c. 17. But the diſtances in that Itinerary are marked ſo inaccurately, and in ſome inſtances are ſo palpably erroneous, that one cannot found upon them with much ſecurity. According to it, Palibothra is ſituated four hundred and twenty-five miles below the confluence of the Jumna and Ganges. The actual diſtance, however, between Allahabad and Patna, is not more than two hundred Britiſh miles. A diſagreement ſo conſiderable cannot be accounted for, without ſuppoſing ſome extraordinary error in the Itinerary, or that the point of conflux of the Jumna with the Ganges has undergone a change. For the former of theſe ſuppoſitions there is no authority (as far as I know) from any manuſcript, or for the latter from any tradition. Major Rennell has produced the reaſons which led him to ſuppoſe the ſite of Palibothra to be the ſame with that of Patna; Memoirs, p. 49—54. Some of the objections which might be made to this ſuppoſition he has foreſeen, and endeavoured to obviate; and after all that I have added to them, I ſhall not be ſurpriſed, if, in a geographical diſcuſſion, my readers are diſpoſed to prefer his deciſion to mine.

NOTE

NOTE XIV. SECT. I. p. 32.

I DO not mention a ſhort inroad into India by Antiochus the Great, about one hundred and ninety-ſeven years poſterior to the invaſion of his anceſtor Seleucus. We know nothing more of this tranſaction, than that the Syrian monarch, after finiſhing the war he carried on againſt the two revolted provinces of Parthia and Bactria, entered India, and concluding a peace with Sophagaſenus, a king of the country, received from him a number of elephants, and a ſum of money; Polyb. lib. x. p. 597, &c. lib. xi. p. 651. edit. Caſaub. Juſtin. lib. xv. c. 4. Bayer's Hiſt. Regn. Græcor. Bactr. p. 69, &c.

NOTE XV. SECT. I. p. 34.

A FACT curſorily related by Strabo, and which has eſcaped the inquiſitive induſtry of M. de Guignes, coincides remarkably with the narrative of the Chineſe writers, and confirms it. The Greeks, he ſays, were deprived of Bactria by tribes or hordes of Scythian Nomades, who came from the country beyond the Jaxartes, and are known by the names of Aſij, Paſiani, Tachari, and Sacarauli; Strab. lib. xi. p. 779. A. The Nomades of the ancients were nations who, like the Tartars, ſubſiſted entirely, or almoſt entirely, as ſhepherds, without agriculture.

NOTE

NOTE XVI. Sect. I. p. 36.

As the diftance of Arfinoe, the modern Suez, from the Nile, is confiderably lefs than that between Berenice and Coptos, it was by this route that all the commodities imported into the Arabian Gulf, might have been conveyed with moft expedition and leaft expence into Egypt. But the navigation of the Arabian Gulf, which even in the prefent improved ftate of nautical fcience is flow and difficult, was in ancient times confidered by the nations around it to be fo extremely perilous, that it led them to give fuch names to feveral of its promontories, bays, and harbours, as convey a ftriking idea of the impreffion which the dread of this danger had made upon their imagination. The entry into the Gulf they called *Babelmandeb*, the gate or port of affliction. To a harbour not far diftant, they gave the name of *Mete*, i. e. Death. A headland adjacent they called *Gardefan*, the Cape of Burial. Other denominations of fimilar import are mentioned by the author to whom I am indebted for this information. Bruce's Travels, vol. i. p. 442, &c. It is not furprifing then, that the ftaple of Indian trade fhould have been transferred from the northern extremity of the Arabian Gulf to Berenice, as by this change a dangerous navigation was greatly fhortened. This feems to have been the chief reafon that induced Ptolemy to eftablifh the port of communication with India at Berenice, as there were other harbours on the Arabian Gulf which were confiderably nearer than it to the Nile. At a later period, after the

the ruin of Coptos by the Emperor Diocletian, we are informed by Abulfeda, Defcript. Egypt. edit. Michaelis, p. 77, that Indian commodities were conveyed from the Red Sea to the Nile, by the fhorteft route, viz. from Coffeir, probably the Philoteras Portus of Ptolemy, to Cous, the Vicus Apollinis, a journey of four days. The fame account of the diftance was given by the natives to Dr. Pococke, Travels, vol. i. p. 87. In confequence of this, Cous, from a fmall village, became the city in upper Egypt next in magnitude to Foftat, or Old Cairo. In procefs of time, from caufes which I cannot explain, the trade from the Red Sea by Coffeir removed to Kene, farther down the river than Cous, Abulf. p. 13. 77. D'Anville Egypte, 196—200. In modern times, all the commodities of India imported into Egypt, are either brought by fea from Gidda to Suez, and thence carried on camels to Cairo, or are conveyed by land carriage by the caravan returning from the pilgrimage to Mecca, Niebuhr Voyage, tom. i. p. 224. Volney, i. 188, &c. This, as far as I have been able to trace it, is a complete account of all the different routes by which the productions of the Eaft have been conveyed to the Nile, from the firft opening of that communication. It is fingular that P. Sicard, Mem. des Miffions dans le Levant, tom. ii. p. 157, and fome other refpectable writers, fhould fuppofe Coffeir to be the Berenice founded by Ptolemy, although Ptolemy has laid down its latitude at 23° 50′, and Strabo has defcribed it as nearly under the fame parallel with that of Syenè, lib. ii. p. 195, D. In confequence of this miftake, Pliny's computation of the diftance between Berenice and Coptos, at two hundred and fifty-eight miles, has been deemed erroneous. Pococke, p. 87. But as Pliny not only

only mentions the total diſtance, but names the different ſtations in the journey, and ſpecifies the number of miles between each; and as the Itinerary of Antoninus coincides exactly with his account, D'Anville Egypte, p. 21, there is no reaſon to call in queſtion the accuracy of it.

NOTE XVII. Sect. I. p. 37.

Major Rennell is of opinion, "that under the Ptolemies, the Egyptians extended their navigation to the extreme point of the Indian continent, and even ſailed up the Ganges to Palibothra," now Patna. Introd. p. xxxvi. But had it been uſual to ſail up the Ganges as high as Patna, the interior parts of India muſt have been better known to the ancients than they ever were, and they would not have continued to derive their information concerning them from Megaſthenes alone. Strabo begins his deſcription of India in a very remarkable manner. He requeſts his readers to peruſe with indulgence the account which he gives of it, as it was a country very remote, and few perſons had viſited it; and of theſe, many having ſeen only a ſmall part of the country, related things either from hear-ſay, or, at the beſt, what they had haſtily remarked while they paſſed through it in the courſe of military ſervice, or on a journey. Strabo, lib. xv. p. 1005. B. He takes notice that few of the traders from the Arabian Gulf ever reached the Ganges. Ibid. 1006. C. He aſſerts, that the Ganges enters

7 the

the ſea by one mouth, ibid. 1011. C.; an error into which he could not have fallen if the navigation of that river had been common in his time. He mentions indeed the ſailing up the Ganges, ibid. 1010, but it is curſorily in a ſingle ſentence; whereas, if ſuch a conſiderable inland voyage of above four hundred miles, through a populous and rich country, had been cuſtomary, or even if it had ever been performed by the Roman, or Greek, or Egyptian traders, it muſt have merited a particular deſcription, and muſt have been mentioned by Pliny and other writers, as there was nothing ſimilar to it in the practice of navigation among the ancients. It is obſerved by Arrian (or whoever is the author of the Periplus Maris Erythræi), that previous to the diſcovery of a new route to India, which ſhall be mentioned afterwards, the commerce with that country was carried on in ſmall veſſels which ſailed round every bay, p. 32. Ap. Hudſ. Geogr. Min. Veſſels of ſuch light conſtruction, and which followed this mode of ſailing, were ill fitted for a voyage ſo diſtant as that round Cape Comorin, and up the bay of Bengal, to Patna. It is not improbable, that the merchants whom Strabo mentions as having reached the Ganges, may have travelled thither by land, either from the countries towards the mouth of the Indus, or from ſome part of the Malabar coaſt, and that the navigation up the Ganges, of which he caſually takes notice, was performed by the natives in veſſels of the country. This opinion derives ſome confirmation from his remarks upon the bad ſtructure of the veſſels which frequented that part of the Indian ocean. From his deſcription of them, p. 1012. C. it is evident that they were veſſels of the country.

NOTE XVIII. Sect. I. p. 39.

The erroneous ideas of many intelligent writers of antiquity with respect to the Caspian Sea, though well known to every man of letters, are so remarkable, and afford such a striking example of the imperfection of their geographical knowledge, that a more full account of them may not only be acceptable to some of my readers, but in endeavouring to trace the various routes by which the commodities of the East were conveyed to the nations of Europe, it becomes necessary to enter into some detail concerning their various sentiments with respect to this matter. 1. According to Strabo, the Caspian is a bay, that communicates with the great Northern ocean, from which it issues at first, by a narrow strait, and then expands into a sea extending in breadth five hundred stadia, lib. xi. p. 773. A. With him Pomponius Mela agrees, and describes the strait by which the Caspian is connected with the ocean, as of considerable length, and so narrow that it had the appearance of a river, lib. iii. c. 5. edit. Pliny likewise gives a similar description of it, Nat. Hist. lib. vi. c. 13. In the age of Justinian, this opinion concerning the communication of the Caspian Sea with the ocean, was still prevalent; Cosm. Indicopl. Topog. Christ. lib. ii. p. 138. C. 2. Some early writers, by a mistake still more singular, have supposed the Caspian Sea to be connected with the Euxine. Quintus Curtius, whose ignorance of geography is notorious, has adopted this error, lib. vii. c. 7. edit. 3. Arrian, though a much more judicious

judicious writer, and who by residing for some time in the Roman province of Cappadocia, of which he was governor, might have obtained more accurate information, declares in one place, the origin of the Caspian Sea to be still unknown, and is doubtful whether it was connected with the Euxine, or with the great Eastern ocean which surrounds India; lib. vii. c. 16. In another place he asserts, that there was a communication between the Caspian and the Eastern ocean; lib. v. c. 26. These errors appear more extraordinary, as a just description had been given of the Caspian by Herodotus, near five hundred years before the age of Strabo. "The Caspian, says he, is a sea by itself, unconnected with any other. Its length is as much as a vessel with oars can sail in fifteen days, its greatest breadth as much as it can sail in eight days;" lib. i. c. 203. Aristotle describes it in the same manner, and with his usual precision contends that it ought to be called a great lake not a sea; Meteorolog. lib. ii. Diodorus Siculus concurs with them in opinion, vol. ii. lib. xviii. p. 261. None of those authors determine whether the greatest length of the Caspian was from North to South, or from East to West. In the ancient maps which illustrate the geography of Ptolemy, it is delineated, as if its greatest length extended from East to West. In modern times the first information concerning the true form of the Caspian which the people of Europe received, was given by Anthony Jenkinson, an English merchant, who with a caravan from Russia travelled along a considerable part of its coast in the year 1558; Hakluyt Collect. vol. i. p. 334. The accuracy of Jenkinson's description was confirmed by an actual survey of that sea made by order of Peter the Great,

4 A. D.

A. D. 1718, and it is now ascertained not only that the Caspian is unconnected with any other sea, but that its length from North to South is considerably more than its greatest breadth from East to West. From this detail, however, we learn how the ill-founded ideas concerning it, which were generally adopted, gave rise to various wild schemes of conveying Indian commodities to Europe by means of its supposed communication with the Euxine sea, or with the Northern ocean. It is an additional proof of the attention of Alexander the Great to every thing conducive to the improvement of commerce, that a short time before his death he gave directions to fit out a squadron in the Caspian, in order to survey that sea, and to discover whether it was connected either with the Euxine or Indian ocean; Arrian. lib. vii. c. 16.

NOTE XIX. SECT. I. p. 49.

FROM this curious detail, we learn how imperfect ancient navigation was, even in its most improved state. The voyage from Berenice to Ocelis, could not have taken thirty days, if any other course had been held than that of servilely following the windings of the coast. The voyage from Ocelis to Musiris would be (according to Major Rennell) fifteen days run for an European ship in the modern stile of navigation, being about seventeen hundred and fifty marine miles, on a streight course; Introd. p. xxxvii. It is remarkable, that though the Periplus Maris Erythræi was written after the voyage of Hippalus, the chief object of the author of it is to describe the

the ancient courſe along the coaſts of Arabia and Perſia, to the mouth of the Indus, and from thence down the weſtern ſhore of the continent to Muſiris. I can account for this, only by ſuppoſing, that from the unwillingneſs of mankind to abandon old habits, the greater part of the traders from Berenice ſtill continued to follow that route to which they were accuſtomed. To go from Alexandria to Muſiris, required (according to Pliny) ninety-four days. In the year 1788, the Boddam, a ſhip belonging to the Engliſh Eaſt-India Company, of a thouſand tuns burthen, took only fourteen days more to complete her voyage from Portſmouth to Madras. Such are the improvements which have been made in navigation.

NOTE XX. SECT. II. p. 50.

It was the opinion of Plato, that in a well-regulated commonwealth the citizens ſhould not engage in commerce, nor the ſtate aim at obtaining maritime power. Commerce, he contends, would corrupt the purity of their morals, and by entering into the ſea-ſervice, they would be accuſtomed to find pretexts for juſtifying conduct ſo inconſiſtent with what was manly and becoming, as would gradually relax the ſtrictneſs of military diſcipline. It had been better for the Athenians, he aſſerts, to have continued to ſend annually the ſons of ſeven of their principal citizens to be devoured by the Minotaur, than to have changed their ancient manners, and to have become a maritime power. In that perfect republic, of which he delineates the form, he ordains that the capital ſhould be ſituated at leaſt

ten.

ten miles from the ſea; De Legibus, lib. iv. ab initio. Theſe ideas of Plato were adopted by other philoſophers. Ariſtotle enters into a formal diſcuſſion of the queſtion, whether a State rightly conſtituted ſhould be commercial or not; and though abundantly diſpoſed to eſpouſe ſentiments oppoſite to thoſe of Plato, he does not venture to decide explicitly with reſpect to it; De Repub. lib. vii. c. 6. In ages when ſuch opinions prevail, little information concerning commerce can be expected.

NOTE XXI. Sect. II. p. 53.

Pliny, lib. ix. c. 35. Principium ergo culmenque omnium rerum prætij Margaritæ tenent. In lib. xxxvii. c. 4. he affirms, Maximum in rebus humanis prætium, non ſolum inter gemmas, habet Adamas. Theſe two paſſages ſtand in ſuch direct contradiction to one another, that it is impoſſible to reconcile them, or to determine which is moſt comformable to truth. I have adhered to the former, becauſe we have many inſtances of the exorbitant price of pearls, but none, as far as I know, of diamonds having been purchaſed at a rate ſo high. In this opinion I am confirmed by a paſſage in Pliny, lib. xix. c. 1.; having mentioned the exorbitant price of *Aſbeſtos*, he ſays, "æquat prætia excellentium Margaritarum;" which implies, that he conſidered them to be of higher price than any other commodity.

NOTE

NOTE XXII. SECT. II. p. 54.

PLINY has devoted two entire books of his Natural Hiſtory, lib. xii. and xiii. to the enumeration and deſcription of the ſpices, aromatics, ointments, and perfumes, the uſe of which luxury had introduced among his countrymen. As many of theſe were the productions of India, or of the countries beyond it, and as the trade with the Eaſt was carried on to a great extent in the age of Pliny, we may form ſome idea of the immenſe demand for them, from the high price at which they continued to be ſold in Rome. To compare the prices of the ſame commodities in ancient Rome, with thoſe now paid in our own country, is not a gratification of curioſity merely, but affords a ſtandard by which we may eſtimate the different degree of ſucceſs with which the Indian trade has been conducted in ancient and modern times. Many remarkable paſſages in ancient authors, concerning the extravagant price of precious ſtones and pearls among the Romans, as well as the general uſe of them by perſons of all ranks, are collected by Meurſius de Lux. Romanorum, cap. 5.; and by Staniſlaus Robierzyckius, in his treatiſe on the ſame ſubject, lib. ii. c. 1. The Engliſh reader will receive ſufficient information from Dr. Arbuthnot, in his valuable Tables of ancient coins, weights, and meaſures, p. 172, &c.

NOTE XXIII. Sect. II. p. 56.

M. Mahudel, in a memoir read in the academy of inſcriptions and belles lettres in the year 1719, has collected the various opinions of the ancients concerning the nature and origin of ſilk, which tend all to prove their ignorance with regard to it. Since the publication of M. Mahudel's memoir, P. du Halde has deſcribed a ſpecies of ſilk, of which I believe he communicated the firſt notice to the moderns. "This is produced by ſmall inſects nearly reſembling ſnails. They do not form cocoons either round or oval like the ſilk-worm, but ſpin very long threads, which faſten themſelves to trees and buſhes as they are driven by the wind. Theſe are gathered, and wrought into ſilk ſtuffs, coarſer than thoſe produced by domeſtic ſilk-worms. The inſects who produce this coarſe ſilk are wild." Deſcription de l'Empire de la Chine, tom. ii. folio, p. 207. This nearly reſembles Virgil's deſcription,

> Velleraque ut foliis depectant tenuia Seres.
>
> Georg. II. 121.

An attentive reader of Virgil will find, that, beſides all the other qualities of a great deſcriptive poet, he poſſeſſed an extenſive knowledge of natural hiſtory. The nature and productions of the wild ſilk-worms are illuſtrated at greater length in the large collection of Memoires concernant l'Hiſtoire, les Sciences, les Arts, &c. des Chinois, tom. ii. p. 575, &c.; and by Pere de Mailla, in his voluminous Hiſtory of China, tom. xiii. p. 434. It is a ſingular circumſtance in the hiſtory of ſilk, that

4 on

on account of its being an excretion of a worm, the Mahomedans conſider it as an unclean dreſs; and it has been decided, with the unanimous aſſent of all the doctors, that a perſon wearing a garment made entirely of ſilk, cannot lawfully offer up the daily prayers enjoined by the Koran. Herbel. Bibl. Orient. artic. *Harir.*

NOTE XXIV. Sect. II. p. 57.

If the uſe of the cotton manufactures of India had been common among the Romans, the various kinds of them would have been enumerated in the Law de Publicanis et Vectigalibus, in the ſame manner as the different kinds of ſpices and precious ſtones. Such a ſpecification would have been equally neceſſary for the direction both of the merchant and of the tax-gatherer.

NOTE XXV. Sect. II. p. 57.

This part of Arrian's Periplus has been examined with great accuracy and learning by Lieutenant Wilford; and from his inveſtigation it is evident, that the Plithana of Arrian is the modern Pultanah, on the ſouthern banks of the river Godvery, two hundred and ſeventeen Britiſh miles ſouth from Baroach; that the poſition of Tagara is the ſame with that of the modern Dowlatabad, and the high grounds acroſs which the goods were conveyed to Baroach, are the Ballagaut mountains. The bearings and diſtances of theſe different places, as ſpecified by Arrian, afford an additional proof (were that neceſſary) of the exact information which he had received concerning this diſtrict of India; Aſiatic Reſearches, vol. i. p. 369, &c.

NOTE XXVI. Sect. II. p. 64.

Strabo acknowledges his neglect of the improvements in geography which Hipparchus had deduced from aſtronomical obſervations, and juſtifies it by one of thoſe logical ſubtleties which the ancients were apt to introduce into all their writings. "A geographer," ſays he, (i. e. a deſcriber of the earth) "is "to pay no attention to what is out of the earth; nor will "men, engaged in conducting the affairs of that part of the "earth which is inhabited, deem the diſtinction and diviſions "of Hipparchus worthy of notice." Lib. ii. 194. C.

NOTE XXVII. Sect. II. p. 64.

What an high opinion the ancients had of Ptolemy, we learn from Agathemerus, who flouriſhed not long after him. "Ptolemy," ſays he, "who reduced geography into a regular "ſyſtem, treats of every thing relating to it, not careleſsly, "or merely according to ideas of his own; but attending to "what had been delivered by more ancient authors, he adopted "from them whatever he found conſonant to truth." Epitome Geogr.

Geogr. lib. i. c. 6. edit. Hudſon. From the ſame admiration of his work, Agathodæmon, an artiſt of Alexandria, prepared a ſeries of maps for the illuſtration of it, in which the poſition of all the places mentioned by Ptolemy, with their longitude and latitude, is laid down preciſely according to his ideas. Fabric. Biblioth. Græc. iii. 412.

NOTE XXVIII. SECT. II. p. 65.

As theſe public Surveys and Itineraries furniſhed the ancient geographers with the beſt information concerning the poſition and diſtances of many places, it may be proper to point out the manner in which they were completed by the Romans. The idea of a general ſurvey of the whole empire was firſt formed by Julius Cæſar, and, having been begun by him under authority of a decree of the ſenate, was finiſhed by Auguſtus. As Rome was ſtill far inferior to Greece in ſcience, the execution of this great undertaking was committed to three Greeks, men of great abilities, and ſkilled in every part of philoſophy. The ſurvey of the eaſtern diviſion of the empire was finiſhed by Zenodoxus in fourteen years five months and nine days. That of the northern diviſion was finiſhed by Theodotus in twenty years eight months and ten days. The ſouthern diviſion was finiſhed in twenty-five years one month and ten days. Æthici Coſmographia apud Geographos, editos à Hen. Stephano, 1577. p. 107. This was an undertaking worthy of thoſe illuſtrious perſons, and ſuited to the magnificence of a great people. Beſides this general ſurvey, every new war produced

duced a new delineation and meaſurement of the countries which were the ſeat of it. We may conclude from Vegetius, Inſtit. Rei Militaris, lib. iii. c. 6., that every governor of a Roman province was furniſhed with a deſcription of it; in which were ſpecified the diſtance of places in miles, the nature of the roads, the bye-roads, the ſhort cuts, the mountains, the rivers, &c.; all theſe, ſays he, were not only deſcribed in words, but were delineated in a map, that, in deliberating concerning his military movements, the eyes of a general might aid the deciſions of his mind.

NOTE XXIX. Sect. II. p. 66.

The conſequence of this miſtake is remarkable. Ptolemy, lib. vii. c. 1., computes the longitude of Barygaza, or Baroach, to be 17° 20′; and that of Cory, or Cape Comorin, to be 13° 20′. which is the difference of four degrees preciſely; whereas the real difference between theſe two places is nearly fourteen degrees.

NOTE XXX. Sect. II. p. 66.

Ramusio, the publiſher of the moſt ancient and perhaps the moſt valuable Collection of Voyages, is the firſt perſon, as far as I know, who takes notice of this ſtrange error of Ptolemy; Viaggi, vol. i. p. 181. He juſtly obſerves, that the Author

Author of the Circumnavigation of the Erythræan Sea had been more accurate, and had deſcribed the peninſula of India as extending from north to ſouth; Peripl. p. 24. 29.

NOTE XXXI. Sect. II. p. 68.

This error of Ptolemy juſtly merits the name of *enormous*, which I have given to it; and it will appear more ſurpriſing when we recollect, that he muſt have been acquainted, not only with what Herodotus relates concerning the circumnavigation of Africa, by order of one of the Egyptian kings, Lib. iv. c. 4., but with the opinion of Eratoſthenes, who held that the great extent of the Atlantic ocean was the only thing which prevented a communication between Europe and India by ſea; Strab. Geogr. lib. i. p. 113. A. This error, however, muſt not be imputed wholly to Ptolemy. Hipparchus, whom we may conſider as his guide, had taught that the earth is not ſurrounded by one continuous ocean, but that it is ſeparated by different iſthmuſes, which divide it into ſeveral large baſons; Strab. lib. i. p. 11. B. Ptolemy, having adopted this opinion, was induced to maintain that an unknown country extended from Cattigara to Praſſum on the ſouth-eaſt coaſt of Africa; Geogr. lib. vii. c. 3 and 5. As Ptolemy's ſyſtem of geography was univerſally received, this error ſpread along with it. In conformity to it the Arabian geographer Edriſſi, who wrote in the twelfth century, taught that a continued tract of land ſtretched eaſtward from Sofala on the African coaſt, until it united with ſome part of the Indian continent; D'Anville, Antiq.

Antiq. p. 187. Annexed to the firſt volume of Geſta Dei per Francos, there is an ancient and very rude map of the habitable globe, delineated according to this idea of Ptolemy. M. Goſſellin, in his map entitled Ptolemæi Syſtema Geographicum, has exhibited this imaginary tract of land which Ptolemy ſuppoſes to have connected Africa with Aſia; Geographie des Grecs analyſée.

NOTE XXXII. Sect. II. p. 69.

In this part of the Diſquiſition, as well as in the map prepared for illuſtrating it, the geographical ideas of M. D'Anville, to which Major Rennell has given the ſanction of his approbation, Introd. p. xxxix. have been generally adopted. But M. Goſſellin has lately publiſhed, "The Geography of the "Greeks analiſed; or, the Syſtems of Eratoſthenes, Strabo, and "Ptolemy, compared with each other, and with the Knowledge "which the Moderns have acquired;" a learned and ingenious work, in which he differs from his countryman with reſpect to many of his determinations. According to M. Goſſellin, the Magnum Promontorium, which M. D'Anville concludes to be Cape Romania, at the ſouthern extremity of the peninſula of Malacca, is the point of Bragu, at the mouth of the great river Ava; near to which he places Zaba, ſuppoſed by M. D'Anville, and by Barros, Decad. ii. liv. vi. c. 1. to be ſituated on the ſtrait of Sincapura or Malacca. The Magnus Sinus of Ptolemy he holds to be the ſame with the Gulf of Martaban, not the Gulf of Siam, according to M. D'Anville's deciſion. The

2 poſition

poſition of Cattigara, as he endeavours to prove, correſponds to that of Mergui, a conſiderable port on the weſt coaſt of the kingdom of Siam, and that Thinæ, or Sinæ Metropolis, which M. D'Anville removes as far as Sin-hoa, in the kingdom of Cochin-China, is ſituated on the ſame river with Mergui, and now bears the name of Tana-ſerim. The Ibadij Inſula of Ptolemy, which M. D'Anville determines to be Sumatra, he contends, is one of that cluſter of ſmall iſles which lie off this part of the coaſt of Siam; p. 137—148. According to M. Goſſellin's ſyſtem, the ancients never ſailed through the Straits of Malacca, had no knowledge of the iſland of Sumatra, and were altogether unacquainted with the Eaſtern Ocean. If to any of my readers theſe opinions appear to be well founded, the navigation and commerce of the ancients in India muſt be circumſcribed within limits ſtill more confined than thoſe which I have allotted to them. From the Ayeen Akbery, vol. ii. p. 7. we learn that Cheen was an ancient name of the kingdom of Pegu; as that country borders upon Ava, where M. Goſſellin places the Great Promontory, this near reſemblance of names may appear, perhaps, to confirm his opinion that Sinæ Metropolis was ſituated on this coaſt, and not ſo far Eaſt as M. D'Anville has placed it.

As Ptolemy's geography of this eaſtern diviſion of Aſia is more erroneous, obſcure, and contradictory than in any other part of his work, and as all the manuſcripts of it, both Greek and Latin, are remarkably incorrect in the two chapters which contain the deſcription of the countries beyond the Ganges, M. D'Anville, in his Memoir concerning the limits of the world known to the ancients beyond the Ganges, has admitted into it a larger portion of conjecture than we find in the other researches of that cautious geographer. He likewise builds more than usual upon the resemblances between the ancient and modern names of places, though at all times he discovers a propensity, perhaps too great, to trace these, and to rest upon them. These resemblances are often, indeed, very striking, and have led him to many happy discoveries. But in perusing his works, it is impossible, I should think, not to perceive that some which he mentions are far fetched and fanciful. Whenever I follow him, I have adopted only such conclusions as seem to be established with his accustomed accuracy.

NOTE XXXIII. Sect. II. p. 78.

The Author of the Circumnavigation of the Erythræan Sea has marked the distances of many of the places which he mentions, with such accuracy as renders it a nearer approach, than what is to be found in any writer of antiquity, to a complete survey of the coast from Myos-hormus, on the west side of the Arabian Gulf, along the shores of Ethiopia, Arabia, Persia, and Caramania, to the mouth of the Indus, and thence down the west coast of the Indian Peninsula to Musiris and Barace. This adds to the value of this short treatise, which, in every other respect, possesses great merit. It may be considered as a remarkable proof of the extent and accuracy of this Author's intelligence concerning India, that he is the only ancient writer who appears in any degree to have been acquainted with the great divifion of the country, which ftill fubfifts, viz. Indoftan Proper, comprehending the northern provinces of the Peninfula, and the Deccan, comprehending the fouthern provinces. "From Barygaza (fays he) the continent "ftretches to the fouth; hence that diftrict is called Dachina-"bades, for, in the language of the country, the fouth is called "Dachanos;" Peripl. p. 29. As the Greeks and Romans, when they adopt any foreign name, always gave it a termination peculiar to their own language, which the grammatical ftructure of both tongues rendered, in fome degree, neceffary, it is evident that Dachanos is the fame with Deccan, which word has ftill the fame fignification, and is ftill the name of that divifion of the Peninfula. The northern limit of the Deccan at prefent is the river Nerbuddah, where our Author likewife fixes it, Peripl. ibid.

NOTE XXXIV. Sect. II. p. 81.

Though, in deducing the latitudes of places from obfervations of the fun or ftars, the ancient aftronomers neglected feveral corrections, which ought to have been applied, their refults were fometimes exact to a few minutes, but at other times they appear to have been erroneous to the extent of two, or even three degrees, and may perhaps be reckoned, one with another, to have come within half a degree of the truth. This part of the ancient geography would therefore have been tolerably accurate, if there had been a ſufficient number of ſuch determinations. Theſe, however, were far from being numerous, and appear to have been confined to ſome of the more remarkable places in the countries which ſurround the Mediterranean ſea.

When, from want of more accurate obſervations, the latitude was inferred from the length of the longeſt or ſhorteſt day, no great degree of preciſion was, in any caſe, to be expected, and leaſt of all in the vicinity of the Equator. An error of a quarter of an hour, which, without ſome mode of meaſuring time more accurate than ancient obſervers could employ, was not eaſily avoided, might produce, in ſuch ſituations, an error of four degrees in the determination of the latitude.

With reſpect to places in the torrid zone, there was another reſource for determining the latitude. This was by obſerving the time of the year when the ſun was vertical to any place, or when bodies that ſtood perpendicular to the horizon had no ſhadow at noon-day; the ſun's diſtance from the Equator at that time, which was known from the principles of aſtronomy, was equal to the latitude of the place. We have inſtances of the application of this method in the determination of the parallels of Syene and Meroe. The accuracy which this method would admit of, ſeems to be limited to about half a degree, and this only on the ſuppoſition that the obſerver was ſtationary; for if he was travelling from one place to another,

6 and

and had not an opportunity of correcting the obſervation of one day by that of the day following, he was likely to deviate much more conſiderably from the truth.

WITH reſpect to the longitude of places, as eclipſes of the moon are not frequent, and could ſeldom be of uſe for determining it, and only when there were aſtronomers to obſerve them with accuracy, they may be left out of the account altogether when we are examining the geography of remote countries. The differences of the meridians of places were therefore anciently aſcertained entirely by the bearings and diſtances of one place from another, and of conſequence all the errors of reckonings, ſurveys, and itineraries, fell chiefly upon the longitude, in the ſame manner as happens at preſent in a ſhip which has no method of determining its longitude, but by comparing the dead-reckoning with the obſervations of the latitude; though with this difference, that the errors, to which the moſt ſkilful of the ancient navigators was liable, were far greater than what the moſt ignorant ſhip-maſter of modern times, provided with a compaſs, can well commit. The length of the Mediterranean meaſured, in degrees of longitude, from the Pillars of Hercules to the Bay of Iſſus, is leſs than forty degrees; but in Ptolemy's maps it is more than ſixty, and, in general, his longitudes, counting from the meridian of Alexandria, eſpecially toward the Eaſt, are erroneous nearly in the ſame proportion. It appears, indeed, that in remote ſeas, the coaſts were often delineated from an imperfect account of the diſtances ſailed, without the leaſt knowledge of the bearings or direction of the ſhip's courſe.

Ptolemy,

Ptolemy, it is true, uſed to make an allowance of about one-third for the winding of a ſhip's courſe, Geogr. lib. i. c. 12.; but it is plain, that the application of this general rule could ſeldom lead to an accurate concluſion. Of this there is a ſtriking inſtance in the form which that geographer has given to the Peninſula of India. From the Barygazenum Promontorium to the place marked Locus unde ſolvunt in Chryſen navigantes, that is, from Surat on the Malabar coaſt, to about Narſapour on the Coromandel coaſt, the diſtance meaſured along the ſea-ſhore is nearly the ſame with what it is in reality; that is, about five hundred and twenty leagues. But the miſtake in the direction is aſtoniſhing, for the Malabar and Coromandel coaſt, inſtead of ſtretching to the ſouth, and interſecting one another at Cape Comorin, in a very acute angle, are extended by Ptolemy almoſt in the ſame ſtraight line from weſt to eaſt, declining a little to the ſouth. This coaſt is, at the ſame time, marked with ſeveral bays and promontories, nearly reſembling, in their poſition, thoſe which actually exiſt on it. All theſe circumſtances compared together, point out very clearly what were the materials from which the ancient map of India was compoſed. The ſhips which had viſited the coaſt of that country, had kept an account of the time which they took to ſail from one place to another, and had marked, as they ſtood along ſhore, on what hand the land lay, when they ſhaped their courſe acroſs a bay, or doubled a promontory. This imperfect journal, with an inaccurate account, perhaps, of the latitude of one or two places, was probably all the information concerning the coaſt of India, which Ptolemy was able to procure. That he ſhould have been able to procure

cure no better information from merchants who failed with no particular view of exploring the coaft, will not appear wonderful, if we confider that even the celebrated Periplus of Hanno would not enable a geographer to lay down the coaft of Africa with more precifion, than Ptolemy has delineated that of India.

NOTE XXXV. Sect. II. p. 89.

The introduction of the filk-worm into Europe, and the effects which this produced, came under the view of Mr. Gibbon, in writing the hiftory of the Emperor Juftinian, and though it was an incident of fubordinate importance only, amidft the multiplicity of great tranfactions which muft have occupied his attention, he has examined this event with an accuracy, and related it with a precifion, which would have done honour to an author who had no higher object of refearch. Vol. iv. p. 71, &c. Nor is it here only that I am called upon to afcribe to him this merit. The fubject of my inquiries has led me feveral times upon ground which he had gone over, and I have uniformly received information from the induftry and difcernment with which he has furveyed it.

NOTE

NOTE XXXVI. Sect. III. p. 94.

This voyage, together with the obſervations of Abu Zeid al Haſan of Siraf, was publiſhed by M. Renaudot, A. D. 1718, under the title of "Anciennes Relations des Indes, et de la "Chine, de deux Voyageurs Mahometans, qui y allerent "dans le Neuvieme Siecle traduites de Arabe, avec des re-"marques ſur les principaux endroits de ces Relations." As M. Renaudot, in his remarks, repreſents the literature and police of the Chineſe, in colours very different from thoſe of the ſplendid deſcriptions which a blind admiration had prompted the Jeſuits to publiſh, two zealous miſſionaries have called in queſtion the authenticity of theſe Relations, and have aſſerted that the authors of them had never been in China; P. Premare Lettr. edifiantes et curieuſes, tom. xix. p. 420, &c. P. Parennin, ibid. tom. xxi. p. 158, &c. Some doubts concerning their authenticity were entertained likewiſe by ſeveral learned men in England, on account of M. Renaudot's having given no notice of the manuſcript which he tranſlated, but that he found it in the library of M. le Comte de Seignelay. As no perſon had ſeen the manuſcript ſince that time, the doubts increaſed, and M. Renaudot was charged with the crime of impoſing upon the public. But the Colbert Manuſcripts having been depoſited in the King's Library, as (fortunately for literature) moſt private collections are in France, M. de Guignes, after a long ſearch, diſcovered the identical manuſcript to which

which M. Renaudot refers. It appears to have been written in the twelfth century; Journal des Scavans, Dec. 1764, p. 315, &c. As I had not the French edition of M. Renaudot's book, my references are made to the English tranſlation. The Relation of the two Arabian Travellers is confirmed, in many points, by their countryman Maſſoudi, who publiſhed his treatiſe on univerſal hiſtory, to which he gives the fantaſtical title of "Meadows of Gold, and Mines of "Jewels," a hundred and ſix years after their time. From him, likewiſe, we receive ſuch an account of India in the tenth century, as renders it evident that the Arabians had then acquired an extenſive knowledge of that country. According to his deſcription, the peninſula of India was divided into four kingdoms. The firſt was compoſed of the provinces ſituated on the Indus, and the rivers which fall into it; the capital of which was Moultan. The capital of the ſecond kingdom was Canoge, which, from the ruins of it ſtill remaining, appears to have been a very large city; Rennell's Memoirs, p. 54. In order to give an idea of its populouſneſs, the Indian hiſtorians aſſert, that it contained thirty thouſand ſhops, in which betel-nut was ſold, and ſixty thouſand ſets of muſicians and ſingers, who paid a tax to government; Feriſhta, tranſlated by Dow, vol. i. p. 32. The third kingdom was Cachemire. Maſſoudi, as far as I know, is the firſt author who mentions this paradiſe of India, of which he gives a ſhort but juſt deſcription. The fourth is the kingdom of Guzerate, which he repreſents as the greateſt and moſt powerful; and he concurs with the two Arabian Travellers, in giving the ſovereigns of it the appellation of Balhara. What Maſſoudi relates concerning India is more

 worthy

worthy of notice, as he himſelf had viſited that country; Notices et Extraits des Manuſcrits de la Bibliotheque du Roi, tom. i. p. 9, 10. Maſſoudi confirms what the two Arabian Travellers relate, concerning the extraordinary progreſs of the Indians in aſtronomical ſcience. According to his account, a temple was built during the reign of Brahman, the firſt monarch of India, with twelve towers, repreſenting the twelve ſigns of the zodiac; and in which was delineated, a view of all the ſtars as they appear in the heavens. In the ſame reign was compoſed the famous Sind-Hind, which ſeems to be the ſtandard treatiſe of Indian aſtronomy; Notices, &c. tom. i. p. 7. Another Arabian author, who wrote about the middle of the fourteenth century, divides India into three parts. The northern, comprehending all the provinces on the Indus. The middle, extending from Guzerate to the Ganges. The ſouthern, which he denominates Comar, from Cape Comorin; Notices, &c. tom. ii. p. 46.

NOTE XXXVII. Sect. III. p. 95.

The naval ſkill of the Chineſe ſeems not to have been ſuperior to that of the Greeks, the Romans, or Arabians. The courſe which they held from Canton to Siraf, near the mouth of the Perſian Gulf, is deſcribed by their own authors. They kept as near as poſſible to the ſhore until they reached the iſland of Ceylon, and then doubling Cape Comorin, they ſailed along the weſt ſide of the Peninſula, as far as the mouth of the Indus,

Indus, and thence ſteered along the coaſt to the place of their deſtination; Mem. de Literat. tom. xxxii. p. 367. Some authors have contended, that both the Arabs and Chineſe were well acquainted with the mariners compaſs, and the uſe of it in navigation; but it is remarkable that in the Arabic, Turkiſh, or Perſian languages there is no original name for the compaſs. They commonly call it *Boſſola*, the Italian name, which ſhews that the thing ſignified is foreign to them as well as the word. There is not one ſingle obſervation, of ancient date, made by the Arabs on the variation of the needle, or any inſtruction deduced from it, for the aſſiſtance of navigators. Sir John Chardin, one of the moſt learned and beſt informed travellers who has viſited the Eaſt, having been conſulted upon this point, returns for anſwer, "I "boldly aſſert, that the Aſiatics are beholden to us for this "wonderful inſtrument, which they had from Europe a long "time before the Portugueſe conqueſts. For, firſt, their "compaſſes are exactly like ours, and they buy them of "Europeans as much as they can, ſcarce daring to meddle with "their needles themſelves. Secondly, It is certain that the "old navigators only coaſted it along, which I impute to their "want of this inſtrument to guide and inſtruct them in the "middle of the ocean. We cannot pretend to ſay that they "were afraid of venturing far from home, for the Arabs, the "firſt navigators in the world, in my opinion, at leaſt for the "Eaſtern ſeas, have, time out of mind, ſailed from the bottom "of the Red Sea, all along the coaſt of Africa; and the "Chineſe have always traded with Java and Sumatra, which

Gg 2 "is

"is a very considerable voyage. So many islands uninhabited "and yet productive, so many lands unknown to the people I "speak of, are a proof that the old navigators had not the "art of sailing on the main sea. I have nothing but argu- "ment to offer touching this matter, having never met with "any person in Persia or the Indies to inform me when the "compass was first known among them, though I made "inquiry of the most learned men in both countries. I have "sailed from the Indies to Persia in Indian ships, when no "European has been aboard but myself. The pilots were "all Indians, and they used the fore-staff and quadrant for "their observations. These instruments they have from us, and "made by our artists, and they do not in the least vary from "ours, except that the characters are Arabic. The Arabs are "the most skilful navigators of all the Asiatics or Africans; "but neither they nor the Indians make use of charts; and "they do not much want them: some they have, but they "are copied from ours, for they are altogether ignorant of per- "spective." Inquiry when the Mahomedans first entered China, p. 141, &c. When M. Niehbuhr was at Cairo, he found a magnetic needle in the possession of a Mahomedan, which served to point out the Kaaba, and he gave it the name of *El Magnatis*, a clear proof of its European origin. Voyage en Arabie, tom. ii. p. 169.

NOTE

NOTE XXXVIII. SECT. III. p. 97.

THE progreſs of Chriſtianity, and of Mahomedaniſm, both in China and India, is atteſted by ſuch evidence as leaves no doubt with reſpect to it. This evidence is collected by Aſſemannus, Biblioth. Orient. vol. iv. p. 437, &c. 521, &c.; and by M. Renaudot, in two Diſſertations annexed to Anciennes Relations; and by M. de la Croze, Hiſtoire de Chriſtianiſme des Indes. In our own age, however, we know that the number of proſelytes to either of theſe religions is extremely ſmall, eſpecially in India. A Gentoo conſiders all the diſtinctions and privileges of his caſt, as belonging to him by an excluſive and incommunicable right. To convert, or to be converted, are ideas equally repugnant to the principles moſt deeply rooted in his mind; nor can either the Catholic or Proteſtant miſſionaries in India boaſt of having overcome theſe prejudices, except among a few in the loweſt caſts, or of ſuch as have loſt their caſt altogether. This laſt circumſtance is a great obſtacle to the progreſs of Chriſtianity in India. As Europeans eat the fleſh of that animal which the Hindoos deem ſacred, and drink intoxicating liquors, in which practices they are imitated by the converts to Chriſtianity, this ſinks them to a level with the Pariars, the moſt contemptible and odious race of men. Some Catholic miſſionaries were ſo ſenſible of this, that they affected to imitate the dreſs and manner of living of Brahmins, and refuſed to aſſociate with the Pariars, or to admit them to the participation of the ſacraments. But this was condemned by the apoſtolic legate

legate Tournon, as inconſiſtent with the ſpirit and precepts of the Chriſtian religion; Voyage aux Indes Orientales, par M. Sonnerat, tom. i. p. 58. note. Notwithſtanding the labours of miſſionaries for upwards of two hundred years, (ſays a late ingenious writer,) and the eſtabliſhments of different Chriſtian nations, who ſupport and protect them, out of, perhaps, one hundred millions of Hindoos, there are not twelve thouſand Chriſtians, and thoſe almoſt entirely *Chancalas*, or outcaſts. Sketches relating to the hiſtory, religion, learning, and manners of the Hindoos, p. 48. The number of Mahomedans, or Moors, now in Indoſtan, is ſuppoſed to be near ten millions; but they are not the original inhabitants of the country, but the deſcendants of adventurers, who have been pouring in from Tartary, Perſia, and Arabia, ever ſince the invaſion of Mahmoud of Gazna, A. D. 1002, the firſt Mahomedan conqueror of India. Orme Hiſt. of Military Tranſact. in Indoſtan, vol. i. p. 24. Herbelot, Biblioth. Orient. artic. *Gaznaviah*. As the manners of the Indians in ancient times ſeem to have been, in every reſpect, the ſame with thoſe of the preſent age, it is probable, that the Chriſtians and Mahomedans, ſaid to be ſo numerous in India and China, were chiefly foreigners, allured thither by a lucrative commerce, or their deſcendants. The number of Mahomedans in China has been conſiderably increaſed by a practice, common among them, of buying children in years of famine, whom they educate in the Mahomedan religion. Hiſt. Genev. des Voyages, tom. vi. p. 357.

NOTE

NOTE XXXIX. Sect. III. p. 102.

From the Chronicle of Andrew Dandulo, Doge of Venice, who was elevated to that high ſtation at a time when his countrymen had eſtabliſhed a regular trade with Alexandria, and imported from it all the productions of the Eaſt, it was natural to expect ſome information concerning their early trade with that country; but, except an idle tale concerning ſome Venetian ſhips which had ſailed to Alexandria about the year 828, contrary to a decree of the ſtate, and which ſtole thence the body of St. Mark; Murat. Script. Rer. Ital. vol. xii. lib. 8. c. 2. p. 170.; I find no other hint concerning the communication between the two countries. On the contrary, circumſtances occur, which ſhew that the reſort of Europeans to Egypt had ceaſed, almoſt entirely, for ſome time. Prior to the ſeventh and eighth centuries, the greater part of the public deeds in Italy, and in other countries of Europe, were written upon paper fabricated of the Egyptian Papyrus; but after that period, as Europeans no longer ventured to trade in Alexandria, almoſt all charters and other deeds are written upon parchment. Murat. Antiq. Ital. Medii Ævi, vol. iii. p. 832. I have been induced, both in the text and in this note, to ſtate theſe particulars concerning the interruption of trade between the Chriſtians and Mahometans ſo fully, in order to correct an error into which ſeveral modern authors have fallen, by ſuppoſing, that ſoon after the firſt conqueſts of the Caliphs, the trade with India returned into its ancient channels, and the merchants

chants of Europe resorted with the same freedom as formerly to the ports of Egypt and Syria.

NOTE XL. Sect. III. p. 106.

It is proper to remark (says Mr. Stewart) that the Indians have an admirable method of rendering their religion lucrative, it being usual for the Faquirs to carry with them, in their pilgrimages from the sea-coasts to the interior parts, pearls, corals, spices, and other precious articles, of small bulk, which they exchange, on their return, for gold-dust, musk, and other things of a similar nature, concealing them easily in their hair, and in the cloths round their middle, carrying on, in proportion to their numbers, no inconsiderable traffic by these means. Account of the Kingdom of Thibet, Philos. Transact. vol. lxvii. part ii. p. 483.

NOTE XLI. Sect. III. p. 113.

Caffa is the most commodious station for trade in the Black Sea. While in the hands of the Genoese, who kept possession of it above two centuries, they rendered it the seat of an extensive and flourishing commerce. Even under all the disadvantages of its subjection, at present, to the Turkish government, it continues to be a place of considerable trade. Sir John Chardin, who visited it A. D. 1672, relates, that, during his

his residence of forty days there, above four hundred ships arrived at Caffa, or sailed from it. Voyages, i. 48. He observed there, several remains of Genoese magnificence. The number of its inhabitants, according to M. Peyssonnel, amounts still to eighty thousand. Commerce de la Mer Noire, tom. i. p. 15. He describes its trade as very great.

NOTE XLII. Sect. III. p. 115.

The rapacity and insolence of the Genoese settled in Constantinople, are painted by Nicephorus Gregoras, an eye-witness of their conduct, in very striking colours. "They," says he, "now," i. e. about the year 1340, "dreamed that they "had acquired the dominion of the sea, and claimed an exclusive "right to the trade of the Euxine, prohibiting the Greeks "to sail to the Mæotis, the Chersonesus, or any part of the "coast beyond the mouth of the Danube, without a licence from "them. This exclusion they extended likewise to the Vene- "tians, and their arrogance proceeded so far as to form a "scheme of imposing a toll upon every vessel passing through "the Bosphorus." Lib. xviii. c. 2. § 1.

NOTE XLIII. SECT. III. p. 115.

A PERMISSION from the Pope was deemed ſo neceſſary to authoriſe a commercial intercourſe with infidels, that long after this period, in the year 1454, Nicolas V. in his famous bull in favour of prince Henry of Portugal, among other privileges, grants him a licence to trade with Mahomedans, and refers to ſimilar conceſſions from Pope Martin V., and Eugenius, to kings of Portugal. Leibnitz Codex Jur. Gent. Diplomat. Pars I. p. 489.

NOTE XLIV. SECT. III. p. 117.

NEITHER Jovius, the profeſſed panegyriſt of the Medici, nor Jo. M. Brutus, their detractor, though both mention the exorbitant wealth of the family, explain the nature of the trade by which it was acquired. Even Machiavel, whoſe genius delighted in the inveſtigation of every circumſtance which contributed to aggrandize or depreſs nations, ſeems not to have viewed the commerce of his country as a ſubject that merited any elucidation. Denina, who has entitled the firſt chapter of his eighteenth book, "The Origin of the Medici, and the Commencement of their Power and Grandeur," furniſhes little information with regard to the trade carried on by them. This ſilence

ſilence of ſo many authors is a proof that hiſtorians had not yet begun to view commerce as an object of ſuch importance in the political ſtate of nations, as to enter into any detail concerning its nature and effects. From the references of different writers to Scipio Ammirato, Iſtorie Fiorentine; to Pagnini, Della Decima ed altri gravezze della Mercatura di Fiorentini, and to Balducci, Practica della Mercatura, I ſhould imagine that ſomething more ſatisfactory may be learned concerning the trade both of the republic and family of the Medici; but I could not find any of theſe books either in Edinburgh or in London.

NOTE XLV. SECT. III. p. 117.

LEIBNITZ has preſerved a curious paper, containing the inſtructions of the republic of Florence to the two ambaſſadors ſent to the Soldan of Egypt, in order to negociate this treaty with him, together with the report of theſe ambaſſadors on their return. The great object of the republic was, to obtain liberty of trading in all parts of the Soldan's dominions, upon the ſame terms with the Venetians. The chief privileges which they ſolicited, were; 1. A perfect freedom of admiſſion into every port belonging to the Soldan, protection while they continued in it, and liberty of departure at what time they choſe. 2. Permiſſion to have a conſul, with the ſame rights and juriſdiction as thoſe of the Venetians; and liberty to build a church, a warehouſe, and a bath, in every place where they ſettled. 3. That they ſhould not pay for goods imported or exported higher duties than were paid by the Venetians. 4. That the effects of any Florentine who died in the dominions of the Soldan should be consigned to the consul. 5. That the gold and silver coin of Florence should be received in payments. All these privileges (which shew on what equal and liberal terms Christians and Mahomedans now carried on trade) the Florentines obtained; but from the causes mentioned in the text, they seem never to have acquired any considerable share in the commerce with India. Leibnitz, Mantissa Cod. Jur. Gent. Diplom. Pars altera, p. 163.

NOTE XLVI. SECT. III. p. 122.

THE Eastern parts of Asia are now so completely explored, that the first imperfect accounts of them, by Marco Polo, attract little of that attention which was originally excited by the publication of his travels; and some circumstances in his narrative have induced different authors to justify this neglect, by calling in question the truth of what he relates, and even to assert that he had never visited those countries which he pretends to describe. He does not, say they, ascertain the position of any one place, by specifying its longitude or latitude. He gives names to provinces and cities, particularly in his description of Cathay, which have no resemblance to those which they now bear. We may observe, however, that as Marco Polo seems to have been, in no degree, a man of science, it was not to be expected that he should fix the position of places with geographical accuracy. As he travelled through China, either in the ſuite of the great Khan, or in execution of his orders, it is probable that the names which he gives to different provinces and cities, are thoſe by which they were known to the Tartars, in whoſe ſervice he was, not their original Chineſe names. Some inaccuracies which have been obſerved in the relation of his travels, may be accounted for, by attending to one circumſtance, that it was not publiſhed from a regular journal, which, perhaps, the viciſſitudes in his ſituation, during ſuch a long ſeries of adventures, did not permit him to keep, or to preſerve. It was compoſed after his return to his native country, and chiefly from recollection. But notwithſtanding this diſadvantage, his account of thoſe regions of the Eaſt, towards which my inquiries have been directed, contains information with reſpect to ſeveral particulars, altogether unknown in Europe at that time, the accuracy of which is now fully confirmed. I ſhall mention ſome of theſe, which, though they relate to matters of no great conſequence, afford the beſt proof of his having viſited theſe countries, and of his having obſerved the manners and cuſtoms of the people with attention. He gives a diſtinct account of the nature and preparation of Sago, the principal article of ſubſiſtence among all the nations of Malayan race, and he brought the firſt ſpecimen of this ſingular production to Venice, Lib. ii. c. 16. He takes notice, likewiſe, of the general cuſtom of chewing Betel, and his deſcription of the mode of preparing it, is the ſame with that ſtill in uſe. Ramus. Viaggi, i. p. 55. D. 56. B. He even deſcends into ſuch detail as to mention the peculiar manner of feeding horſes in India, which ſtill continues. Ramus. p. 53. F. What is of more importance, we learn from him, that the trade with Alexandria continued when

he

he travelled through India, to be carried on in the ſame manner as I conjectured it to have been in ancient times. The commodities of the Eaſt were ſtill brought to the Malabar coaſt by veſſels of the country, and conveyed thence, together with pepper, and other productions peculiar to that part of India, by ſhips which arrived from the Red Sea. Lib. iii. c. 27. This, perhaps, may account for the ſuperior quality which Sanudo aſcribes to the goods brought to the coaſt of Syria from the Perſian Gulf, above thoſe imported into Egypt by the Red Sea. The former were choſen and purchaſed in the places where they grew, or where they were manufactured, by the merchants of Perſia, who ſtill continued their voyages to every part of the Eaſt; while the Egyptian merchants, in making up their cargoes, depended upon the aſſortment of goods brought to the Malabar coaſt by the natives. To ſome perſons in his own age, what Marco Polo related concerning the numerous armies and immenſe revenues of the Eaſtern princes, appeared ſo extravagant, (though perfectly conſonant to what we now know concerning the population of China, and the wealth of Indoſtan,) that they gave him the name of *Meſſer Marco Millioni.* Prefat. de Ramus. p. 4. But among perſons better informed, the reception he met with was very different. Columbus, as well as the men of ſcience with whom he correſponded, placed ſuch confidence in the veracity of his relations, that upon them, the ſpeculations and theories, which led to the diſcovery of the New World, were in a great meaſure founded. Life of Columbus by his Son, c. 7, and 8.

NOTE

NOTE XLVII. Sect. III. p. 128.

In the year 1301, Joanna of Navarre, the wife of Philip le Bel, king of France, having been ſome days in Bruges, was ſo much ſtruck with the grandeur and wealth of that city, and particularly with the ſplendid appearance of the citizens wives, that ſhe was moved (ſays Guicciardini) by female envy to exclaim with indignation, "I thought that I had been the only "queen here, but I find there are many hundreds more." Deſcrit. de Paeſi Baſſi, p. 408.

NOTE XLVIII. Sect. III. p. 130.

In the hiſtory of the reign of Charles V. vol. i. p. 163. I obſerved, that, during the war excited by the famous League of Cambray, while Charles VIII. of France could not procure money at a leſs premium than forty-two per cent., the Venetians raiſed what ſums they pleaſed at five per cent. But this, I imagine, is not to be conſidered as the uſual commercial rate of intereſt at that period, but as a voluntary and public-ſpirited effort of the citizens, in order to ſupport their country at a dangerous criſis. Of ſuch laudable exertions, there are ſeveral ſtriking inſtances in the hiſtory of the republic. In the year 1379, when the Genoeſe, after obtaining a great naval victory

7 over

over the Venetians, were ready to attack their capital, the citizens, by a voluntary contribution, enabled the ſenate to fit out ſuch a powerful armament as ſaved their country. Sabellicus, Hiſt. Rer. Venet. Dec. ii. lib. vi. p. 385. 390. In the war with Ferrara, which began in the year 1472, the ſenate, relying upon the attachment of the citizens to their country, required them to bring all their gold and ſilver plate, and jewels, into the public treaſury, upon promiſe of paying the value of them at the concluſion of the war, with five per cent. of intereſt; and this requiſition was complied with cheerfully. Petr. Cyrnæus de Bello Ferrar. ap. Murat. Script. Rer. Ital. vol. xxi. p. 1016.

NOTE XLIX. Sect. III. p. 130.

Two facts may be mentioned as proofs of an extraordinary extenſion of the Venetian trade at this period.——1. There is in Rymer's Great Collection, a ſeries of grants from the kings of England, of various privileges and immunities to Venetian merchants trading in England, as well as ſeveral commercial treaties with the republic, which plainly indicate a conſiderable increaſe of their tranſactions in that country. Theſe are mentioned in their order by Mr. Anderſon, to whoſe patient induſtry and ſound underſtanding, every perſon engaged in any commercial reſearch muſt have felt himſelf greatly indebted on many occaſions.——2. The eſtabliſhment of a Bank by public authority, the credit of which was founded on on that of the ſtate. In an age and nation ſo well acquainted with the advantages which commerce derives from the inſtitution of banks, it is unneceſſary to enumerate them. Mercantile tranſactions muſt have been numerous and extenſive before the utility of ſuch an inſtitution could be fully perceived, or the principles of trade could be ſo fully underſtood as to form the regulations proper for conducting it with ſucceſs. Venice may boaſt of having given the firſt example to Europe of an eſtabliſhment altogether unknown to the ancients, and which is the pride of the modern commercial ſyſtem. The conſtitution of the bank of Venice was originally founded on ſuch juſt principles, that it has ſerved as a model in the eſtabliſhment of banks in other countries, and the adminiſtration of its affairs has been conducted with ſo much integrity, that its credit has never been ſhaken. I cannot ſpecify the preciſe year in which the bank of Venice was eſtabliſhed by a law of the State. Anderſon ſuppoſes it to have been A. D. 1157. Chron. Deduct. vol. i. p. 84. Sandi Stor. Civil. Venez. part II. vol. ii. p. 768. Part III. vol. ii. p. 892.

NOTE L. Sect. III. p. 132.

An Italian author of good credit, and a diligent inquirer into the ancient hiſtory of its different governments, affirms, that if the ſeveral States which traded in the Mediterranean had united together, Venice alone would have been ſuperior to them all, in naval power, and in extent of commerce.

 Denina

Denina Revolutions d'Italie traduits par l'Abbè Jardin, lib. xviii. c. 6. tom. vi. p. 339. About the year 1420, the Doge Mocenigo gives a view of the naval force of the republic, which confirms this decision of Denina. At that time it consisted of three thousand trading vessels, of various dimensions, on board which were employed seventeen thousand sailors; of three hundred ships of greater force, manned by eight thousand sailors; and of forty-five large galeasses, or caracks, navigated by eleven thousand sailors. In public and private arsenals sixteen thousand carpenters were employed. Mar. Sanuto Vite de Duchi di Venezia, ap. Mur. Script. Rer. Ital. vol. xxii. p. 959.

NOTE LI. Sect. III. p. 146.

When we take a view of the form and position of the habitable parts of Asia and Africa, we shall see good reasons for considering the camel as the most useful of all the animals over which the inhabitants of these great continents have acquired dominion. In both, some of the most fertile districts are separated from each other by such extensive tracts of barren sands, the seats of desolation and drought, as seem to exclude the possibility of communication between them. But as the ocean, which appears, at first view, to be placed as an insuperable barrier between different regions of the earth, has been rendered, by navigation, subservient to their mutual intercourse; so, by means of the camel, which the Arabians emphatically call *The Ship of the Desert*,

Desert, the most dreary wastes are traversed, and the nations which they disjoin are enabled to trade with one another. Those painful journies, impracticable by any other animal, the camel performs with astonishing dispatch. Under heavy burdens of six, seven, and eight hundred weight, they can continue their march during a long period of time, with little food or rest, and sometimes without tasting water for eight or nine days. By the wise œconomy of Providence, the camel seems formed of purpose to be the beast of burden in those regions where he is placed, and where his service is most wanted. In all the districts of Asia and Africa, where deserts are most frequent and extensive, the camel abounds. This is his proper station, and beyond this the sphere of his activity does not extend far. He dreads alike the excesses of heat and of cold, and does not agree even with the mild climate of our temperate zone. As the first trade in Indian commodities, of which we have any authentic account, was carried on by means of camels, Genesis, xxxvii. 25, and as it is by employing them that the conveyance of these commodities has been so widely extended over Asia and Africa, the particulars which I have mentioned concerning this singular animal appeared to me necessary towards illustrating this part of my subject. If any of my readers desire more full information, and wish to know how the ingenuity and art of man have seconded the intentions of Nature, in training the camel, from his birth, for that life of exertion and hardship to which he is destined, he may consult Histoire Naturelle, by M. le Comte de Buffon, artic. *Chameau et Dromedaire*, one of the most eloquent, and, as far as I can judge from examining the authorities which he has quoted, one of the moſt accurate, deſcriptions given by that celebrated writer. M. Volney, whoſe accuracy is well known, gives a deſcription of the manner in which the camel performs its journeys, which may be agreeable to ſome of my readers. " In travelling through the deſert, camels " are chiefly employed, becauſe they conſume little, and carry " a great load. His ordinary burden is about ſeven hundred " and fifty pounds; his food, whatever is given him, ſtraw, " thiſtles, the ſtones of dates, beans, barley, &c. With a " pound of food a day, and as much water, he will travel for " weeks. In the journey from Cairo to Suez, which is forty " or forty-ſix hours, they neither eat nor drink; but theſe " long faſts, if often repeated, wear them out. Their uſual " rate of travelling is very ſlow, hardly above two miles an " hour; it is vain to puſh them, they will not quicken their " pace, but, if allowed ſome ſhort reſt, they will travel fifteen " eighteen hours a day." Voyage, tom. ii. p. 383.

NOTE LII. SECT. III. p. 148.

IN order to give an adequate idea of the extenſive circulation of Indian commodities by land carriage, it would be neceſſary to trace the route, and to eſtimate the number, of the various caravans by which they are conveyed. Could this be executed with accuracy, it would be a curious object of geographical reſearch, as well as a valuable addition to commercial hiſtory. Though it is inconſiſtent with the brevity which I have uniformly ſtudied in conducting this Diſquiſition, to enter into a detail

detail of ſo great length, it may be proper here, for illuſtrating this part of my ſubject, to take ſuch a view of two caravans which viſit Mecca, as may enable my readers to eſtimate more juſtly the magnitude of their commercial tranſactions. The firſt is the caravan which takes its departure from Cairo in Egypt, and the other from Damaſcus in Syria; and I ſelect theſe, both becauſe they are the moſt conſiderable, and becauſe they are deſcribed by authors of undoubted credit, who had the beſt opportunities of receiving full information concerning them. The former is compoſed not only of pilgrims from every part of Egypt, but of thoſe which arrive from all the ſmall Mahomedan ſtates on the African coaſt of the Mediterranean, from the empire of Morocco, and even from the Negroe kingdoms on the Atlantic. When aſſembled, the caravan conſiſts at leaſt of fifty thouſand perſons, and the number of camels employed in carrying water, proviſions, and merchandize, is ſtill greater. The journey, which, in going from Cairo and returning thither, is not completed in leſs than a hundred days, is performed wholly by land; and as the route lies moſtly through ſandy deſerts, or barren uninhabited wilds, which ſeldom afford any ſubſiſtence, and where often no ſources of water can be found, the pilgrims always undergo much fatigue, and ſometimes muſt endure incredible hardſhips. An early and good deſcription of this caravan is publiſhed by Hakluyt, vol. ii. p. 202, &c. Maillet has entered into a minute and curious detail with regard to it; Deſcript. de l'Egypte, part ii. p. 212, &c. Pocock has given a route, together with the length of each day's march, which he received from a perſon who had been fourteen times at Mecca, vol. i. pp. 188, 261, &c.—The caravan from

from Damafcus, compofed of pilgrims from almoft every province of the Turkifh empire, is little inferior to the former in number, and the commerce which it carries on is hardly lefs valuable. Voyage de Volney, tom. ii. p. 251, &c. This pilgrimage was performed in the year 1741, by Khizeh Abdulkurreem, whom I formerly mentioned, Note IV. p. 186. He gives the ufual route from Damafcus to Mecca, computed by hours, the common mode of reckoning a journey in the Eaft through countries little frequented. According to the moft moderate eftimate, the diftance between the two cities, by his account, muft be above a thoufand miles; a great part of the journey is through a defert, and the pilgrims not only endure much fatigue, but are often expofed to great danger from the wild Arabs. Memoirs, p. 114, &c. It is a fingular proof of the predatory fpirit of the Arabs, that although all their independent tribes are zealous Mahomedans, yet they make no fcruple of plundering the caravans of pilgrims, while engaged in performing one of the moft indifpenfable duties of their religion. Great as thefe caravans are, we muft not fuppofe that all the pilgrims who vifit Mecca belong to them; fuch confiderable additions are received from the extenfive dominions of Perfia, from every province of Indoftan, and the countries to the Eaft of it, from Abyffinia, from various ftates on the Southern coaft of Africa, and from all parts of Arabia, that when the whole are affembled they have been computed to amount to two hundred thoufand. In fome years the number is farther increafed by fmall bands of pilgrims from feveral interior provinces of Africa, the names and fituations of which are juft beginning to be known in Europe. For this laft fact we are indebted

indebted to the Aſſociation for promoting the Diſcovery of the Interior Parts of Africa, formed by ſome Britiſh Gentlemen upon principles ſo liberal, and with views ſo public-ſpirited, as do honour to themſelves and to their country. Proceedings, &c. p. 174.

In the Report of the Committee of the Privy Council on the Slave Trade, other particulars are contained; and it appears that the commerce carried on by caravans in the interior parts of Africa is not only widely extended, but of conſiderable value. Beſides the great caravan which proceeds to Cairo, and is joined by Mahomedan pilgrims from every part of Africa, there are caravans which have no object but commerce, which ſet out from Fez, Algiers, Tunis, Tripoli, and other States on the ſea-coaſt, and penetrate far into the interior country. Some of them take no leſs than fifty days to reach the place of their deſtination; and, as the medium of their rate of travelling may be eſtimated at about eighteen miles a day, the extent of their journey may be eaſily computed. As both the time of their out-ſet, and their route, are known, they are met by the people of all the countries through which they travel, who trade with them. Indian goods of every kind form a conſiderable article in this traffic, in exchange for which the chief commodity they can give is Slaves. Part vi.

As the journeys of the caravans, which are purely commercial, do not commence at ſtated ſeaſons, and their routes vary according to the convenience or fancy of the merchants of whom they are compoſed, a deſcription cannot be given of them with the ſame degree of accuracy. But by attending to the

the accounts of ſome authors, and the occaſional hints of others, ſufficient information may be gathered to ſatisfy us, that the circulation of Eaſtern goods by theſe caravans is very extenſive. The ſame intercourſe which was anciently kept up by the provinces in the North-eaſt of Aſia with Indoſtan and China, and which I formerly deſcribed, ſtill ſubſiſts. Among all the numerous tribes of Tartars, even of thoſe which retain their paſtoral manners in greateſt purity, the demand for the productions of theſe two countries is very conſiderable. Voyages de Pallas, tom. i. p. 357, &c. tom. ii. p. 422. In order to ſupply them with theſe, caravans ſet out annually from Boghar, (Hackluyt, vol. i. p. 332.) Samarcand, Thibet, and ſeveral other places, and return with large cargoes of Indian and Chineſe goods. But the trade carried on between Ruſſia and China in this part of Aſia is by far the moſt extenſive and beſt known. Some connection of this kind, it is probable, was kept up between them from the earlieſt period, but it increaſed greatly after the interior parts of Ruſſia were rendered more acceſſible by the conqueſts of Zingis Khan and Tamerlane. The commercial nations of Europe were ſo well acquainted with the mode of carrying on this trade, that ſoon after the Portugueſe had opened the communication with the Eaſt by the Cape of Good Hope, an attempt was made in order to diminiſh the advantages which they derived from this diſcovery, to prevail on the Ruſſians to convey Indian and Chineſe commodities through the whole extent of their empire, partly by land-carriage and partly by means of navigable rivers, to ſome port on the Baltic, from which they might be diſtributed through every part of Europe. Ramuſio Raccolto da Viaggi, vol. i. p. 374. B.

2 This

This ſcheme, too great for the monarch then on the throne of Ruſſia to carry into execution, was rendered practicable by the conqueſts of Ivan Baſilowitz, and the genius of Peter the Great. Though the capitals of the two empires were ſituated at the immenſe diſtance of ſix thouſand three hundred and ſeventy-eight miles from each other, and the route lay for above four hundred miles through an uninhabited deſert, (Bell's Travels, vol. ii. p. 167.) caravans travelled from the one to the other. But though it had been ſtipulated when this intercourſe was eſtabliſhed, that the number of perſons in each caravan ſhould not exceed two hundred, and though they were ſhut up within the walls of a Caravanſerai during the ſhort time they remained in Pekin, and were allowed to deal only with a few merchants, to whom a monopoly of the trade with them had been granted ; yet, notwithſtanding all theſe reſtraints and precautions, the jealous vigilance with which the Chineſe government excludes foreigners from a free intercourſe with its ſubjects was alarmed, and the admiſſion of the Ruſſian caravans into the empire was ſoon prohibited. After various negociations, an expedient was at length deviſed, by which the advantages of mutual commerce were ſecured, without infringing the cautious arrangements of Chineſe policy. On the boundary of the two empires, two ſmall towns were built almoſt contiguous, the one inhabited by Ruſſians, the other by Chineſe. To theſe all the marketable productions of their reſpective countries are brought by the ſubjects of each empire ; and the furs, the linen and woollen cloth, the leather, the glaſs, &c. of Ruſſia, are exchanged for the ſilk, the cotton, the tea, the rice, the toys, &c. of China. By ſome well-judged conceſſions of the ſovereign now ſeated on the throne of Ruſſia, whoſe enlarged mind is ſuperior to the illiberal maxims of ſome of her predeceſſors, this trade is rendered ſo flouriſhing, that its amount annually is not leſs than eight hundred thouſand pounds ſterling, and it is the only trade with China carried on almoſt entirely by barter. Mr. Coxe, in his account of the Ruſſian diſcoveries, has collected, with his uſual attention and diſcernment, every thing relative to this branch of trade, the nature and extent of which were little known in Europe. Chap. ii. iii. iv. Nor is this the only place where Ruſſia receives Chineſe and Indian commodities. A conſiderable ſupply of both is brought by caravans of independent Tartars to Orenburg, on the river Jaik, Voyage de Pallas, tom. i. p. 355, &c. to Troitzkaia, on the river Oui, and to other places which I might mention. I have entered into this long detail concerning the mode in which the productions in India and China are circulated through Ruſſia, as it affords the moſt ſtriking inſtance, I know, of the great extent to which valuable commodities may be conveyed by land carriage.

NOTE LIII. SECT. IV. p. 152.

THE only voyage of diſcovery in the Atlantic Ocean towards the South, by any of the ancient commercial ſtates in the Mediterranean, is that of Hanno, undertaken by order of the republic of Carthage. As the ſituation of that city, ſo much nearer the Straits than Tyre, Alexandria, and the other ſeats

5 of

of ancient trade which I have mentioned, gave it more immediate accefs to the ocean ; that circumftance, together with the various fettlements which the Carthaginians had made in different provinces of Spain, naturally fuggefted to them this enterprife, and afforded them the profpect of confiderable advantages from its fuccefs. The voyage of Hanno, inftead of invalidating, feems to confirm the juftnefs of the reafons which I have given, why no fimilar attempt was made by the other commercial ftates in the Mediterranean.

NOTE LIV. Sect. IV. p. 153.

Though the intelligent authors whom I have quoted confidered this voyage of the Phenicians as fabulous, Herodotus mentions a circumftance concerning it, which feems to prove that it had really been performed. "The Phenicians," fays he, "affirmed that, in failing round Africa, they had the fun on "their right hand, which to me appears not to be credible, "though it may be deemed fo by others." Lib. iv. c. 42. This, it is certain, muft have happened, if they really accomplifhed fuch a voyage. The fcience of aftronomy, however, was in that early period fo imperfect, that it was by experience only that the Phenicians could come at the knowledge of this fact ; they durft not, without this, have ventured to affert what would have appeared to be an improbable fiction. Even after what they related, Herodotus difbelieved it.

NOTE LV. Sect. IV. p. 161.

Notwithstanding this increaſing demand for the productions of India, it is remarkable, that during the ſixteenth century ſome commodities which are now the chief articles of importation from the Eaſt, were either altogether unknown, or of little account. Tea, the importation of which, at preſent, far exceeds that of any other production of the Eaſt, has not been in general uſe, in any country of Europe, a full century; and yet, during that ſhort period, from ſome ſingular caprice of taſte, or power of faſhion, the infuſion of a leaf brought from the fartheſt extremity of the earth, of which it is perhaps the higheſt praiſe to ſay that it is innoxious, has become almoſt a neceſſary of life in ſeveral parts of Europe, and the paſſion for it deſcends from the moſt elevated to the loweſt orders in ſociety. In 1785 it was computed that the whole quantity of tea imported into Europe from China was about nineteen millions of pounds, of which it is conjectured that twelve millions were conſumed in Great Britain and the dominions depending upon it. Dodſley's Annual Regiſter for 1784 and 1785, p. 156. The porcelane of China, now as common in many parts of Europe as if it were of domeſtic manufacture, was not known to the ancients. Marco Polo is the firſt among the moderns who mentions it. The Portugueſe began to import it not long after their firſt voyage to China, A. D. 1517; but it was a conſiderable time before the uſe of it became extenſive.

APPENDIX.

A P P E N D I X.

I SHALL now endeavour to fulfil an engagement which I came under [a], to make ſome obſervations upon the genius, the manners, and inſtitutions of the people of India, as far as they can be traced from the earlieſt ages to which our knowledge of them extends. Were I to enter upon this wide field with an intention of ſurveying its whole extent; were I to view each object which it preſents to a philoſophical inquirer, under all its different aſpects, it would lead me into reſearches and ſpeculations, not only of immenſe length, but altogether foreign from the ſubject of this Diſquiſition. My inquiries and reflections ſhall therefore be confined to what is intimately connected with the deſign of this work. I ſhall collect the facts

[a] See page 21.

which

which the ancients have tranſmitted to us concerning the inſtitutions peculiar to the natives of India, and, by comparing them with what we know of that country, endeavour to deduce ſuch concluſions as tend to point out the circumſtances which have induced the reſt of mankind, in every age, to carry on commercial intercourſe to ſo great an extent with that country.

Of this intercourſe there are conſpicuous proofs in the earlieſt periods concerning which hiſtory affords information. Not only the people contiguous to India, but remote nations, ſeem to have been acquainted, from time immemorial, with its commodities, and to have valued them ſo highly, that in order to procure them they undertook fatiguing, expenſive, and dangerous journeys. Whenever men give a decided preference to the commodities of any particular country, this muſt be owing either to its poſſeſſing ſome valuable natural productions peculiar to its ſoil and climate, or to ſome ſuperior progreſs which its inhabitants have made in induſtry, art, and elegance. It is not to any peculiar excellence in the natural productions of India, that we muſt aſcribe entirely the predilection of ancient nations for its commodities; for, pepper excepted, an article, it muſt be allowed, of great importance, they are little different from thoſe of other tropical countries; and Ethiopia or Arabia might have fully ſupplied the Phenicians, and other trading people of antiquity, with the ſpices, the perfumes, the precious ſtones, the gold and ſilver, which formed the principal articles of their commerce.

Whoever

WHOEVER then wiſhes to trace the commerce with India to its ſource, muſt ſearch for it, not ſo much in any peculiarity of the natural productions of that country, as in the ſuperior improvement of its inhabitants. Many facts have been tranſmitted to us, which, if they are examined with proper attention, clearly demonſtrate, that the natives of India were not only more early civilized, but had made greater progreſs in civilization than any other people. Theſe I ſhall endeavour to enumerate, and to place them in ſuch a point of view as may ſerve both to throw light upon the inſtitutions, manners, and arts of the Indians, and to account for the eagerneſs of all nations to obtain the productions of their ingenious induſtry.

BY the ancient Heathen writers, the Indians were reckoned among thoſe races of men which they denominated *Autochthones* or *Aborigines*, whom they conſidered as natives of the ſoil, whoſe origin could not be traced[b]. By the inſpired writers, the wiſdom of the Eaſt (an expreſſion which is to be underſtood as a deſcription of their extraordinary progreſs in ſcience and arts) was early celebrated[c]. In order to illuſtrate and confirm theſe explicit teſtimonies concerning the ancient and high civilization of the inhabitants of India, I ſhall take a view of their rank and condition as individuals; of their civil policy; of their laws and judicial proceedings; of their uſeful and elegant arts; of their ſciences; and of their religious inſtitutions; as far as information can be gathered from the ac-

[b] Diod. Sic. lib. ii. p. 151.

[c] 1 Kings, iv. 31.

counts of the Greek and Roman writers, compared with what ſtill remains of their ancient acquirements and inſtitutions.

I. FROM the moſt ancient accounts of India we learn, that the diſtinction of ranks and ſeparation of profeſſions were completely eſtabliſhed there. This is one of the moſt undoubted proofs of a ſociety conſiderably advanced in its progreſs. Arts in the early ſtages of ſocial life are ſo few, and ſo ſimple, that each man is ſufficiently maſter of them all, to gratify every demand of his own limited deſires. A ſavage can form his bow, point his arrows, rear his hut, and hollow his canoe, without calling in the aid of any hand more ſkilful than his own [d]. But when time has augmented the wants of men, the productions of art become ſo complicated in their ſtructure, or ſo curious in their fabric, that a particular courſe of education is requiſite towards forming the artiſt to ingenuity in contrivance and expertneſs in execution. In proportion as refinement ſpreads, the diſtinction of profeſſions increaſes, and they branch out into more numerous and minute ſubdiviſions. Prior to the records of authentic hiſtory, and even before the moſt remote æra to which their own traditions pretend to reach, this ſeparation of profeſſions had not only taken place among the natives of India, but the perpetuity of it was ſecured by an inſtitution which muſt be conſidered as the fundamental article in the ſyſtem of their policy. The whole body of the people was divided into four orders or caſts. The members of the firſt, deemed the moſt ſacred, had it for their province, to

[d] Hiſt. of Amer. vol. iii. 165.

ſtudy

ſtudy the principles of religion; to perform its functions; and to cultivate the ſciences. They were the prieſts, the inſtructors, and philoſophers of the nation. The members of the ſecond order were entruſted with the government and defence of the ſtate. In peace they were its rulers and magiſtrates, in war they were the ſoldiers who fought its battles. The third was compoſed of huſbandmen and merchants; and the fourth of artiſans, labourers, and ſervants. None of theſe can ever quit his own caſt, or be admitted into another [e]. The ſtation of every individual is unalterably fixed; his deſtiny is irrevocable; and the walk of life is marked out, from which he muſt never deviate. This line of ſeparation is not only eſtabliſhed by civil authority, but confirmed and ſanctioned by religion; and each order or caſt is ſaid to have proceeded from the Divinity in ſuch a different manner, that to mingle and confound them would be deemed an act of moſt daring impiety [f]. Nor is it between the four different tribes alone that ſuch inſuperable barriers are fixed; the members of each caſt adhere invariably to the profeſſion of their forefathers. From generation to generation, the ſame families have followed, and will always continue to follow, one uniform line of life.

SUCH arbitrary arrangements of the various members which compoſe a community, ſeems, at firſt view, to be adverſe to improvement either in ſcience or in arts; and by forming

[e] Ayeen Akbery, iii. 81, &c. Sketches relating to the Hiſtory, &c. of the Hindoos, p. 107, &c.

[f] See NOTE I.

around the different orders of men, artificial barriers, which it would be impious to paſs, tends to circumſcribe the operations of the human mind within a narrower ſphere than nature has allotted to them. When every man is at full liberty to direct his efforts towards thoſe objects and that end which the impulſe of his own mind prompts him to prefer, he may be expected to attain that high degree of eminence to which the uncontrouled exertions of genius and induſtry naturally conduct. The regulations of Indian policy, with reſpect to the different orders of men, muſt neceſſarily, at ſome times, check genius in its career, and confine to the functions of an inferior caſt, talents fitted to ſhine in an higher ſphere. But the arrangements of civil government are made, not for what is extraordinary, but for what is common; not for the few, but for the many. The object of the firſt Indian legiſlators was to employ the moſt effectual means of providing for the ſubſiſtence, the ſecurity, and happineſs of all the members of the community over which they preſided. With this view they ſet apart certain races of men for each of the various profeſſions and arts neceſſary in a well-ordered ſociety, and appointed the exerciſe of them to be tranſmitted from father to ſon in ſucceſſion. This ſyſtem, though extremely repugnant to the ideas which we, by being placed in a very different ſtate of ſociety, have formed, will be found, upon attentive inſpection, better adapted to attain the end in view, than a careleſs obſerver is, on a firſt view, apt to imagine. The human mind bends to the law of neceſſity, and is accuſtomed, not only to accommodate itſelf to the reſtraints which the condition of its nature, or the inſtitutions of its country, impoſe, but to acquieſce in them. From

5 his

his entrance into life, an Indian knows the ſtation allotted to him, and the functions to which he is deſtined by his birth. The objects which relate to theſe are the firſt that preſent themſelves to his view. They occupy his thoughts, or employ his hands; and, from his earlieſt years, he is trained to the habit of doing with eaſe and pleaſure that which he muſt continue through life to do. To this may be aſcribed that high degree of perfection conſpicuous in many of the Indian manufactures; and though veneration for the practices of their anceſtors may check the ſpirit of invention, yet, by adhering to theſe, they acquire ſuch an expertneſs and delicacy of hand, that Europeans, with all the advantages of ſuperior ſcience, and the aid of more complete inſtruments, have never been able to equal the exquiſite execution of their workmanſhip. While this high improvement of their more curious manufactures excited the admiration, and attracted the commerce, of other nations, the ſeparation of profeſſions in India, and the early diſtribution of the people into claſſes, attached to particular kinds of labour, ſecured ſuch abundance of the more common and uſeful commodities, as not only ſupplied their own wants, but miniſtered to thoſe of the countries around them.

To this early diviſion of the people into caſts, we muſt likewiſe aſcribe a ſtriking peculiarity in the ſtate of India; the permanence of its inſtitutions, and the immutability in the manners of its inhabitants. What now is in India, always was there, and is likely ſtill to continue: neither the ferocious violence and illiberal fanaticiſm of its Mahomedan conquerors, nor the

the power of its European masters, have effected any considerable alteration [g]. The same distinctions of condition take place, the same arrangements in civil and domestic society remain, the same maxims of religion are held in veneration, and the same sciences and arts are cultivated. Hence, in all ages, the trade with India has been the same; gold and silver have uniformly been carried thither in order to purchase the same commodities with which it now supplies all nations; and from the age of Pliny to the present times, it has been always considered and execrated as a gulf which swallows up the wealth of every other country, that flows incessantly towards it, and from which it never returns [h]. According to the accounts which I have given of the cargoes anciently imported from India, they appear to have consisted of nearly the same articles with those of the investments in our own times; and whatever difference we may observe in them seems to have arisen, not so much from any diversity in the nature of the commodities which the Indians prepared for sale, as from a variety in the tastes, or in the wants, of the nations which demanded them.

II. ANOTHER proof of the early and high civilization of the people of India, may be deduced from considering their political constitution and form of government. The Indians trace back the history of their own country through an immense succession of ages, and assert, that all Asia, from the mouth of the Indus on the west, to the confines of China on the east, and from the mountains of Thibet on the north, to Cape Comorin on the south, formed a vast empire,

[g] See NOTE II. [h] See NOTE III.

subject

ſubject to one mighty ſovereign, under whom ruled ſeveral hereditary Princes and Rajahs. But their chronology, which meaſures the life of man in ancient times by thouſands of years, and computes the length of the ſeveral periods, during which it ſuppoſes the world to have exiſted, by millions, is ſo wildly extravagant, as not to merit any ſerious diſcuſſion. We muſt reſt ſatisfied, then, until ſome more certain information is obtained with reſpect to the ancient hiſtory of India, with taking the firſt accounts of that country, which can be deemed authentic, from the Greeks, who ſerved under Alexander the Great. They found kingdoms of conſiderable magnitude eſtabliſhed in that country. The territories of Porus and of Taxiles comprehended a great part of the Panjab, one of the moſt fertile and beſt cultivated countries in India. The kingdom of the Praſij, or Gandaridæ, ſtretched to a great extent on both ſides of the Ganges. All the three, as appears from the ancient Greek writers, were powerful and populous.

THIS deſcription of the partition of India into ſtates of ſuch magnitude, is alone a convincing proof of its having advanced far in civilization. In whatever region of the earth there has been an opportunity of obſerving the progreſs of men in ſocial life, they appear at firſt in ſmall independent tribes or communities. Their common wants prompt them to unite; and their mutual jealouſies, as well as the neceſſity of ſecuring ſubſiſtence, compel them to drive to a diſtance every rival who might encroach on thoſe domains which they conſider as their own. Many ages elapſe before they coaleſce, or acquire ſufficient foreſight to provide for the wants, or ſufficient wiſdom to conduct the affairs of

I a numea numerous society. Even under the genial climate, and in the rich soil of India, more favourable perhaps to the union and increase of the human species than any other part of the globe, the formation of such extensive states, as were established in that country when first visited by Europeans, must have been a work of long time; and the members of them must have been long accustomed to exertions of useful industry.

THOUGH monarchical government was established in all the countries of India to which the knowledge of the ancients extended, the sovereigns were far from possessing uncontrouled or despotic power. No trace, indeed, is discovered there of any assembly or public body, the members of which, either in their own right, or as representatives of their fellow-citizens, could interpose in enacting laws, or in superintending the execution of them. Institutions destined to assert and guard the rights belonging to men in a social state, how familiar soever the idea may be to the people of Europe, never formed a part of the political constitution in any great Asiatic kingdom. It was to different principles that the natives of India were indebted for restrictions which limited the exercise of regal power. The rank of individuals was unalterably fixed, and the privileges of the different casts were deemed inviolable. The monarchs of India, who are all taken from the second of the four classes formerly described, which is intrusted with the functions of government and exercise of war, behold among their subjects an order of men far superior to themselves in dignity, and so conscious of their own pre-eminence, both in rank and in sanctity, that they would deem it degradation and pollution, if they were

were to eat of the ſame food with their ſovereign[k]. Their perſons are ſacred, and even for the moſt heinous crimes they cannot be capitally puniſhed; their blood muſt never be ſhed[l]. To men in this exalted ſtation monarchs muſt look up with reſpect, and reverence them as the miniſters of religion, and the teachers of wiſdom. On important occaſions, it is the duty of ſovereigns to conſult them, and to be directed by their advice. Their admonitions, and even their cenſures, muſt be received with ſubmiſſive reſpect. This right of the Brahmins to offer their opinion with reſpect to the adminiſtration of public affairs was not unknown to the ancients[m]; and in ſome accounts preſerved in India of the events which happened in their own country, princes are mentioned, who, having violated the privileges of the caſts, and diſregarded the remonſtrances of the Brahmins, were depoſed by their authority, and put to death[n].

WHILE the ſacred rights of the Brahmins oppoſed a barrier againſt the encroachments of regal power on one hand, it was circumſcribed on the other by the ideas which thoſe who occupied the higheſt ſtations in ſociety entertained of their own dignity and privileges. As none but the members of the caſt next in rank to that which religion has rendered ſacred, could be employed in any function of the ſtate, the ſovereigns of the

[k] Orme's Diſſert. vol. i. p. 4. Sketches, &c. p. 113.

[l] Code of Gentoo Laws, ch. xxi. § 10. p. 275. 283, &c.

[m] Strabo, lib. xv. p. 1029. C.

[n] Account of the Qualities requiſite in a Magiſtrate, prefixed by the Pundits to the Code of Gentoo Laws, p. cii and cxvi.

Mm extenſive

extensive kingdoms anciently established in India, found it necessary to entrust them with the superintendence of the cities and provinces too remote to be under their own immediate inspection. In these stations they often acquired such wealth and influence, that offices conferred during pleasure, continued in their families, and they came gradually to form an intermediate order between the sovereign and his subjects; and by the vigilant jealousy with which they maintained their own dignity and privileges, they constrained their rulers to respect them, and to govern with equity.

Nor were the benefits of these restraints upon the power of the sovereign confined wholly to the two superior orders in the state; they extended, in some degree, to the third class employed in agriculture. The labours of that numerous and useful body of men are so essential to the preservation and happiness of society, that the greatest attention was paid to render their condition secure and comfortable. According to the ideas which prevailed among the natives of India (as we are informed by the first Europeans who visited their country), the sovereign is considered as the sole universal proprietor of all the land in his dominions, and from him is derived every species of tenure by which his subjects can hold it. These lands were let out to the farmers who cultivated them, at a stipulated rent, amounting usually to a fourth part of their annual produce paid in kind [a]. In a country where the price of work is extremely low, and where the labour of cultivation is very inconsiderable, the earth yielding its productions almost spontaneously,

[a] Strabo, lib. xv. p. 1030. A. Diod. Sic. lib. ii. p. 53.

where

where ſubſiſtence is amazingly cheap, where few clothes are needed, and houſes are built and furniſhed at little expence, this rate cannot be deemed exorbitant or oppreſſive. As long as the huſbandman continued to pay the eſtabliſhed rent, he retained poſſeſſion of the farm, which deſcended, like property, from father to ſon.

THESE accounts given by ancient authors of the condition and tenure of the renters of land in India, agree ſo perfectly with what now takes place, that it may be conſidered almoſt as a deſcription of the preſent ſtate of its cultivation. In every part of India, where the native Hindoo Princes retain dominion, the *Ryots*, the modern name by which the renters of land are diſtinguiſhed, hold their poſſeſſions by a leaſe, which may be conſidered as perpetual, and at a rate fixed by ancient ſurveys and valuations. This arrangement has been ſo long eſtabliſhed, and accords ſo well with the ideas of the natives, concerning the diſtinctions of caſts, and the functions allotted to each, that it has been inviolably maintained in all the provinces ſubject either to Mahomedans or Europeans; and, to both, it ſerves as the baſis on which their whole ſyſtem of finance is founded [p]. In a more remote period, before the original inſtitutions of India were ſubverted by foreign invaders, the induſtry of the huſbandman, on which every member of the community depended for ſubſiſtence, was as ſecure as the tenure by which he held his lands was equitable. Even war did not interrupt his labours or endanger his property. It was not

[p] See NOTE IV.

uncommon, we are informed, that while two hoſtile armies were fighting a battle in one field, the peaſants were ploughing or reaping in the next field in perfect tranquillity [q]. Theſe maxims and regulations of the ancient legiſlators of India have a near reſemblance to the ſyſtem of thoſe ingenious modern ſpeculators on political œconomy, who repreſent the produce of land as the ſole ſource of wealth in every country; and who conſider the diſcovery of this principle, according to which they contend that the government of nations ſhould be conducted, as one of the greateſt efforts of human wiſdom. Under a form of government, which paid ſuch attention to all the different orders of which the ſociety is compoſed, particularly the cultivators of the earth, it is not wonderful that the ancients ſhould deſcribe the Indians as a moſt happy race of men; and that the moſt intelligent modern obſervers ſhould celebrate the equity, the humanity, and mildneſs of Indian policy. A Hindoo Rajah, as I have been informed by perſons well acquainted with the ſtate of India, reſembles more a father preſiding in a numerous family of his own children, than a ſovereign ruling over inferiors, ſubject to his dominion. He endeavours to ſecure their happineſs with vigilant ſolicitude; they are attached to him with the moſt tender affection and inviolable fidelity. We can hardly conceive men to be placed in any ſtate more favourable to their acquiring all the advantages derived from ſocial union. It is only when the mind is perfectly at eaſe, and neither feels nor dreads oppreſſion, that it employs its active powers in forming numerous arrangements of police,

[q] Strab. lib. xv. p. 1030. A.

for

for ſecuring its enjoyments and increaſing them. Many arrangements of this nature the Greeks, though accuſtomed to their own inſtitutions, the moſt perfect at that time in Europe, obſerved and admired among the Indians, and mention them as inſtances of high civilization and improvement. There were eſtabliſhed among the Indians three diſtinct claſſes of officers, one of which had it in charge to inſpect agriculture, and every kind of country work. They meaſured the portions of land allotted to each renter. They had the cuſtody of the *Tanks*, or public reſervoirs of water, without a regular diſtribution of which, the fields in a torrid climate cannot be rendered fertile. They marked out the courſe of the highways, along which, at certain diſtances, they erected ſtones, to meaſure the road and direct travellers [r]. To officers of a ſecond claſs was committed the inſpection of the police in cities, and their functions, of courſe, were many and various; ſome of which only I ſhall ſpecify. They appropriated houſes for the reception of ſtrangers; they protected them from injury, provided for their ſubſiſtence, and, when ſeized with any diſeaſe, they appointed phyſicians to attend them; and, on the event of their death, they not only buried them with decency, but took charge of their effects, and reſtored them to their relations. They kept exact regiſters of births and of deaths. They viſited the public markets, and examined weights and meaſures. The third claſs of officers ſuperintended the military department; but, as the objects to which their attention was directed are foreign from the ſubject of my

[r] See NOTE V.

inquiries,

inquiries, it is unneceſſary to enter into any detail with reſpect to them[a].

As manners and cuſtoms in India deſcend almoſt without variation from age to age, many of the peculiar inſtitutions which I have enumerated ſtill ſubſiſt there. There is ſtill the ſame attention to the conſtruction and preſervation of tanks, and the diſtribution of their waters. The direction of roads, and placing ſtones along them, is ſtill an object of police. *Choultries*, or houſes built for the accommodation of travellers, are frequent in every part of the country, and are uſeful as well as noble monuments of Indian munificence and humanity. It is only among men in the moſt improved ſtate of ſociety, and under the beſt forms of government, that we diſcover inſtitutions ſimilar to thoſe which I have deſcribed; and many nations have advanced far in their progreſs, without eſtabliſhing arrangements of police equally perfect.

III. In eſtimating the progreſs which any nation has made in civilization, the object that merits the greateſt degree of attention, next to its political conſtitution, is the ſpirit of the laws and nature of the forms by which its judicial proceedings are regulated. In the early and rude ages of ſociety, the few diſputes with reſpect to property which ariſe, are terminated by the interpoſition of the old men, or by the authority of the chiefs in every ſmall tribe or community; their deciſions are dictated by their own diſcretion, or founded on plain and

[a] Strabo, lib. xv. p. 1034. A, &c. Diod. Sicul. lib. ii. p. 154.

obvious

obvious maxims of equity. But as controversies multiply, cases similar to such as have been formerly determined must recur, and the awards upon these grow gradually into precedents, which serve to regulate future judgments. Thus, long before the nature of property is defined by positive statutes, or any rules prescribed concerning the mode of acquiring or conveying it, there is gradually formed, in every state, a body of customary or common law, by which judicial proceedings are directed, and every decision conformable to it is submitted to with reverence, as the result of the accumulated wisdom and experience of ages.

In this state the administration of justice seems to have been in India when first visited by Europeans. Though the Indians, according to their account, had no written laws, but determined every controverted point, by recollecting what had been formerly decided[t]; they assert, that justice was dispensed among them with great accuracy, and that crimes were most severely punished[u]. But in this general observation is contained all the intelligence which the ancients furnish concerning the nature and forms of judicial proceedings in India. From the time of Megasthenes, no Greek or Roman of any note appears to have resided long enough in the country, or to have been so much acquainted with the customs of the natives, as to be capable of entering into any detail with respect to a point of so much importance in their policy. Fortunately, the defects of their information have been amply supplied by the more

[t] Strabo, lib. xv. 1035. D.

[u] Diod. Sicul. lib. ii. p. 154.

5 accurate

accurate and extenſive reſearches of the moderns. During the courſe of almoſt three centuries, the number of perſons who have reſorted from Europe to India has been great. Many of them, who have remained long in the country, and were perſons of liberal education and enlarged minds, have lived in ſuch familiar intercourſe with the natives, and acquired ſo competent a knowledge of their languages, as enabled them to obſerve their inſtitutions with attention, and to deſcribe them with fidelity. Reſpectable as their authority may be, I ſhall not, in what I offer for illuſtrating the judicial proceedings of the Hindoos, reſt upon it alone, but ſhall derive my information from ſources higher and more pure.

TOWARDS the middle of the ſixteenth century, Akber the ſixth, in deſcent from Tamerlane, mounted the throne of Indoſtan. He is one of the few ſovereigns intitled to the appellation both of Great and Good, and the only one of Mahomedan race, whoſe mind appears to have riſen ſo far above all the illiberal prejudices of that fanatical religion in which he was educated, as to be capable of forming a plan worthy of a monarch who loved his people, and was ſolicitous to render them happy. As, in every province of his extenſive dominions, the Hindoos formed the great body of his ſubjects, he laboured to acquire a perfect knowledge of their religion, their ſciences, their laws and inſtitutions; in order that he might conduct every part of his government, particularly the adminiſtration of juſtice, in a manner as much accommodated as poſſible to their own ideas[x]. In this generous undertaking he

[x] See NOTE VI.

was ſeconded with zeal by his vizier Abul Fazel, a miniſter whoſe underſtanding was not leſs enlightened than that of his maſter. By their aſſiduous reſearches, and conſultation of learned men [y], ſuch information was obtained as enabled Abul Fazel to publiſh a brief compendium of Hindoo juriſprudence in the Ayeen Akbery [z], which may be conſidered as the firſt genuine communication of its principles to perſons of a different religion. About two centuries afterwards, the illuſtrious example of Akber was imitated and ſurpaſſed by Mr. Haſtings, the Governor General of the Britiſh Settlements in India. By his authority, and under his inſpection, the moſt eminent Pundits, or Brahmins learned in the laws, of the provinces over which he preſided, were aſſembled at Calcutta; and, in the courſe of two years, compiled, from their moſt ancient and approved authors, ſentence by ſentence, without addition or diminution, a full code of Hindoo laws [a]; which is, undoubtedly, the moſt valuable and authentic elucidation of Indian policy and manners that has been hitherto communicated to Europe. A.D. 1773.

According to the Pundits, ſome of the writers upon whoſe authority they found the decrees which they have inſerted in the Code, lived ſeveral millions of years before their time [b]; and they boaſt of having a ſucceſſion of expounders of their laws from that period to the preſent. Without entering into any

[y] Ayeen Akbery, A. vol. iii. p. 95.
[z] Vol. iii. p. 197, &c.
[a] Preface to the Code, p. x.
[b] Ibid. p. xxxviii.

examination of what is ſo extravagant, we may conclude, that the Hindoos have in their poſſeſſion treatiſes concerning the laws and juriſprudence of their country, of more remote antiquity than are to be found in any other nation. The truth of this depends not upon their own teſtimony alone, but it is put beyond doubt by one circumſtance, that all theſe treatiſes are written in the Sanſkreet language, which has not been ſpoken for many ages in any part of Indoſtan, and is now underſtood by none but the moſt learned Brahmins. That the Hindoos were a people highly civilized, at the time when their laws were compoſed, is moſt clearly eſtabliſhed by internal evidence contained in the Code itſelf. Among nations beginning to emerge from barbariſm, the regulations of law are extremely ſimple, and applicable only to a few obvious caſes of daily occurrence. Men muſt have been long united in a ſocial ſtate, their tranſactions muſt have been numerous and complex, and judges muſt have determined an immenſe variety of controverſies to which theſe give riſe, before the ſyſtem of law becomes ſo voluminous and comprehenſive as to direct the judicial proceedings of a nation far advanced in improvement. In that early age of the Roman republic, when the laws of the Twelve Tables were promulgated, nothing more was required than the laconic injunctions which they contain for regulating the deciſions of courts of juſtice; but, in a later period, the body of civil law, ample as its contents are, was found hardly ſufficient for that purpoſe. To the jejune brevity of the Twelve Tables, the Hindoo Code has no reſemblance, but with reſpect to the number and variety of points it conſiders, it will bear a compariſon parifon with the celebrated digeft of Juftinian; or with the fyftems of jurifprudence in nations moft highly civilized. The articles of which the Hindoo Code is compofed, are arranged in natural and luminous order. They are numerous and comprehenfive, and inveftigated with that minute attention and difcernment which are natural to a people diftinguifhed for acutenefs and fubtility of underftanding, who have been long accuftomed to the accuracy of judicial proceedings, and acquainted with all the refinements of legal practice. The decifions concerning every point (with a few exceptions occafioned by local prejudices and peculiar cuftoms) are founded upon the great and immutable principles of juftice which the human mind acknowledges and refpects, in every age, and in all parts of the earth. Whoever examines the whole work, cannot entertain a doubt of its containing the jurifprudence of an enlightened and commercial people. Whoever looks into any particular title, will be furprifed with a minutenefs of detail and nicety of diftinction, which, in many inftances, feem to go beyond the attention of European legiflation; and it is remarkable that fome of the regulations which indicate the greateft degree of refinement, were eftablifhed in periods of the moft remote antiquity. "In the firft of the facred law tracts, (as is obferved by a perfon "to whom Oriental literature, in all its branches, has been "greatly indebted,) which the Hindoos fuppofe to have been "revealed by Menu fome millions of years ago, there is a "curious paffage on the legal intereft of money, and the "limited rate of it in different cafes, with an exception in re"gard to adventures at fea; an exception which the fenfe of "mankind approves, and which commerce abfolutely requires, "though it was not before the reign of Charles I. that our "English jurisſprudence fully admitted it in reſpect of maritime "contracts [c]." It is likewiſe worthy of notice, that though the natives of India have been diſtinguiſhed in every age for the humanity and mildneſs of their diſpoſition, yet ſuch is the ſolicitude of their law-givers to preſerve the order and tranquillity of ſociety, that the puniſhments which they inflict on criminals, are (agreeably to an obſervation of the ancients already mentioned) extremely rigorous. "Puniſhment (according to a ſtriking "perſonification in the Hindoo code) is the magiſtrate; puniſhment is the inſpirer of terror; puniſhment is the nouriſher of the ſubjects; puniſhment is the defender from calamity; puniſhment is the guardian of thoſe that ſleep; puniſhment, with a black aſpect, and a red eye, terrifies "the guilty [d]."

IV. As the condition of the ancient inhabitants of India, whether we conſider them as individuals, or as members of ſociety, appears, from the preceding inveſtigation, to have been extremely favourable to the cultivation of uſeful and elegant arts; we are naturally led to enquire, whether the progreſs which they actually made in them, was ſuch as might have been expected from a people in that ſituation. In attempting to trace this progreſs, we have not the benefit of guidance equal to that which conducted our reſearches concerning the former articles of enquiry. The ancients, from their ſlender acquaintance

[c] Sir William Jones's Third Diſcourſe, Aſiat. Reſearch. p. 428.
[d] Code, ch. xxi. § 8.

with

with the interior ſtate of India, have been able to communicate little information with reſpect to the arts cultivated there; and though the moderns, during their continued intercourſe with India for three centuries, have had acceſs to obſerve them with greater attention, it is of late only, that by ſtudying the languages now and formerly ſpoken in India, and by conſulting and tranſlating their moſt eminent authors, they have begun to enter into that path of enquiry which leads with certainty to a thorough knowledge of the ſtate of arts cultivated in that country.

One of the firſt arts which human ingenuity aimed at improving, beyond what mere neceſſity requires, was that of building. In the brief remarks which the ſubject of my inquiries leads me to make on the progreſs of this art in India, I ſhall confine my attention wholly to thoſe of higheſt antiquity. The moſt durable monuments of human induſtry are public buildings. The productions of art, formed for the common purpoſes of life, waſte and periſh in uſing them; but works deſtined for the benefit of poſterity ſubſiſt through ages, and it is according to the manner in which theſe are executed, that we form a judgment with reſpect to the degree of power, ſkill, and improvement to which the people by whom they were erected had attained. In every part of India monuments of high antiquity are found. Theſe are of two kinds, ſuch as were conſecrated to the offices of religion, or fortreſſes built for the ſecurity of the country. In the former of theſe, to which Europeans, whatever their ſtructure may be, give the general name of *Pagodas*, we may obſerve a diverſity of ſtile, which both

both marks the gradual progreſs of architecture, and throws light on the general ſtate of arts and manners in different periods. The moſt early Pagodas appear to have been nothing more than excavations in mountainous parts of the country, formed probably in imitation of the natural caverns to which the firſt inhabitants of the earth retired for ſafety during the night, and where they found ſhelter from the inclemency of the ſeaſons. The moſt celebrated, and, as there is reaſon to believe, the moſt ancient of all theſe, is the Pagoda in the iſland Elephanta, at no great diſtance from Bombay. It has been hewn by the hands of man out of a ſolid rock, about half way up a high mountain, and formed into a ſpacious area, nearly 120 feet ſquare. In order to ſupport the roof, and the weight of the mountain that lies above it, a number of maſſy pillars, and of a form not inelegant, have been cut out of the ſame rock, at ſuch regular diſtances, as on the firſt entrance preſents to the eye of the ſpectator an appearance both of beauty and of ſtrength. Great part of the inſide is covered with human figures in high relief, of gigantic ſize as well as ſingular forms, and diſtinguiſhed by a variety of ſymbols, repreſenting, it is probable, the attributes of the deities whom they worſhipped, or the actions of the heroes whom they admired. In the iſle of Salſette, ſtill nearer to Bombay, are excavations in a ſimilar ſtile, hardly inferior in magnificence, and deſtined for the ſame religious purpoſes.

THESE ſtupendous works are of ſuch high antiquity, that as the natives cannot, either from hiſtory or tradition, give any information concerning the time in which they were executed, they

they univerfally afcribe the formation of them to the power of fuperior beings. From the extent and grandeur of thefe fubterraneous manfions, which intelligent travellers compare to the moft celebrated monuments of human power and art in any part of the earth, it is manifeft that they could not have been formed in that ftage of focial life where men continue divided into fmall tribes, unaccuftomed to the efforts of perfevering induftry. It is only in States of confiderable extent, and among people long habituated to fubordination, and to act with concert, that the idea of fuch magnificent works is conceived, or the power of accomplifhing them can be found.

THAT fome fuch powerful ftate was eftablifhed in India at the time when the excavations in the iflands of Elephanta and Salfette were formed, is not the only conclufion to be drawn from a furvey of them; the ftile in which the fculptures with which they are adorned is executed, indicates a confiderable improvement in art at that early period. Sculpture is the imitative art in which man feems to have made the firft trial of his own talents. But even in thofe countries where it has attained to the higheft degree of perfection, its progrefs has been extremely flow. Whoever has attended to the hiftory of this art in Greece, knows how far removed the firft rude effay to reprefent the human form, was from any complete delineation of it [e]. But the different groupes of figures which ftill remain entire in the Pagoda of Elephanta, however low they muft rank if they be compared with the more elegant works of

[e] Winkelman's Hift. de l'Art chez les Anciens, tom. i. p. 32, &c.

Grecian

Grecian or even Etruſcan artiſts, are finiſhed in a ſtile conſiderably ſuperior to the hard inexpreſſive manner of the Egyptians, or the figures in the celebrated palace of Perſepolis. In this light they have appeared to perſons abundantly qualified to appretiate their merit, and from different drawings, particularly thoſe of Niebuhr, a traveller equally accurate in obſerving, and faithful in deſcribing, we muſt form a favourable opinion of the ſtate of arts in India at that period.

It is worthy of notice, that although ſeveral of the figures in the caverns at Elephanta be ſo different from thoſe now exhibited in the Pagodas as objects of veneration, that ſome learned Europeans have imagined they repreſent the rites of a religion more ancient than that now eſtabliſhed in Indoſtan, yet by the Hindoos themſelves the caverns are conſidered as hallowed places of their own worſhip, and they ſtill reſort thither to perform their devotions, and honour the figures there in the ſame manner with thoſe in their own Pagodas. In confirmation of this, I have been informed by an intelligent perſon, who viſited this ſubterraneous ſanctuary in the year 1782, that he was accompanied by a ſagacious Brahmin, a native of Benares, who, though he had never been in it before that time, was well acquainted with the parentage, education, and life of every deity or human figure there repreſented, and explained with fluency the meaning of the various ſymbols by which the images were diſtinguiſhed. This may be conſidered as a clear proof that the ſyſtem of mythology now prevalent in Benares, is not different from that delineated in the caverns of Elephanta. Mr. Hunter, who viſited Elephanta in the year 1784, ſeems to conſider the figures ſigures there as repreſenting deities who are ſtill objects of worſhip among the Hindoos [f]. One circumſtance ſerves to confirm the juſtneſs of this opinion. Several of the moſt conſpicuous perſonages in the groupes at Elephanta are decorated with the *Zennar*, the ſacred ſtring or cord peculiar to the order of Brahmins, an authentic evidence of the diſtinction of caſts having been eſtabliſhed in India at the time when theſe works were finiſhed.

2. INSTEAD of caverns, the original places of worſhip, which could be formed only in particular ſituations, the devotion of the people ſoon began to raiſe temples in honour of their deities in other parts of India. The ſtructure of theſe was at firſt extremely ſimple. They were pyramids of large dimenſion, and had no light within but what came from a ſmall door. After having been long accuſtomed to perform all the rites of religion in the gloom of caverns, the Indians were naturally led to conſider the ſolemn darkneſs of ſuch a manſion as ſacred. Some Pagodas in this firſt ſtile of building ſtill remain in Indoſtan. Drawings of two of theſe at Deogur, and of a third near Tanjore in the Carnatic, all fabrics of great antiquity, have been publiſhed by Mr. Hodges [g], and though they are rude ſtructures, they are of ſuch magnitude as muſt have required the power of ſome conſiderable ſtate to rear them.

3. IN proportion to the progreſs of the different countries of India in opulence and refinement, the ſtructure of their temples

[f] Archæologia, vol. vii. p. 286, &c.

[g] N° VI.

O o gradually

gradually improved. From plain buildings they became highly ornamented fabrics, and, both by their extent and magnificence, are monuments of the power and taſte of the people by whom they were erected. In this highly finiſhed ſtile there are Pagodas of great antiquity in different parts of Indoſtan, particularly in the Southern provinces, which were not expoſed to the deſtructive violence of Mahomedan zeal [h]. In order to aſſiſt my readers in forming ſuch an idea of theſe buildings as may enable them to judge with reſpect to the early ſtate of arts in India, I ſhall briefly deſcribe two, of which we have the moſt accurate accounts. The entry to the Pagoda of Chillambrum, near Porto Novo, on the Coromandel coaſt, held in high veneration on account of its antiquity, is by a ſtately gate under a pyramid an hundred and twenty-two feet in height, built with large ſtones above forty feet long, and more than five feet ſquare, and all covered with plates of copper, adorned with an immenſe variety of figures neatly executed. The whole ſtructure extends one thouſand three hundred and thirty-two feet in one direction, and nine hundred and thirty-ſix in another. Some of the ornamental parts are finiſhed with an elegance intitled to the admiration of the moſt ingenious artiſts [i]. The Pagoda of Seringham, ſuperior in ſanctity to that of Chillambrum, ſurpaſſes it as much in grandeur; and, fortunately, I can convey a more perfect idea of it by adopting the words of an elegant and accurate hiſtorian. This Pagoda is ſituated about a mile from the weſtern extremity of the iſland of Seringham, formed by the diviſion of the great river Caveri into two channels.

[h] See NOTE VII.

[i] Mem. de Literat. tom. xxxi. p. 44, &c. Voy. de M. Sonnerat, tom. i. p. 217.

13

channels. " It is composed of seven square inclosures, one " within the other, the walls of which are twenty-five feet high, " and four thick. These inclosures are three hundred and fifty feet " distant from one another, and each has four large gates with a " high tower; which are placed, one in the middle of each side " of the inclosure, and opposite to the four cardinal points. The " outward wall is near four miles in circumference, and its gate- " way to the South is ornamented with pillars, several of which " are single stones thirty-three feet long, and nearly five in " diameter; and those which form the roof are still larger: " in the inmost inclosures are the chapels. About half a mile " to the East of Seringham, and nearer to the Caveri than the " Coleroon, is another large Pagoda, called Jembikisma; but this " has only one inclosure. The extreme veneration in which " Seringham is held, arises from a belief that it contains that " identical image of the god Wistchnu, which used to be " worshipped by the god Brahma. Pilgrims from all parts of " the peninsula come here to obtain absolution, and none come " without an offering of money; and a large part of the reve- " nue of the island is allotted for the maintenance of the Brah- " mins who inhabit the Pagoda; and these, with their families, " formerly composed a multitude not less than forty thousand " souls, maintained, without labour, by the liberality of su- " perstition. Here, as in all the other great Pagodas of India, " the Brahmins live in a subordination which knows no resist- " ance, and slumber in a voluptuousness which knows no " wants *."

* Orme's Hist. of Milit. Transact. of Indostan, vol. i. p. 178.

The other species of public buildings which I mentioned, were those erected for the defence of the country. From the immense plains of Indostan there arise, in different parts, eminences and rocks formed by nature to be places of strength. Of these the natives early took possession, and fortifying them with works of various kinds, rendered them almost impregnable stations. There seems to have been in some distant age, a period of general turbulence and danger in India, when such retreats were deemed essentially necessary to public safety; for among the duties of magistrates prescribed by the Pundits, one is, "that he shall erect a strong fort in the place "where he chuses to reside; and shall build a wall on all the "four sides of it, with towers and battlements, and shall make "a full ditch around it[l]." Of these fortresses several remain, which, both from the appearance of the buildings, and from the tradition of the natives, must have been constructed in very remote times. Mr. Hodges has published views of three of these, one of Chunar Gur, situated upon the river Ganges, about sixteen miles above the city of Benares[m]; the second, of Gwallior, about eighty miles to the south of Agra[n]; the third of Bidjegur, in the territory of Benares[o]. They are all, particularly Gwallior, works of considerable magnitude and strength. The fortresses in Bengal, however, are not to be compared with several in the Deccan. Asseergur, Burhampour, and Dowlatabad, are deemed by the natives to be impregnable[p]; and I am assured, by a good judge, that Asseergur is indeed a most stu-

[l] Introd. to Code of Gentoo Laws, p. cxi.

[m] N° I. [n] N° II. [o] N° III.

[p] Rennel. Mem. p. 133. 139.

pendous

pendous work, and so advantageously situated that it would be extremely difficult to reduce it by force.

Nor is it only from surveying their public works that we are justified in asserting the early proficiency of the Indians in elegant and useful arts: we are led to form the same conclusion by a view of those productions of their ingenuity, which were the chief articles of their trade with foreign nations. Of these the labours of the Indian loom and needle have, in every age, been the most celebrated; and fine linen is conjectured, with some probability, to have been called by the ancients *Sindon*, from the name of the river Indus or Sindus, near which it was wrought in the highest perfection [q]. The cotton manufactures of India seem anciently to have been as much admired as they are at present, not only for their delicate texture, but for the elegance with which some of them are embroidered, and the beautiful colour of the flowers with which others are adorned. From the earliest period of European intercourse with India, that country has been distinguished for the number and excellence of the substances for dying various colours, with which it abounded [r]. The dye of the deep blue colour in highest estimation among the Romans bore the name of *Indicum* [s]. From India too, the substance used in dying a bright red colour, seems to have been imported [t];

[q] Sir William Jones's Third Discourse, p. 428.

[r] Strab. lib. xv. p. 1018 A. 1024 B.

[s] Plin. Nat. Hist. lib. xxxv. c. 6. § 27.

[t] Salmasius Exercit. Plinianæ in Solin. 180, &c. 810. Salmasius de Homionymis Hyles Jatrica, c. 107. See NOTE VIII.

and

and it is well known that both in the cotton and ſilk ſtuffs which we now receive from India, the blue and the red are the colours of moſt conſpicuous luſtre and beauty. But however much the ancients may have admired theſe productions of Indian art, ſome circumſtances, which I have already mentioned, rendered their demand for the cotton manufactures of India, far inferior to that of modern times; and this has occaſioned the information concerning them which we receive from the Greek and Roman writers to be very imperfect. We may conclude, however, from the wonderful reſemblance of the ancient ſtate of India to the modern, that, in every period, the productions of their looms were as various as beautiful. The ingenuity of the Indians in other kinds of workmanſhip, particularly in metals and in ivory, is mentioned with praiſe by ancient authors, but without any particular deſcription of their nature [u]. Of theſe early productions of Indian artiſts, there are now ſome ſpecimens in Europe, from which it appears that they were acquainted with the method of engraving upon the hardeſt ſtones and gems; and, both in the elegance of their deſigns and in neatneſs of execution, had arrived at a conſiderable degree of excellence. An ingenious writer maintains, that the art of engraving on gems was probably an Indian invention, and certainly was early improved there, and he ſupports this opinion by ſeveral plauſible arguments [x]. The Indian engraved gems, of which he has publiſhed deſcriptions, appear to be the work-

[u] Strabo, lib. xv. p. 1044. B. Dionyſ. Periegies, verſ. 1016.

[x] Raſpe's Introd. to Taſſie's Deſcript. Catal. of engraved Gems, &c. p. xii. &c.

manſhip

manſhip of a very remote period, as the legends on them are in the Sanſkreet language [y].

But it is not only from the improved ſtate of mechanic arts in India, that we conclude its inhabitants to have been highly civilized; a proof of this, ſtill more convincing, may be deduced from the early and extraordinary productions of their genius in the fine arts. This evidence is rendered more intereſting, by being derived from a ſource of knowledge which the laudable curioſity of our countrymen has opened to the people of Europe within theſe few years. That all the ſcience and literature poſſeſſed by the Brahmins, were contained in books written in a language, underſtood by a few only of the moſt learned among them, is a fact which has long been known; and all the Europeans ſettled in India during three centuries, have complained that the Brahmins obſtinately refuſed to inſtruct any perſon in this language. But at length, by addreſs, mild treatment, and a perſuaſion, that the earneſtneſs with which inſtruction was ſolicited, proceeded not from any intention of turning their religion into deriſion, but from a deſire of acquiring a perfect knowledge of their ſciences and literature, their ſcruples have been overcome. Several Britiſh gentlemen are now completely maſters of the Sanſkreet language. The myſterious veil, formerly deemed impenetrable, is removed; and, in the courſe of five years, the curioſity of the public has been gratified by two publications as ſingular as they were unexpected.

[y] Raſpe's Introd. to Taſſie's Deſcript. Catal. of engraved Gems, vol i. p. 74. vol. ii. plate xiii.

pected. The one is a translation, by Mr. Wilkins, of an Episode from the *Mahabarat*, an Epic poem, in high estimation among the Hindoos, composed, according to their account, by Kreeshna Dwypayen Veias, the most eminent of all their Brahmins, above three thousand years before the Christian æra. The other is *Sacontala*, a dramatic poem, written about a century before the birth of Christ, translated by Sir William Jones. I shall endeavour to give my readers such a view of the subject and composition of each of these, as may enable them to estimate the degree of merit which they possess.

The Mahabarat is a voluminous poem, consisting of upwards of four hundred thousand lines. Mr. Wilkins has translated more than a third of it; but only a short episode, intitled Baghvat-Geeta, is hitherto published, and from this specimen we must form an opinion with respect to the whole. The subject of the poem is a famous civil war between two branches of the royal house of Bhaurat. When the forces on each side were formed in the field, and ready to decide the contest by the sword, Arjoon, the favourite and pupil of the god Kreeshna, who accompanied him in this hour of danger, requested of him to cause his chariot advance between the two hostile armies. He looked at both armies, and beheld, on either side, none but grandsires, uncles, cousins, tutors, sons, and brothers, near relations or bosom friends; and when he had gazed for a while, and saw these prepared for the fight, he was seized with extreme pity and compunction, and uttered his sorrow in the following words:—" Having beheld, O *Kreeshna!* my kindred

6 " thus

"thus waiting anxious for the fight, my members fail me, "my countenance withereth, the hair ſtandeth an end upon my "body, and all my frame trembleth with horror! Even *Gan-* "*deev*, my bow, eſcapeth from my hand, and my ſkin is parched "and dried up.—When I have deſtroyed my kindred, ſhall I "longer look for happineſs? I wiſh not for victory, *Kreeſhna*; "I want not dominion; I want not pleaſure; for what is do- "minion and the enjoyments of life, or even life itſelf, when "thoſe for whom dominion, pleaſure, and enjoyment were to "be coveted, have abandoned life and fortune, and ſtand here "in the field ready for the battle. Tutors, ſons, and fathers, "grandſires and grandſons, uncles, nephews, couſins, kindred, "and friends! Although they would kill me, I wiſh not to "fight them; no not even for the dominion of the three re- "gions of the univerſe, much leſs for this little earth [*]." In order to remove his ſcruples, Kreeſhna informs him what was the duty of a prince of the Chehteree, or military caſt, when called to act in ſuch a ſituation, and incites him to perform it by a variety of moral and philoſophical arguments, the nature of which I ſhall have occaſion to conſider particularly in another part of this Diſſertation. In this dialogue between Kreeſhna and his pupil, there are ſeveral paſſages which give an high idea of the genius of the poet. The ſpeech of Arjoon I have quoted, in which he expreſſes the anguiſh of his ſoul, muſt have ſtruck every reader as beautiful and pathetic; and I ſhall afterwards produce a deſcription of the Supreme Being, and of the reverence wherewith he ſhould be worſhipped, which is ſublime. But while theſe ex-

[*] Baghvat Geeta, p. 30, 31.

cite our admiration, and confirm us in the belief of a high degree of civilization in that country where fuch a work was produced, we are furprifed at the defect of tafte and of art in the manner of introducing this Epifode. Two powerful armies are drawn up in battle-array, eager for the fight; a young hero and his inftructor are defcribed as ftanding in a chariot of war between them; that furely was not the moment for teaching him the principles of philofophy, and delivering eighteen lectures of metaphyfics and theology.

WITH regard, however, both to the dramatic and epic poetry of the Hindoos, we labour under the difadvantage of being obliged to form an opinion from a fingle fpecimen of each, and that of the latter, too, (as it is only a part of a large work,) an imperfect one. But if, from fuch fcanty materials, we may venture upon any decifion, it muft be, that of the two, the drama feems to have been conducted with the moft correct tafte. This will appear from the obfervations which I now proceed to make upon Sacontala.

IT is only to nations confiderably advanced in refinement, that the drama is a favourite entertainment. The Greeks had been for a good time a polifhed people; Alcæus and Sappho had compofed their Odes, and Thales and Anaximander had opened their fchools, before Tragedy made its firft rude effay in the cart of Thefpis; and a good time elapfed before it attained to any confiderable degree of excellence. From the drama of Sacontala, then, we muft form an advantageous idea of the ftate of improvement in that fociety to whofe tafte it was fuited. In eftimating its merit, however,

however, we muſt not apply to it rules of criticiſm drawn from the literature and taſte of nations with which its author was altogether unacquainted; we muſt not expect the unities of the Greek theatre; we muſt not meaſure it by our own ſtandard of propriety. Allowance muſt be made for local cuſtoms, and ſingular manners, ariſing from a ſtate of domeſtic ſociety, an order of civil policy, and a ſyſtem of religious opinions, very different from thoſe eſtabliſhed in Europe. Sacontala is not a regular drama, but, like ſome of the plays early exhibited on the Spaniſh and Engliſh theatres, is an hiſtory in dialogue, unfolding events which happened in different places, and during a ſeries of years. When viewed in this light, the fable is in general well arranged, the incidents are happily choſen, and the viciſſitudes in the ſituation of the principal perſonages are ſudden and unexpected. The unravelling of the piece, however, though ſome of the circumſtances preparatory to it be introduced with ſkill, is at laſt brought about by the intervention of ſuperior beings, which has always a bad effect, and diſcovers ſome want of art. But as Sacontala was deſcended of a celeſtial nymph, and under the protection of a holy hermit, this heavenly interpoſition may appear leſs marvellous, and is extremely agreeable to the Oriental taſte. In many places of this drama it is ſimple and tender, in ſome pathetic; in others there is a mixture of comic with what is more ſerious. Of each, examples might be given. I ſhall ſelect a few of the firſt, both becauſe ſimplicity and tenderneſs are the characteriſtic beauties of the piece, and becauſe they ſo little reſemble the extravagant imagery and turgid ſtyle of Oriental poetry.

Pp 2 SACONTALA,

SACONTALA, the heroine of the drama, a princeſs of high birth, had been educated by an holy hermit in a hallowed grove, and had paſſed the early part of her life in rural occupations and paſtoral innocence. When ſhe was about to quit this beloved retreat, and repair to the court of a great monarch, to whom ſhe had been married, Cana, her foſter-father, and her youthful companions, thus bewail their own loſs, and expreſs their wiſhes for her happineſs, in a ſtrain of ſentiment and language perfectly ſuited to their paſtoral character.

"HEAR, O ye trees of this hallowed foreſt, hear and proclaim "that Sacontala is going to the palace of her wedded lord; "ſhe, who drank not, though thirſty, before you were wa- "tered; ſhe, who cropped not, through affection for you, "one of your freſh leaves, though ſhe would have been "pleaſed with ſuch an ornament for her locks; ſhe, whoſe "chief delight was in the ſeaſon when your branches are "ſpangled with flowers!"

CHORUS of Wood Nymphs.—"May her way be attended "with proſperity! May propitious breezes ſprinkle, for her "delight, the odoriferous duſt of rich bloſſoms. May pools "of clear water, green with the leaves of the lotos, refreſh "her as ſhe walks; and may ſhady branches be her defence "from the ſcorching ſun-beams!"

SACONTALA, juſt as ſhe was departing from the grove, turns to Cana: "Suffer me, venerable father! to addreſs "this Madhavi-creeper, whoſe red bloſſoms inflame the grove."

——Cana.

——Cana. "My child I know thy affection for it."——Sacont. "O most radiant of shining plants, receive my embraces, and "return them with thy flexible arms! from this day, though "removed at a fatal distance, I shall for ever be thine.—O "beloved father, consider this creeper as myself!" As she advances, she again addresses Cana: "Father! when yon "female antelope, who now moves slowly from the weight of "the young ones with which she is pregnant, shall be deli-"vered of them, send me, I beg, a kind message with tidings "of her safety.—Do not forget."——Cana. "My beloved! "I will not forget it."——Sacont. [*stopping.*] "Ah! what is "it that clings to the skirts of my robe, and detains me?"——Cana. "It is thy adopted child, the little fawn, whose mouth, "when the sharp points of Cusa grass had wounded it, has "been so often smeared by thee with the healing oil of Ingudi; "who has been so often fed by thee with a handful of Synmaka "grains, and now will not leave the footsteps of his protectress."——Sacont. "Why dost thou weep, tender fawn, for me who "must leave our common dwelling-place?—As thou wast "reared by me when thou hadst lost thy mother, who died "soon after thy birth, so will my foster-father attend thee, "when we are separated, with anxious care.—Return, poor "thing, return——we must part." [*She bursts into tears.*]——Cana. "Thy tears, my child, ill suit the occasion, we shall "all meet again; be firm; see the direct road before thee, "and follow it. When the big tear lurks beneath thy beau-"tiful eye-lashes, let thy resolution check its first efforts to "disengage itself.—In thy passage over this earth, where "the paths are now high, now low, and the true path sel-

"dom

5

"dom diſtinguiſhed, the traces of thy feet muſt needs be un-
"equal; but virtue will preſs thee right onward [b]."

From this ſpecimen of the Indian drama, every reader of good taſte, I ſhould imagine, will be ſatisfied, that it is only among a people of poliſhed manners and delicate ſentiments that a compoſition ſo ſimple and correct could be produced or reliſhed. I obſerve one inſtance in this drama of that wild extravagance ſo frequent in Oriental poetry. The monarch, in replacing a bracelet which had dropped from the arm of Sacontala, thus addreſſes her: "Look, my darling, this is the "new moon which left the firmament in honour of ſuperior "beauty, and having deſcended on your enchanting wriſt, "hath joined both its horns round it in the ſhape of a "bracelet [c]." But this is the ſpeech of an enraptured young man to his miſtreſs, and in every age and nation exaggerated praiſe is expected from the mouth of lovers. Dramatic exhibitions ſeem to have been a favourite amuſement of the Hindoos as well as of other civilized nations. "The "tragedies, comedies, farces, and muſical pieces of the In-"dian theatre, would fill as many volumes as that of any "nation in ancient or modern Europe. They are all in verſe "where the dialogue is elevated, and in proſe where it is "familiar; the men of rank and learning are repreſented "ſpeaking pure Sanſcrit, and the women Pracrit, which is "little more than the language of the Brahmins, melted down "by a delicate articulation to the ſoftneſs of Italian; while the

[b] Act IV. p. 47, &c. [c] Act III. p. 36.

6 "low

"low persons of the drama ſpeak the vulgar dialects of the "ſeveral provinces which they are ſuppoſed to inhabit [d]."

V. The attainments of the Indians in ſcience, furniſh an additional proof of their early civilization. By every perſon who has viſited India in ancient or modern times, its inhabitants, either in tranſactions of private buſineſs, or in the conduct of political affairs, have been deemed not inferior to the people of any nation in ſagacity, acuteneſs of underſtanding, or addreſs. From the application of ſuch talents to the cultivation of ſcience, an extraordinary degree of proficiency might have been expected. The Indians were, accordingly, early celebrated on that account, and ſome of the moſt eminent of the Greek philoſophers travelled into India, that, by converſing with the ſages of that country, they might acquire ſome portion of the knowledge for which they were diſtinguiſhed [e]. The accounts, however, which we receive from the Greeks and Romans, of the ſciences which attracted the attention of the Indian philoſophers, or of the diſcoveries which they had made in them, are very imperfect. To the reſearches of a few intelligent perſons, who have viſited India during the courſe of the three laſt centuries, we are indebted for more ample and authentic information. But from the reluctance with which the Brahmins communicate their ſciences to ſtrangers, and the inability of Europeans to acquire much knowledge of them, while, like the myſteries of their religion, they were concealed from vulgar

[d] Preface to Sacont. by Sir William Jones, p. ix. See NOTE IX.

[e] Bruckeri Hiſt. Philoſoph. vol. i. p. 190.

gar eyes in an unknown tongue, this information was acquired ſlowly and with great difficulty. The ſame obſervation, however, which I made concerning our knowledge of the ſtate of the fine arts among the people of India, is applicable to that of their progreſs in ſcience, and the preſent age is the firſt furniſhed with ſufficient evidence upon which to found a deciſive judgment with reſpect to either.

SCIENCE, when viewed as disjoined from religion, the conſideration of which I reſerve for another head, is employed in contemplating either the operations of the underſtanding, the exerciſe of our moral powers, or the nature and qualities of external objects. The firſt is denominated logic; the ſecond ethics; the third phyſics, or the knowledge of nature. With reſpect to the early progreſs in cultivating each of theſe ſciences in India, we are in poſſeſſion of facts which merit attention.

BUT, prior to the conſideration of them, it is proper to examine the ideas of the Brahmins with reſpect to mind itſelf, for if theſe were not juſt, all their theories concerning its operations muſt have been erroneous and fanciful. The diſtinction between matter and ſpirit appears to have been early known by the philoſophers of India, and to the latter they aſcribed many powers, of which they deemed the former to be incapable; and when we recollect how inadequate our conceptions are of every object that does not fall under the cognizance of the ſenſes, we may affirm (if allowance be made for a peculiar notion of the Hindoos which ſhall be afterwards explained) that no deſcription of the human ſoul is more ſuited to the dignity of of its nature than that given by the author of the Mahabarat. "Some," ſays he, "regard the ſoul as a wonder, others hear "of it with aſtoniſhment, but no one knoweth it. The wea-"pon divideth it not; the fire burneth it not; the water cor-"rupteth it not; the wind drieth it not away; for it is indi-"viſible, inconſumable, incorruptible; it is eternal, univerſal, "permanent, immovable; it is inviſible, inconceivable, and "unalterable[f]." After this view of the ſentiments of the Brahmins concerning mind itſelf, we may proceed to conſider their ideas with reſpect to each of the ſciences, in that tripartite arrangement which I mentioned.

1ſt, LOGIC and Metaphyſics. On no ſubject has the human underſtanding been more exerciſed than in analyſing its own operations. The various powers of the mind have been examined and defined. The origin and progreſs of our ideas have been traced; and proper rules have been preſcribed, of proceeding from the obſervation of facts to the eſtabliſhment of principles, or from the knowledge of principles to form arrangements of ſcience. The philoſophers of ancient Greece were highly celebrated for their proficiency in theſe abſtruſe ſpeculations; and, in their diſcuſſions and arrangements, diſcovered ſuch depth of thought, and acuteneſs of diſcernment, that their ſyſtems of Logic, particularly that of the Peripatetick School, have been deemed moſt diſtinguiſhed efforts of human reaſon.

[f] Baghvat-Geeta, p. 37.

But ſince we became acquainted, in ſome degree, with the literature and ſcience of the Hindoos, we find that as ſoon as men arrive at that ſtage in ſocial life, when they can turn their attention to ſpeculative inquiries, the human mind will, in every region of the earth, diſplay nearly the ſame powers, and proceed in its inveſtigations and diſcoveries by nearly ſimilar ſteps. From Abul Fazel's compendium of the philoſophy [g] of the Hindoos, the knowledge of which he acquired, as he informs us, by aſſociating intimately with the moſt learned men of the nation; from the ſpecimen of their logical diſcuſſions contained in that portion of the Shaſter publiſhed by Colonel Dow [h], and from many paſſages in the Baghvat-Geeta, it appears that the ſame ſpeculations which occupied the philoſophers of Greece had engaged the attention of the Indian Brahmins; and the theories of the former, either concerning the qualities of external objects, or the nature of our own ideas, were not more ingenious than thoſe of the latter. To define with accuracy, to diſtinguiſh with acuteneſs, and to reaſon with ſubtlety, are characteriſtics of both; and in both, the ſame exceſs of refinement, in attempting to analyſe thoſe operations of mind which the faculties of man were not formed to comprehend, led ſometimes to the moſt falſe and dangerous concluſions. That ſceptical philoſophy, which denies the exiſtence of the material world, and aſſerts nothing to be real but our own ideas, ſeems to have been known in India as well as in Europe [i]; and the ſages of the Eaſt, as they were indebted to philoſophy for the

[g] Ayeen Akbery, vol. iii. p. 95, &c. [h] Diſſertation, p. xxxix, &c.
[i] Dow's Diſſertation, p. lvii. Ayeen Akbery, vol. iii. p. 128.

5 knowledge

knowledge of many important truths, were not more exempt than those of the West from its delusions and errors.

2d, ETHICS. This science, which has for its object, to ascertain what distinguishes virtue from vice, to investigate what motives should prompt men to act, and to prescribe rules for the conduct of life, as it is of all other the most interesting, seems to have deeply engaged the attention of the Brahmins. Their sentiments with respect to these points were various, and, like the philosophers of Greece, the Brahmins were divided into sects, distinguished by maxims and tenets often diametrically opposite. That sect with whose opinions we are, fortunately, best acquainted, had established a system of morals, founded on principles the most generous and dignified which unassisted reason is capable of discovering. Man, they taught, was formed, not for speculation or indolence, but for action. He is born, not for himself alone, but for his fellow men. The happiness of the society of which he is a member, the good of mankind, are his ultimate and highest objects. In chusing what to prefer or to reject, the justness and propriety of his choice are the only considerations to which he should attend. The events which may follow his actions are not in his own power, and whether they be prosperous or adverse, as long as he is satisfied with the purity of the motives which induced him to act, he can enjoy that approbation of his own mind, which constitutes genuine happiness, independent of the power of fortune or the opinions of other men. "Man (says the author of the Mahabarat) "enjoyeth not freedom from action. Every man is involuntarily urged to act by those principles which are inherent in "his nature. He who restraineth his active faculties, and sitteth down with his mind attentive to the objects of his senses, may be called one of an astrayed soul. The man is praised, who having subdued all his passions, performeth with his active faculties all the functions of life unconcerned about the event[k]. Let the motive be in the deed, and not in the event. Be not one whose motive for action is the hope of reward. Let not thy life be spent in inaction. Depend upon application, perform thy duty, abandon all thought of the consequence, and make the event equal, whether it terminate in good or in evil; for such an equality is called *Yog* [i. e. attention to what is spiritual]. Seek an asylum then in wisdom alone; for the miserable and unhappy are so on account of the event of things. Men who are endued with true wisdom are unmindful of good or evil in this world. Study then to obtain this application of thy understanding, for such application in business is a precious art. Wise men who have abandoned all thought of the fruit which is produced from their actions, are freed from the chains of birth; and go to the regions of eternal happiness[l]."

FROM these, and other passages which I might have quoted, we learn that the distinguishing doctrines of the Stoical School were taught in India many ages before the birth of Zeno, and inculcated with a persuasive earnestness nearly resembling that of Epictetus; and it is not without astonishment that we find the tenets of this manly active philosophy, which seem to be

k Baghvat-Geeta, p. 44.

l Ibid. p. 40.

formed

formed only for men of the most vigorous spirit, prescribed as the rule of conduct to a race of people more eminent for the gentleness of their disposition than for the elevation of their minds.

3d, PHYSICS. In all the sciences which contribute towards extending our knowledge of nature, in mathematics, mechanics, and astronomy, Arithmetic is of elementary use. In whatever country then we find that such attention has been paid to the improvement of arithmetic as to render its operations most easy and correct, we may presume that the sciences depending upon it have attained a superior degree of perfection. Such improvement of this science we find in India. While, among the Greeks and Romans, the only method used for the notation of numbers was by the letters of the alphabet, which necessarily rendered arithmetical calculation extremely tedious and operose, the Indians had, from time immemorial, employed for the same purpose the ten cyphers, or figures, now universally known, and by means of them performed every operation in arithmetic with the greatest facility and expedition. By the happy invention of giving a different value to each figure according to its change of place, no more than ten figures are needed in calculations the most complex, and of any given extent; and arithmetic is the most perfect of all the sciences. The Arabians, not long after their settlement in Spain, introduced this mode of notation into Europe, and were candid enough to acknowledge that they had derived the knowledge of it from the Indians. Though the advantages of this mode of notation are obvious and great, yet so slowly do mankind adopt new inventions, that the uſe of it was for ſome time confined to ſcience; by degrees, however, men of buſineſs relinquiſhed the former cumberſome method of computation by letters, and the Indian arithmetic came into general uſe throughout Europe[m]. It is now ſo familiar and ſimple, that the ingenuity of the people, to whom we are indebted for the invention, is leſs obſerved and leſs celebrated than it merits.

THE Aſtronomy of the Indians is a proof ſtill more conſpicuous of their extraordinary progreſs in ſcience. The attention and ſucceſs with which they ſtudied the motions of the heavenly bodies were ſo little known to the Greeks and Romans that it is hardly mentioned by them but in the moſt curſory manner[n]. But as ſoon as the Mahomedans eſtabliſhed an intercourſe with the natives of India, they obſerved and celebrated the ſuperiority of their aſtronomical knowledge. Of the Europeans who viſited India after the communication with it by the Cape of Good Hope was diſcovered, M. Bernier, an inquiſitive and philoſophical traveller, was one of the firſt who learned that the Indians had long applied to the ſtudy of aſtronomy, and had made conſiderable progreſs in that ſcience[o]. His information, however, ſeems to have been very general and imperfect. We are indebted for the firſt ſcientific proof of the great proficiency of the Indians in aſtronomical knowledge, to M. de la Loubere, who, on his return from his embaſſy to Siam,

[m] Montucla Hiſt. des Mathemat. tom. i. p. 360, &c.

[n] Strabo, lib. xv. p. 1047 A. Dirn. Perieg. v. 1173.

[o] Voyages, tom. ii. p. 145, &c.

brought

brought with him an extract from a Siamese manuscript, which A. D. 1687.
contained tables and rules for calculating the places of the sun and moon. The manner in which these tables were constructed rendered the principles on which they were founded extremely obscure, and it required a commentator as conversant in astronomical calculation as the celebrated Cassini, to explain the meaning of this curious fragment. The epoch of the Siamese tables corresponds to the 21st of March, A. D. 638. Another set of tables was transmitted from Chrisnabouram, in the Carnatic, the epoch of which answers to the 10th of March, A. D. 1491. A third set of tables came from Narsapour, and the epoch of them goes no farther back than A. D. 1569. The fourth and most curious set of tables was published by M. le Gentil, to whom they were communicated by a learned Brahmin of Tirvalore, a small town on the Coromandel coast, about twelve miles west of Negapatam. The epoch of these tables is of high antiquity, and coincides with the beginning of the celebrated æra of the Calyougham or Collee Jogue, which commenced, according to the Indian account, three thousand one hundred and two years before the birth of Christ [p].

These four sets of tables have been examined and compared by M. Bailly, who with singular felicity of genius has conjoined an uncommon degree of eloquence with the patient researches of an astronomer, and the profound investigations of a geometrician. His calculations have been verified, and his reasonings have been illustrated and extended by Mr. Playfair,

[p] See NOTE X.

in

in a very masterly Dissertation, published in the Transactions of the Royal Society of Edinburgh [q].

INSTEAD of attempting to follow them in reasonings and calculations, which, from their nature, are often abstruse and intricate, I shall satisfy myself with giving such a general view of them as is suited to a popular work. This, I hope, may convey a proper idea of what has been published concerning the astronomy of India, a subject too curious and important to be omitted in any account of the state of science in that country; and, without interposing any judgment of my own, I shall leave each of my readers to form his own opinion.

IT may be considered as the general result of all the inquiries, reasonings, and calculations, with respect to Indian astronomy, which have hitherto been made public, "That the "motion of the heavenly bodies, and more particularly their "situation at the commencement of the different epochs to "which the four sets of tables refer, are ascertained with "great accuracy; and that many of the elements of their cal-"culations, especially for very remote ages, are verified by an "astonishing coincidence with the tables of the modern astro-"nomy of Europe, when improved by the latest and most nice "deductions from the theory of gravitation." These conclusions are rendered peculiarly interesting, by the evidence which they afford of an advancement in science unexampled in the history

[q] Vol. ii. p. 135.

of

of rude nations. The Indian Brahmins, who annually circulate a kind of almanack, containing aſtronomical predictions of ſome of the more remarkable phenomena in the heavens, ſuch as the new and full moons, the eclipſes of the ſun and moon, are in poſſeſſion of certain methods of calculation, which, upon examination, are found to involve in them a very extenſive ſyſtem of aſtronomical knowledge. M. le Gentil, a French aſtronomer, had an opportunity, while in India, of obſerving two eclipſes of the moon, which had been calculated by a Brahmin, and he found the error in either to be very inconſiderable.

THE accuracy of theſe reſults is leſs ſurpriſing than the juſtneſs and ſcientific nature of the principles on which the tables, by which they calculate, are conſtructed. For the method of predicting eclipſes which is followed by the Brahmins, is of a kind altogether different from any that has been found in the poſſeſſion of rude nations in the infancy of aſtronomy. In Chaldæa, and even in Greece, in the early ages, the method of calculating eclipſes was founded on the obſervation of a certain period or cycle, after which the eclipſes of the ſun and moon return nearly in the ſame order; but there was no attempt to analyſe the different circumſtances on which the eclipſe depends, or to deduce its phenomena from a preciſe knowledge of the motions of the ſun and moon. This laſt was reſerved for a more advanced period, when geometry, as well as arithmetic, were called in to the aſſiſtance of aſtronomy, and if it was attempted at all, ſeems not to have been attempted with ſucceſs before the age of Hipparchus. It is a method of this ſuperior kind, founded on principles, and on an analyſis of the motions of the ſun and moon, which guides the calculations of the Brahmins, and they never employ any of the groſſer eſtimations, which were the pride of the firſt aſtronomers in Egypt and Chaldæa.

THE Brahmins of the preſent times are guided in their calculations by theſe principles, though they do not now underſtand them; they know only the uſe of the tables which are in their poſſeſſion, but are unacquainted with the method of their conſtruction. The Brahmin who viſited M. le Gentil at Pondicherry, and inſtructed him in the uſe of the Indian tables, had no knowledge of the principles of his art, and diſcovered no curioſity concerning the nature of M. le Gentil's obſervations, or about the inſtruments which he employed. He was equally ignorant with reſpect to the authors of theſe tables; and whatever is to be learnt concerning the time or place of their conſtruction, muſt be deduced from the tables themſelves. One ſet of theſe tables (as was formerly obſerved) profeſs to be as old as the beginning of the Calyougham, or to go back to the year 3102 before the Chriſtian æra; but as nothing (it may be ſuppoſed) is eaſier than for an aſtronomer to give to his tables what date he pleaſes, and, by calculating backwards, to eſtabliſh an epoch of any aſſigned antiquity, the pretenſions of the Indian aſtronomy to ſo remote an origin are not to be admitted without examination.

THAT examination has accordingly been inſtituted by M. Bailly, and the reſult of his inquiries is aſſerted to be, that the aſtronomy

nomy of India is founded on obſervations which cannot be of a much later date than the period above mentioned. For the Indian tables repreſent the ſtate of the heavens at that period with aſtoniſhing exactneſs; and there is between them and the calculations of our modern aſtronomy ſuch a conformity, with reſpect to thoſe ages, as could reſult from nothing, but from the authors of the former having accurately copied from nature, and having delineated truly the face of the heavens, in the age wherein they lived. In order to give ſome idea of the high degree of accuracy in the Indian tables, I ſhall ſelect a few inſtances of it, out of many that might be produced. The place of the ſun for the aſtronomical epoch at the beginning of the Calyougham, as ſtated in the tables of Tirvalore, is only forty-ſeven minutes greater than by the tables of M. de la Caille, when corrected by the calculations of M. de la Grange. The place of the moon, in the ſame tables, for the ſame epoch, is only thirty-ſeven minutes different from the tables of Mayer. The tables of Ptolemy, for that epoch, are erroneous no leſs than ten degrees with reſpect to the place of the ſun, and eleven degrees with reſpect to that of the moon. The acceleration of the moon's motion, reckoning from the beginning of the Calyougham to the preſent time, agrees, in the Indian tables, with thoſe of Mayer to a ſingle minute. The inequality of the ſun's motion, and the obliquity of the ecliptic, which were both greater in former ages than they are now, as repreſented in the tables of Tirvalore, are almoſt of the preciſe quantity that the theory of gravitation aſſigns to them three thouſand years before the Chriſtian æra. It is accordingly for thoſe very remote ages (about 5000 years diſtant from the present) that their aſtronomy is moſt accurate, and the nearer we come down to our own times, the conformity of its reſults with ours diminiſhes. It ſeems reaſonable to ſuppoſe, that the time when its rules are moſt accurate, is the time when the obſervations were made on which theſe rules are founded.

In ſupport of this concluſion, M. Bailly maintains that none of all the aſtronomical ſyſtems of Greece or Perſia, or of Tartary, from ſome of which it might be ſuſpected that the Indian tables were copied, can be made to agree with them, eſpecially when we calculate for very remote ages. The ſuperior perfection of the Indian tables becomes always more conſpicuous as we go farther back into antiquity. This ſhews, likewiſe, how difficult it is to conſtruct any aſtronomical tables, which will agree with the ſtate of the heavens for a period ſo remote from the time when the tables were conſtructed, as four or five thouſand years. It is only from aſtronomy in its moſt advanced ſtate, ſuch as it has attained in modern Europe, that ſuch accuracy is to be expected.

When an eſtimate is endeavoured to be made of the geometrical ſkill neceſſary for the conſtruction of the Indian tables and rules, it is found to be very conſiderable; and, beſide the knowledge of elementary geometry, it muſt have required plain and ſpherical trigonometry, or ſomething equivalent to them, together with certain methods of approximating to the values of geometrical magnitudes, which ſeem to riſe very far above the elements of any of thoſe ſciences. Some of theſe laſt mark alſo very clearly (although this has not been obſerved by M. Bailly)

Bailly) that the places to which theſe tables are adapted, muſt be ſituated between the Tropics, becauſe they are altogether inapplicable at a greater diſtance from the Equator.

FROM this long induction, the concluſion which ſeems obviouſly to reſult is, that the Indian aſtronomy is founded upon obſervations which were made at a very early period; and when we conſider the exact agreement of the places which they aſſign to the ſun and moon, and other heavenly bodies, at that epoch, with thoſe deduced from the tables of De la Caille and Mayer, it ſtrongly confirms the truth of the poſition which I have been endeavouring to eſtabliſh, concerning the early and high ſtate of civilization in India.

BEFORE I quit this ſubject, there is one circumſtance which merits particular attention. All the knowledge which we have hitherto acquired of the principles and concluſions of Indian aſtronomy is derived from the ſouthern part of the Carnatic, and the tables are adapted to places ſituated between the meridian of Cape Comorin and that which paſſes through the eaſtern part of Ceylon [r]. The Brahmins in the Carnatic acknowledge that their ſcience of aſtronomy was derived from the North, and that their method of calculation is denominated *Fakiam*, or New, to diſtinguiſh it from the *Siddantam*, or ancient method eſtabliſhed at Benares, which they allow to be much more perfect; and we learn from Abul Fazel, that all the aſtronomers of Indoſtan rely entirely upon the precepts con-

[r] Bailly, Diſc. Prelim. p. xvii.

tained

tained in a book called *Soorej Sudhant*, composed in a very remote period [s]. It is manifestly from this book that the method to which the Brahmins of the South gave the name of Siddantam is taken. Benares has been from time immemorial the Athens of India, the residence of the most learned Brahmins, and the seat both of science and literature. There, it is highly probable, whatever remains of the ancient astronomical knowledge and discoveries of the Brahmins is still preserved [t]. In an enlightened age and nation, and during a reign distinguished by a succession of the most splendid and successful undertakings to extend the knowledge of nature, it is an object worthy of public attention, to take measures for obtaining possession of all that time has spared of the philosophy and inventions of the most early and most highly civilized people of the East. It is with peculiar advantages Great Britain may engage in this laudable undertaking. Benares is subject to its dominion; the confidence of the Brahmins has been so far gained as to render them communicative; some of our countrymen are acquainted with that sacred language in which the mysteries both of religion and of science are recorded; movement and activity has been given to a spirit of inquiry throughout all the British establishments in India; persons who visited that country with other views, though engaged in occupations of a very different kind, are now carrying on scientific and literary researches with ardour and success. Nothing seems now to be wanting but that those entrusted with the administration of the British empire in

[s] Ayeen Akbery, iii. p. 8.

[t] M. Bernier, in the year 1668, saw a large hall in Benares filled with the works of the Indian philosophers, physicians, and poets. Voy. ii. p. 148.

6 India,

India, ſhould enable ſome perſon, capable, by his talents and liberality of ſentiment, of inveſtigating and explaining the more abſtruſe parts of Indian philoſophy, to devote his whole time to that important object. Thus Great Britain may have the glory of exploring fully that extenſive field of unknown ſcience, which the Academicians of France had the merit of firſt opening to the people of Europe [u].

VI. THE laſt evidence which I ſhall mention of the early and high civilization of the ancient Indians, is deduced from the conſideration of their religious tenets and practices. The inſtitutions of religion, publicly eſtabliſhed in all the extenſive countries ſtretching from the Banks of the Indus to Cape Comorin, preſent to view an aſpect nearly ſimilar. They form a regular and complete ſyſtem of ſuperſtition, ſtrengthened and upheld by every thing which can excite the reverence and ſecure the attachment of the people. The temples, conſecrated to their deities, are magnificent, and adorned not only with rich offerings, but with the moſt exquiſite works in painting and ſculpture, which the artiſts, higheſt in eſtimation among them, were capable of executing. The rites and ceremonies of their worſhip are pompous and ſplendid, and the performance of them not only mingles in all the tranſactions of common life, but conſtitutes an eſſential part of them. The Brahmins, who, as miniſters of religion, preſide in all its functions, are elevated above every other order of men, by an origin deemed not only more noble, but acknowledged to be ſacred. They have eſtabliſhed among themſelves a regular hierarchy and gradation of ranks, which, by ſecuring ſubordination in their own order,

[u] See NOTE XI.

adds

adds weight to their authority, and gives them a more abſolute dominion over the minds of the people. This dominion they ſupport by the command of the immenſe revenues with which the liberality of princes, and the zeal of pilgrims and devotees, have enriched their Pagodas [u].

It is far from my intention to enter into any minute detail with reſpect to this vaſt and complicated ſyſtem of ſuperſtition. An attempt to enumerate the multitude of deities which are the objects of adoration in India; to deſcribe the ſplendour of worſhip in their Pagodas, and the immenſe variety of their rites and ceremonies; to recount the various attributes and functions which the craft of prieſts, or the credulity of the people, have aſcribed to their divinities; eſpecially if I were to accompany all this with a review of the numerous and often fanciful ſpeculations and theories of learned men on this ſubject, would require a work of great magnitude. I ſhall, therefore, on this, as on ſome of the former heads, confine myſelf to the preciſe point which I have kept uniformly in view, and by conſidering the ſtate of religion in India, I ſhall endeavour not only to throw additional light on the ſtate of civilization in that country, but I flatter myſelf that, at the ſame time, I ſhall be able to give what may be conſidered as a ſketch and outline of the hiſtory and progreſs of ſuperſtition and falſe religion in every region of the earth.

I. We may obſerve, that, in every country, the received mythology, or ſyſtem of ſuperſtitious belief, with all the rites

[u] Roger. Porte Ouverte, p. 39. 209, &c.

and ceremonies which it prefcribes is formed in the infancy of fociety, in rude and barbarous times. True religion is as different from fuperftition in its origin, as in its nature. The former is the offspring of reafon cherifhed by fcience, and attains to its higheft perfection in ages of light and improvement. Ignorance and fear give birth to the latter, and it is always in the darkeft periods that it acquires the greateft vigour. That numerous part of the human fpecies whofe lot is labour, whofe principal and almoft fole occupation is to fecure fubfiftence, has neither leifure nor capacity for entering into that path of intricate and refined fpeculation, which conducts to the knowledge of the principles of rational religion. When the intellectual powers are juft beginning to unfold, and their firft feeble exertions are directed towards a few objects of primary neceffity and ufe; when the faculties of the mind are fo limited as not to have formed general and abftract ideas; when language is fo barren as to be deftitute of names to diftinguifh any thing not perceivable by fome of the fenfes; it is prepofterous to expect that men fhould be capable of tracing the relation between effects and their caufes; or to fuppofe that they fhould rife from the contemplation of the former to the difcovery of the latter, and form juft conceptions of one Supreme Being, as the Creator and Governor of the univerfe. The idea of creation is fo familiar, wherever the mind is enlarged by fcience, and illuminated by revelation, that we feldom reflect how profound and abftrufe the idea is, or confider what progrefs man muft have made in obfervation and refearch, before he could arrive at any diftinct knowledge of this elementary principle in religion. But even in its rude ftate, the human mind, formed for reli-

S s gion,

gion, opens to the reception of ideas, which are deſtined, when corrected and refined, to be the great ſource of conſolation amidſt the calamities of life. Theſe apprehenſions, however, are originally indiſtinct and perplexed, and ſeem to be ſuggeſted rather by the dread of impending evils, than to flow from gratitude for bleſſings received. While nature holds on her courſe with uniform and undiſturbed regularity, men enjoy the benefits reſulting from it, without much inquiry concerning its cauſe. But every deviation from this regular courſe rouſes and aſtoniſhes them. When they behold events to which they are not accuſtomed, they ſearch for the cauſes of them with eager curioſity. Their underſtanding is often unable to diſcover theſe, but imagination, a more forward and ardent faculty of the mind, decides without heſitation. It aſcribes the extraordinary occurrences in nature to the influence of inviſible beings, and ſuppoſes the thunder, the hurricane, and the earthquake, to be the immediate effect of their agency. Alarmed by theſe natural evils, and expoſed, at the ſame time, to many dangers and diſaſters, which are unavoidable in the early and uncivilized ſtate of ſociety, men have recourſe for protection to power ſuperior to what is human, and the firſt rites or practices which bear any reſemblance to acts of religion have it for their object to avert evils which they ſuffer or dread [x].

[x] In the ſecond volume of the Hiſtory of America, p. 183, of fifth edition, I gave nearly a ſimilar account of the origin of falſe religion. Inſtead of labouring to convey the ſame ideas in different language, I have inſerted here ſome paragraphs in the ſame words I then uſed.

II. As

II. As superstition and false religion take their rise, in every country, from nearly the same sentiments and apprehensions, the invisible beings, who are the first objects of veneration, have every where a near resemblance. To conceive an idea of one superintending mind, capable of arranging and directing all the various operations of nature, seems to be an attainment far beyond the powers of man in the more early stages of his progress. His theories, more suited to the limited sphere of his own observation, are not so refined. He supposes that there is a distinct cause of every remarkable effect, and ascribes to a separate power every event which attracts his attention, or excites his terror. He fancies that it is the province of one deity to point the lightning, and, with an awful sound, to hurl the irresistible thunderbolt at the head of the guilty; that another rides in the whirlwind, and, at his pleasure, raises or stills the tempest; that a third rules over the ocean; that a fourth is the god of battles; that while malevolent powers scatter the seeds of animosity and discord, and kindle in the breast those angry passions which give rise to war, and terminate in destruction, others, of a nature more benign, by inspiring the hearts of men with kindness and love, strengthen the bonds of social union, augment the happiness, and increase the number of the human race.

WITHOUT descending farther into detail, or attempting to enumerate that infinite multitude of deities to which the fancy or the fears of men have allotted the direction of the several departments in nature, we may recognise a striking uniformity of features in the systems of superstition established throughout every part of the earth. The lefs men have advanced beyond the ftate of favage life, and the more flender their acquaintance with the operations of nature, the fewer were their deities in number, and the more compendious was their theological creed; but as their mind gradually opened, and their knowledge continued to extend, the objects of their veneration multiplied, and the articles of their faith became more numerous. This took place remarkably among the Greeks in Europe, and the Indians in Afia, the two people, in thofe great divifions of the earth, who were moft early civilized, and to whom, for that reafon, I fhall confine all my obfervations. They believed, that over every movement in the natural world, and over every function in civil or domeftic life, even the moft common and trivial, a particular deity prefided. The manner in which they arranged the ftations of thefe fuperintending powers, and the offices which they allotted to each, were in many refpects the fame. What is fuppofed to be performed by the power of Jupiter, of Neptune, of Æolus, of Mars, of Venus, according to the mythology of the Weft, is afcribed in the Eaft to the agency of Agnée, the god of fire; Varoon, the god of oceans; Vayoo, the god of wind [y]; Cama, the god of love; and a variety of other divinities.

The ignorance and credulity of men having thus peopled the heavens with imaginary beings, they afcribed to them fuch qualities and actions as they deemed fuitable to their character and functions. It is one of the benefits derived from true re-

[y] Baghvat-Geeta, p. 94.

ligion,

ligion, that by ſetting before men a ſtandard of perfect excellence, which they ſhould have always in their eye, and endeavour to reſemble, it may be ſaid to bring down virtue from heaven to earth, and to form the human mind after a divine model. In fabricating ſyſtems of falſe religion the procedure is directly the reverſe. Men aſcribe to the beings whom they have deified, ſuch actions as they themſelves admire and celebrate. The qualities of the gods who are the objects of adoration, are copied from thoſe of the worſhippers who bow down before them; and thus many of the imperfections peculiar to men have found admittance into heaven. By knowing the adventures and attributes of any falſe deity, we can pronounce, with ſome degree of certainty, what muſt have been the ſtate of ſociety and manners when he was elevated to that dignity. The mythology of Greece plainly indicates the character of the age in which it was formed. It muſt have been in times of the greateſt licentiouſneſs, anarchy, and violence, that divinities of the higheſt rank could be ſuppoſed capable of perpetrating actions, or of being influenced by paſſions, which, in more enlightened periods, would be deemed a diſgrace to human nature; it muſt have been when the earth was ſtill infeſted with deſtructive monſters, and mankind, under forms of government too feeble to afford them protection, were expoſed to the depredations of lawleſs robbers, or the cruelty of ſavage oppreſſors, that the well-known labours of Hercules, by which he was raiſed from earth to heaven, could have been neceſſary, or would have been deemed ſo highly meritorious. The ſame obſervation is applicable to the ancient mythology of India. Many of the adventures and exploits of the Indian deities are ſuited to the rudeſt ages of turbulence and rapine. It was to check diſorder, to redreſs wrongs, and to clear the earth of powerful oppreſſors, that Viſhnou, a divinity of the higheſt order, is ſaid to have become ſucceſſively incarnate, and to have appeared on earth in various forms [z].

III. THE character and functions of thoſe deities which ſuperſtition created to itſelf as objects of its veneration, having every where a near reſemblance, the rites of their worſhip were every where extremely ſimilar. Accordingly as deities were diſtinguiſhed, either by ferocity of character or licentiouſneſs of conduct, it is obvious what ſervices muſt have been deemed moſt acceptable to them. In order to conciliate the favour, or to appeaſe the wrath, of the former, faſts, mortifications, and penances, all rigid, and many of them excruciating to an extreme degree, were the means employed. Their altars were always bathed in blood, the moſt coſtly victims were offered, whole hecatombs were ſlaughtered, even human ſacrifices were not unknown, and were held to be the moſt powerful expiations. In order to gain the good-will of the deities of the latter deſcription, recourſe was had to inſtitutions of a very different kind, to ſplendid ceremonies, gay feſtivals, heightened by all the pleaſures of poetry, muſick, and dancing, but often terminating in ſcenes of indulgence too indecent to be deſcribed. Of both theſe, inſtances occur in the rites of Greek and Roman worſhip, which I need not mention to my learned readers [a]. In

[z] Voyage de Sonnerat. tom. i. p. 158, &c.
[a] Strab. lib. viii. p. 581. A. Lib. xii. p. 837. C.

6 the

the East the ceremonial of superstition is nearly the same. The manners of the Indians, though distinguished, from the time when they became known to the people of the West, for mildness, seem, in a more remote period, to have been, in a greater degree, similar to those of other nations. Several of their deities were fierce and awful in their nature, and were represented in their temples under the most terrific forms. If we did not know the dominion of superstition over the human mind, we should hardly believe, that a ritual of worship suited to the character of such deities could have been established among a gentle people. Every act of religion, performed in honour of some of their gods, seems to have been prescribed by fear. Mortifications and penances so rigorous, so painful, and so long continued, that we read the accounts of them with astonishment and horror, were multiplied. Repugnant as it is to the feelings of an Hindoo, to shed the blood of any creature that has life, many different animals, even the most useful, the horse and the cow, were offered up as victims upon the altars of some of their gods[b]; and what is still more strange, the Pagodas of the East were polluted with human sacrifices, as well as the temples of the West[c]. But religious institutions, and ceremonies of a less severe kind, were more adapted to the genius of a people, formed, by the extreme sensibility both of their mental and corporeal frame, to an immoderate love of pleasure. In no part of the earth was a connection between

[b] Ayeen Akberry, vol. iii. p. 241. Roger Porte Ouverte, p. 251.

[c] Heeto-pades, p. 185—322. Asiat. Researches, p. 265. Voyage de Sonnerat, vol. i. p. 207. Roger, p. 251.

the

the gratification of ſenſual deſire and the rites of public religion, diſplayed with more avowed indecency than in India. In every Pagoda there was a band of women ſet apart for the ſervice of the idol honoured there, and devoted from their early years to a life of pleaſure; for which the Brahmins prepared them by an education which added ſo many elegant accompliſhments to their natural charms, that what they gained by their profligacy, often brought no inconſiderable acceſſion to the revenue of the temple. In every function performed in the Pagodas, as well as in every public proceſſion, it is the office of theſe women to dance before the idol, and to ſing hymns in his praiſe; and it is difficult to ſay, whether they treſpaſs moſt againſt decency by the geſtures they exhibit, or by the verſes which they recite. The walls of the Pagoda are covered with paintings, in a ſtile no leſs indelicate[d]; and in the innermoſt receſs of the temple, for it would be profane to call it the ſanctuary, is placed the *Lingam*, an emblem of productive power too groſs to be explained[e].

IV. How abſurd ſoever the articles of faith may be which ſuperſtition has adopted, or how unhallowed the rites which it preſcribes, the former are received in every age and country with unheſitating aſſent, by the great body of the people, and the latter obſerved with ſcrupulous exactneſs. In our reaſon-

[d] Voyage de Gentil. vol. i. p. 244. 260. Preface to Code of Gentoo Laws, p. lvii.

[e] Roger Porte Ouverte, p. 157. Voyage de Sonnerat, vol. i. p. 41. 175. Sketches, p. 168. Hamilton's Trav. vol. i. p. 379.

ings

ings concerning religious opinions and practices which differ widely from our own, we are extremely apt to err. Having been instructed ourselves in the principles of a religion, worthy in every respect of that divine wisdom by which they were dictated, we frequently express wonder at the credulity of nations in embracing systems of belief which appear to us so directly repugnant to right reason, and sometimes suspect that tenets so wild and extravagant do not really gain credit with them. But experience may satisfy us, that neither our wonder nor suspicions are well founded. No article of the public religion was called in question by those people of ancient Europe with whose history we are best acquainted, and no practice which it enjoined appeared improper to them. On the other hand, every opinion that tended to diminish the reverence of men for the gods of their country, or to alienate them from their worship, excited among the Greeks and Romans, that indignant zeal which is natural to every people attached to their religion, by a firm persuasion of its truth. The attachment of the Indians, both in ancient and modern times, to the tenets and rites of their ancestors, has been, if possible, still greater. In no country, of which we have any account, were precautions taken with so much solicitude, to place the great body of the people beyond the reach of any temptation to doubt or disbelief. They not only were prevented, (as I have already observed the great bulk of mankind must always be in every country,) from entering upon any speculative inquiry, by the various occupations of active and laborious life, but any attempt to extend the sphere of their knowledge was expressly prohibited. If one of the Sooder cast, by far the most numerous of the four into which the

Tt whole

whole nation was divided, presumed to read any portion of the sacred books, in which all the science known in India is contained, he was severely punished; if he ventured to get it by heart, he was put to death [f]. To aspire after any higher degree of knowledge than the Brahmins have been pleased to teach, would be deemed not only presumption but impiety. Even the higher Casts depended entirely for instruction on the Brahmins, and could acquire no portion of science but what they deigned to communicate. By means of this, a devout reverence was universally maintained for those institutions which were considered as sacred; and, though the faith of the Hindoos has been often tried by severe persecutions, excited by the bigotry of their Mahomedan conquerors, no people ever adhered with greater fidelity to the tenets and rites of their ancestors [g].

V. We may observe, that when science and philosophy are diffused through any country, the system of superstition is subjected to a scrutiny from which it was formerly exempt, and opinions spread which imperceptibly diminish its influence over the minds of men. A free and full examination is always favourable to truth, but fatal to error. What is received with implicit faith in ages of darkness, will excite contempt or indignation in an enlightened period. The history of religion in Greece and Italy, the only countries of Europe which, in ancient times, were distinguished for their attainments in science,

[f] Code of Gentoo Laws, ch. xxi. § 7.

[g] Orme's Fragment, p. 102. Sonnerat. vol. i. p. 194.

confirms

confirms the truth of this obſervation. As ſoon as ſcience made ſuch progreſs in Greece as rendered men capable of diſcerning the wiſdom, the foreſight, and the goodneſs diſplayed in creating, preſerving, and governing the world, they muſt have perceived, that the characters of the divinities which were propoſed as the objects of adoration in their temples, could not entitle them to be conſidered as the preſiding powers in nature. A poet might addreſs Jupiter as the father of gods and men, who governed both by eternal laws; but, to a philoſopher, the ſon of Saturn, the ſtory of whoſe life is a ſeries of violent and licentious deeds, which would render any man odious or deſpicable, muſt have appeared altogether unworthy of that ſtation. The nature of the religious ſervice celebrated in their temples muſt have been no leſs offenſive to an enlightened mind, than the character of the deities in honour of whom it was performed. Inſtead of inſtitutions, tending to reclaim men from vice, to form or to ſtrengthen habits of virtue, or to elevate the mind to a ſenſe of its proper dignity, ſuperſtition either occupied its votaries in frivolous unmeaning ceremonies, or preſcribed rites, which operated, with fatal influence, in inflaming the paſſions and corrupting the heart.

It is with timidity, however, and caution, that men venture to attack the eſtabliſhed religion of their country, or to impugn opinions which have been long held ſacred. At firſt, ſome philoſophers endeavoured, by allegorical interpretations and refined comments, to explain the popular mythology, as if it had been a deſcription of the powers of nature, and of the various events and revolutions which take place in the ſyſtem of the material world, and endeavoured, by this expedient, to palliate many of its abſurdities. By degrees, bolder theories concerning religion were admitted into the ſchools of ſcience. Philoſophers of enlarged views, ſenſible of the impiety of the popular ſuperſtition, formed ideas concerning the perfections of one Supreme Being, the Creator and Ruler of the univerſe, as juſt and rational as have ever been attained by the unaſſiſted powers of the human mind.

If from Europe we now turn to Aſia, we ſhall find, that the obſervation which I have made upon the hiſtory of falſe religion holds equally true there. In India as well as in Greece, it was by cultivating ſcience that men were firſt led to examine and to entertain doubts with reſpect to the eſtabliſhed ſyſtems of ſuperſtition; and when we conſider the great difference between the eccleſiaſtical conſtitution (if I may uſe that expreſſion) of the two countries, we are apt to imagine that the eſtabliſhed ſyſtem lay more open to examination in the latter than in the former. In Greece there was not any diſtinct race or order of men ſet apart for performing the functions of religion, or to ſerve as hereditary and intereſted guardians of its tenets and inſtitutions. But in India the Brahmins were born the miniſters of religion, and they had an excluſive right of preſiding in all the numerous rites of worſhip which ſuperſtition preſcribed as neceſſary to avert the wrath of Heaven, or to render it propitious. Theſe diſtinctions and privileges ſecured to them a wonderful aſcendant over their countrymen; and every conſideration that can influence the human mind, the honour, the intereſt, the power of their order, called upon them to ſupport the

the tenets, and to maintain the institutions and rites, with which the preservation of this ascendant was so intimately connected.

But as the most eminent persons of the cast devoted their lives to the cultivation of science, the progress which they made in all the branches of it (of which I have given some account), was great, and enabled them to form such a just idea of the system of nature, and of the power, wisdom, and goodness displayed in the formation and government of it, as elevated their minds above the popular superstition, and led them to acknowledge and reverence one Supreme Being, "the Creator "of all things (to use their own expressions), and from whom "all things proceed [h]."

This is the idea which Abul Fazel, who examined the opinions of the Brahmins with the greatest attention and candour, gives of their theology. "They all," says he, "believe in "the unity of the Godhead, and although they hold images "in high veneration, it is only because they represent celestial "beings, and prevent their thoughts from wandering [i]." The sentiments of the most intelligent Europeans who have visited India, coincide perfectly with his, in respect to this point. The accounts which Mr. Bernier received from the Pundits of Benares, both of their external worship, and of one Sovereign Lord being the sole object of their devotion, is precisely the same with that given by Abul Fazel [k]. Mr. Wilkins, better

[h] Baghvat-Geeta, p. 84.

[i] Ayeen Akbery, vol. iii. p. 3.

[k] Voyage, tom. ii. p. 159.

qualified perhaps than any European ever was to judge with respect to this subject, represents the learned Brahmins of the present times as Theists, believers in the unity of God[l]. Of the same opinion is M. Sonnerat, who resided in India seven years in order to inquire into the manners, sciences, and religion of the Hindoos[m]. The Pundits, who translated the Code of Gentoo Laws, declare, "that it was the Supreme Being, "who, by his power, formed all creatures of the animal, vegetable, and material world, from the four elements of fire, "water, air, and earth, to be an ornament to the magazine of "creation; and whose comprehensive benevolence selected "man, the center of knowledge, to have dominion and "authority over the rest; and, having bestowed upon this favourite object judgment and understanding, gave him supremacy over the corners of the world[n]."

Nor are these to be regarded as refined sentiments of latter times. The Brahmins being considered by the Mahomedan conquerors of India as the guardians of the national religion, have been so studiously depressed by their fanatical zeal, that the modern members of that order are as far inferior to their ancestors in science as in power. It is from the writings of their ancient Pundits that they derive the most liberal sentiments which they entertain at present, and the wisdom for which they are now celebrated has been transmitted to them from ages very remote.

[l] Preface to Baghvat-Geeta, p. 24. [m] Voyage, tom. i. p. 198.
[n] Prelim. Discours. p. lxxiii.

THAT

THAT this aſſertion is well founded we are enabled to pronounce with certainty, as the moſt profound myſteries of Hindoo theology, concealed with the greateſt care from the body of the people, have been unveiled by the tranſlations from the Sanſkreet language lately publiſhed. The principal deſign of the Baghvat-Geeta, an epiſode in the Mahabarat, a poem of the higheſt antiquity, and of the greateſt authority in India, ſeems to have been to eſtabliſh the doctrine of the unity of the Godhead, and from a juſt view of the divine nature, to deduce an idea of what worſhip will be moſt acceptable to a perfect Being. In it, amidſt much obſcure metaphyſical diſcuſſion, ſome ornaments of fancy unſuited to our taſte, and ſome thoughts elevated to a tract of ſublimity into which our habits of judgment will find it difficult to purſue them°, we find deſcriptions of the Supreme Being entitled to equal praiſe with thoſe of the Greek philoſophers which I have celebrated. Of theſe I ſhall now produce one which I formerly mentioned, and refer my readers for others to the work itſelf: "O mighty "Being," ſays Arjoon, "who art the prime Creator, eternal God "of Gods, the World's Manſion. Thou art the incorruptible "Being, diſtinct from all things tranſient. Thou art before "all Gods, the ancient *Poorooſh* [i. e. vital ſoul], and the "Supreme Supporter of the univerſe. Thou knoweſt all things, "and art worthy to be known; thou art the Supreme Man"ſion, and by thee, O infinite Form, the univerſe was ſpread "abroad.—Reverence be unto thee before and behind; reve"rence be unto thee on all ſides; O thou who art all in all.

° Mr. Haſtings's Letter, prefixed to the Baghvat-Geeta, p. 7.

5 "Infinite

"Infinite is thy power and thy glory.—Thou art the father of "all things, animate and inanimate. Thou art the wise in-"structor of the whole, worthy to be adored. There is "none like unto thee; where then, in the three worlds, "is there one above thee? Wherefore I bow down; and, "with my body prostrate upon the ground, crave thy mercy, "Lord! Worthy to be adored; for thou shouldest bear with "me, even as a father with his son, a friend with his friend, "a lover with his beloved [p]." A description of the Supreme Being is given in one of the sacred books of the Hindoos, from which it is evident what were the general sentiments of the learned Brahmins concerning the divine nature and perfections: "As God is immaterial, he is above all conception; "as he is invisible, he can have no form; but from what we "behold of his works we may conclude, that he is eternal, om-"nipotent, knowing all things, and present every where [q]."

To men capable of forming such ideas of the Deity, the public service in the Pagodas must have appeared to be an idolatrous worship of images, by a superstitious multiplication of frivolous or immoral rites; and they must have seen that it was only by sanctity of heart, and purity of manners, men could hope to gain the approbation of a Being perfect in goodness. This truth Veias labours to inculcate in the Mahabarat, but with the prudent reserve, and artful precautions, natural to a Brahmin, studious neither to offend his countrymen, nor to diminish the influence of his own order. His ideas concerning

[p] Baghvat-Geeta, p. 94. 95.

[q] Dow's Differt. p. xl.

the

the mode of worſhipping the Deity, are explained in many ſtriking paſſages of the poem, but, unwilling to multiply quotations, I ſatisfy myſelf with referring to them[r].

When we recollect how ſlowly the mind of man opens to abſtract ideas, and how difficult (according to an obſervation in the Mahabarat) an inviſible path is to corporeal beings, it is evident that the Hindoos muſt have attained an high degree of improvement before their ſentiments roſe ſo far ſuperior to the popular ſuperſtition of their country. The different ſtates of Greece had ſubſiſted long, and had made conſiderable progreſs in refinement, before the errors of falſe religion began to be detected. It was not until the age of Socrates, and in the ſchools of philoſophy eſtabliſhed by his diſciples, that principles adverſe to the tenets of the popular ſuperſtition were much propagated.

A longer period of time elapſed before the Romans, a nation of warriors and ſtateſmen, were enlightened by ſcience, or ventured upon any free diſquiſition concerning the objects or the rites of worſhip authorized by their anceſtors. But in India the happy effects of progreſs in ſcience were much more early conſpicuous. Without adopting the wild computations of Indian chronology, according to which, the Mahabarat was compoſed above four thouſand years ago, we muſt allow, that it is a work of very great antiquity, and the author of it diſcovers an acquaintance with the principles of theology, of mo-

[r] Baghvat Geeta, p. 55. 67. 75. 97. 119.

U u rals,

rals, and of metaphyſics, more juſt and rational, than ſeems to have been attained, at that period, by any nation whoſe hiſtory is known.

But ſo unable are the limited powers of the human mind to form an adequate idea of the perfections and operations of the Supreme Being, that in all the theories concerning them, of the moſt eminent philoſophers in the moſt enlightened nations, we find a lamentable mixture of ignorance and error. From theſe the Brahmins were not more exempt than the ſages of other countries. As they held that the ſyſtem of nature was not only originally arranged by the power and wiſdom of God, but that every event which happened was brought about by his immediate interpoſition, and as they could not comprehend how a being could act in any place unleſs where it was preſent, they ſuppoſed the Deity to be a vivifying principle diffuſed through the whole creation, an univerſal ſoul that animated each part of it [s]. Every intelligent nature, particularly the ſouls of men, they conceived to be portions ſeparated from this great ſpirit [t], to which, after fulfilling their deſtiny on earth, and attaining a proper degree of purity, they would be again reunited. In order to efface the ſtains with which a ſoul, during its reſidence on earth, has been defiled, by the indulgence of ſenſual and corrupt appetites, they taught that it muſt paſs, in a long ſucceſſion of tranſmigrations, through the bodies of different animals, until, by what it ſuffers and what it learns in

[s] Baghvat-Geeta, p. 65. 78. 85. Bernier, tom. ii. p. 163.

[t] Dow's Diſſert. p. xliii.

the

the various forms of its exiſtence, it ſhall be ſo thoroughly refined from all pollution as to be rendered meet for being abſorbed into the divine eſſence, and returns like a drop into that unbounded ocean from which it originally iſſued [u]. Theſe doctrines of the Brahmins, concerning the Deity, as the ſoul which pervades all nature, giving activity and vigour to every part of it, as well as the final re-union of all intelligent creatures to their primæval ſource, coincide perfectly with the tenets of the Stoical School. It is remarkable, that after having obſerved a near reſemblance in the moſt ſublime ſentiments of their moral doctrine, we ſhould likewiſe diſcover ſuch a ſimilarity in the errors of their theological ſpeculations [x].

The human mind, however, when deſtitute of ſuperior guidance, is apt to fall into a practical error with reſpect to religion, of a tendency ſtill more dangerous. When philoſophers, by their attainments in ſcience, began to acquire ſuch juſt ideas of the nature and perfections of the Supreme Being, as convinced them that the popular ſyſtem of ſuperſtition was not only abſurd but impious, they were fully aware of all the danger which might ariſe from communicating what they had diſcovered to the people, incapable of comprehending the force of thoſe reaſons which had ſwayed with them, and ſo zealouſly attached to eſtabliſhed opinions, as to revolt againſt any attempt to detect their falſehood. Inſtead, therefore, of allowing any ray of that know-

[u] Voy. de Sonnerat, vol. i. p. 192. 200. Baghvat-Geeta, p. 39. 115. Dow's Diſſert. p. xliii.

[x] Lipſij Phyſiol. Stoicor. lib. i. diſſert. viii. xxi. Seneca, Antoninus, Epictetus, paſſim.

Uu2 ledge

ledge which illuminated their own minds to reach them, they formed a theory to juſtify their own conduct, and to prevent the darkneſs of that cloud which hung over the minds of their fellow-men from being ever diſpelled. The vulgar and unlearned, they contended, had no right to truth. Doomed by their condition to remain in ignorance, they were to be kept in order by deluſion, and allured to do what is right, or deterred from venturing upon what is wrong, by the hope of thoſe imaginary rewards which ſuperſtition promiſes, and the dread of thoſe puniſhments which it threatens. In confirmation of this, I might quote the doctrine of moſt of the philoſophic ſects, and produce the words of almoſt every eminent Greek and Roman writer. It will be ſufficient, however, to lay before my readers a remarkable paſſage in Strabo, to whom I have been ſo often indebted in the courſe of my reſearches, and who was no leſs qualified to judge with reſpect to the political opinions of his contemporaries, than to deſcribe the countries which they inhabited. "What is marvellous in fable, is employed," ſays he, "ſometimes to pleaſe, and ſometimes to inſpire terror, and "both theſe are of uſe, not only with children, but with per-"ſons of mature age. To children we propoſe delightful fic-"tions, in order to encourage them to act well, and ſuch as "as are terrible, in order to reſtrain them from evil. Thus "when men are united in ſociety, they are incited to what "is laudable, by hearing the poets celebrate the ſplendid actions "of fabulous ſtory, ſuch as the labours of Hercules and The-"ſeus, in reward for which they are now honoured as divini-"ties, or by beholding their illuſtrious deeds exhibited to "public view in painting and ſculpture. On the other hand,

 "they

" they are deterred from vice, when the punishments inflicted " by the gods upon evil-doers are related, and threats are de- " nounced against them in awful words, or represented by " frightful figures, and when men believe that these threats " have been really executed upon the guilty. For it is impossi- " ble to conduct women and the gross multitude, and to " render them holy, pious, and upright, by the precepts of " reason and philosophy; superstition, or the fear of the gods, " must be called in aid, the influence of which is founded on " fictions and prodigies. For the thunder of Jupiter, the ægis " of Minerva, the trident of Neptune, the torches and snakes " of the furies, the spears of the gods, adorned with ivy, " and the whole ancient theology, are all fables, which the " legislators who formed the political constitution of states " employ as bugbears to overawe the credulous and simple [y]."

THESE ideas of the philosophers of Europe were precisely the same which the Brahmins had adopted in India, and according to which they regulated their conduct with respect to the great body of the people. As their order had an exclusive right to read the sacred books, to cultivate and to teach science, they could more effectually prevent all who were not members of it from acquiring any portion of information beyond what they were pleased to impart. When the free circulation of knowledge is not circumscribed by such restrictions, the whole community derives benefit from every new acquisition in science, the influence of which, both upon sentiment and conduct, extends insensibly from the few to the many, from the learned to

[y] Strab. lib. i. p. 36. B.

the

the ignorant. But wherever the dominion of falſe religion is completely eſtabliſhed, the body of the people gain nothing by the greateſt improvements in knowledge. Their philoſophers conceal from them, with the utmoſt ſolicitude, the truths which they have diſcovered, and labour to ſupport that fabric of ſuperſtition which it was their duty to have overturned. They not only enjoin others to reſpect the religious rites preſcribed by the laws of their country, but conform to them in their own practice, and, with every external appearance of reverence and devotion, bow down before the altars of deities, who muſt inwardly be the objects of their contempt. Inſtead of reſembling the teachers of true religion in the benevolent ardour with which they have always communicated to their fellow-men the knowledge of thoſe important truths with which their own minds were enlightened and rendered happy, the ſages of Greece, and the Brahmins of India, carried on, with ſtudied artifice, a ſcheme of deceit, and, according to an emphatic expreſſion of an inſpired writer, they *detained* the truth in unrighteouſneſs [z]. They knew and approved what was true, but among the reſt of mankind they laboured to ſupport and to perpetuate what is falſe.

Thus I have gone through all the particulars which I originally propoſed to examine, and have endeavoured to diſcover the ſtate of the inhabitants of India with reſpect to each of them. If I had aimed at nothing elſe than to deſcribe the civil policy, the arts, the ſciences, and religious inſtitutions of one of the moſt ancient and moſt numerous races of men,

[z] Rom. i. 18.

that

that alone would have led me into inquiries and discussions both curious and instructive. I own, however, that I have all along kept in view an object more interesting, as well as of greater importance, and entertain hopes, that if the account which I have given of the early and high civilization of India, and of the wonderful progress of its inhabitants in elegant arts and useful science, shall be received as just and well-established, it may have some influence upon the behaviour of Europeans towards that people. Unfortunately for the human species, in whatever quarter of the globe the people of Europe have acquired dominion, they have found the inhabitants not only in a state of society and improvement far inferior to their own, but different in their complexion, and in all their habits of life. Men in every stage of their career are so satisfied with the progress made by the community of which they are members, that it becomes to them a standard of perfection, and they are apt to regard people, whose condition is not similar, with contempt, and even aversion. In Africa and America, the dissimilitude is so conspicuous, that, in the pride of their superiority, Europeans thought themselves entitled to reduce the natives of the former to slavery, and to exterminate those of the latter. Even in India, though far advanced beyond the two other quarters of the globe in improvement, the colour of the inhabitants, their effeminate appearance, their unwarlike spirit, the wild extravagance of their religious tenets and ceremonies, and many other circumstances, confirmed Europeans in such an opinion of their own pre-eminence, that they have always viewed and treated them as an inferior race of men. Happy would it be if any of the four European nations, who have, successively, acquired extensive territories and power in India, could altogether

5 vindicate

vindicate itſelf from having acted in this manner. Nothing, however, can have a more direct and powerful tendency to inſpire Europeans, proud of their own ſuperior attainments in policy, ſcience, and arts, with proper ſentiments concerning the people of India, and to teach them a due regard for their natural rights as men, than their being accuſtomed, not only to conſider the Hindoos of the preſent times as a knowing and ingenious race of men, but to view them as deſcended from anceſtors who had attained to a very high degree of improvement, many ages before the leaſt ſtep towards civilization had been taken in any part in Europe. It was by an impartial and candid inquiry into their manners, that the Emperor Akber was led to conſider the Hindoos as no leſs entitled to protection and favour than his other ſubjects, and to govern them with ſuch equity and mildneſs, as to merit from a grateful people the honourable appellation of "The Guardian of Mankind." It was from a thorough knowledge of their character and acquirements, that his Vizier, Abul Fazel, with a liberality of mind unexampled among Mahomedans, pronounces an high encomium on the virtues of the Hindoos, both as individuals and as members of ſociety, and celebrates their attainments in arts and ſciences of every kind[a]. If I might preſume to hope that the deſcription which I have given of the manners and inſtitutions of the people of India could contribute in the ſmalleſt degree, and with the moſt remote influence, to render their character more reſpectable, and their condition more happy, I ſhall cloſe my literary labours with the ſatisfaction of thinking that I have not lived or written in vain.

[a] Ayeen Akbery, vol. iii. p. 2. 81. 95.

NOTES

TO THE

APPENDIX.

NOTE I. p. 259.

ACCORDING to all the writers of antiquity, the Indians are ſaid to be divided into ſeven tribes or caſts. Strabo, lib. xv. p. 1029. C, &c. Diod. Sicul. lib. ii. p. 153, &c. Arrian. Indic. c. 10. They were led into this error, it is probable, by conſidering ſome of the ſubdiviſions of the caſts, as if they had been a diſtinct independent order. But that there were no more than four original caſts, we learn from the concurrent teſtimony of the beſt informed modern travellers. A moſt diſtinct account of theſe we have in "La Porte Ouverte, "ou la vraye Repreſentation de la Vie, des Mœurs, de la Re- "ligion, et du Service des Bramines, qui demeurent ſur les

"Coſtes de Choromandel," &c. This was compiled, before the middle of laſt century, by Abraham Roger, chaplain of the Dutch factory at Pullicate. By gaining the confidence of an intelligent Brahmin, he acquired information concerning the manners and religion of the Indians, more authentic and extenſive than was known to Europeans prior to the late tranſlations from the Sanſkreet language. I mention this book, becauſe it ſeems to be leſs known than it deſerves to be. There remains now no doubt with reſpect either to the number or the functions of the caſts, as both are aſcertained from the moſt ancient and ſacred books of the Hindoos, and confirmed by the accounts of their own inſtitutions, given by Brahmins eminent for their learning. According to them, the different caſts proceeded from Brahma, the immediate agent of the creation under the Supreme Power, in the following manner, which eſtabliſhes both the rank which they were to hold, and the office which they were required to perform.

The *Brahmin*, from the mouth (wiſdom): To pray, to read, to inſtruct.

The *Chehteree*, from the arms (ſtrength): To draw the bow, to fight, to govern.

The *Bice*, from the belly or thighs (nouriſhment): To provide the neceſſaries of life by agriculture and traffick.

The *Sooder*, from the feet (ſubjection): To labour, to ſerve.

THE

THE prescribed occupations of all these classes are essential in a well-regulated state. Subordinate to them is a fifth, or adventitious class, denominated *Burrun Sunker*, supposed to be the offspring of an unlawful union between persons of different casts. These are mostly dealers in petty articles of retail trade. Preface to the Code of Gentoo Laws, p. xlvi. and xcix. This adventitious cast is not mentioned, as far as I know, by any European author. The distinction was too nice to be observed by them, and they seem to consider the members of this cast, as belonging to the Sooder. Besides these acknowledged casts, there is a race of unhappy men, denominated, on the Coromandel coast, *Pariars*, and, in other parts of India, *Chandalas*. These are out-casts from their original order, who, by their misconduct, have forfeited all the privileges of it. Their condition is, undoubtedly, the lowest degradation of human nature. No person of any cast will have the least communication with them. Sonnerat, tom. i. p. 55, 56. If a Pariar approach a *Nayr*, *i. e.* a warrior of high cast, on the Malabar coast, he may put him to death with impunity. Water or milk are considered as defiled even by their shadow passing over them, and cannot be used until they are purified. Ayeen Akbery, vol. iii. p. 243. It is almost impossible for words to express the sensation of vileness that the name of Pariar or Chandala conveys to the mind of a Hindoo. Every Hindoo who violates the rules or institutions of his cast sinks into this degraded situation. This it is which renders Hindoos so resolute in adhering to the institutions of their tribe, because the loss of cast is, to them, the loss of all human comfort and respectability; and is a punishment, beyond comparifon, more fevere than excommunication, in the moft triumphant period of Papal power.

The four original cafts are named, and their functions defcribed in the Mahabarat, the moft ancient book of the Hindoos, and of higher authority than any with which Europeans are hitherto acquainted. Baghvat-Geeta, p. 130. The fame diftinction of cafts was known to the author of Heeto-pades, another work of confiderable antiquity, tranflated from the Sanfkreet, p. 251.

The mention of one circumftance refpecting the diftinction of cafts has been omitted in the text. Though the line of feparation be fo drawn, as to render the afcent from an inferior to a higher caft abfolutely impoffible, and it would be regarded as a moft enormous impiety, if one in a lower order fhould prefume to perform any function belonging to thofe of a fuperior caft; yet, in certain cafes, the Pundits declare it to be lawful for perfons of a high clafs to exercife fome of the occupations allotted to a clafs below their own, without lofing their caft by doing fo. Pref. of Pundits to the Code of Gentoo Laws, p. 100. Accordingly we find Brahmins employed in the fervice of their princes, not only as minifters of ftate, Orme's Fragments, p. 207, but in fubordinate ftations. Moft of the officers of high rank in the army of Sevagi, the founder of the Mahratta ftate, were Brahmins, and fome of them Pundits or learned Brahmins. Ibid. p. 97. Many Seapoys in the fervice of the Eaft India Company, particularly in the Bengal prefidency, are of the Brahmin caft.

Another

ANOTHER fact concerning the casts deserves notice. An immense number of pilgrims, amounting, in some years, to more than 150,000, visit the Pagoda of Jaggernaut, in Orissa, (one of the most ancient and most revered places of Hindoo worship,) at the time of the annual festival in honour of the deity to whom the temple is consecrated. The members of all the four casts are allowed promiscuously to approach the altar of the idol, and seating themselves without distinction, eat indiscriminately of the same food. This seems to indicate some remembrance of a state prior to the institution of casts, when all men were considered as equal. I have not such information as enables me to account for a practice so repugnant to the first ideas and principles of the Hindoos, either sacred or civil. Bernier, tom. ii. p. 102. Tavernier, book ii. c. 9. Anquetil. Disc. Prelim. p. 81. Sketches, p. 96.

SOME of my readers must have observed, that I have given no account of the numerous orders of Indian devotees, to all of whom European writers give the appellation of *Faquirs*; a name by which the Mahomedans distinguish fanatical monks of their own religion. The light in which I have viewed the religious institutions of the Hindoos, did not render it necessary that I should consider the Indian Faquirs particularly. Their number, the rigour of their mortifications, the excruciating penances which they voluntarily undergo, and the high opinion which the people entertain of their sanctity, have struck all travellers who have visited India, and their descriptions of them are well known. The powerful influence of enthusiasm, the love of distinction, and the desire of obtaining some portion.

tion of that reverence and thoſe honours which the Brahmins are born to enjoy, may account for all the extraordinary things which they do and ſuffer. One particular concerning them merits notice. This order of devotees appears to have been very ancient in India. The deſcription of the *Germani*, which Strabo takes from Megaſthenes, applies, almoſt in every circumſtance, to the modern Faquirs. Lib. xv. p. 1040. B.

NOTE II. p. 262.

WHAT I have aſſerted in the text is in general well-founded. It is the opinion, however, of gentlemen who have ſeen much of India, and who obſerved all they ſaw with a diſcerning eye, that the conqueſts both of the Mahomedans and of the Europeans have had ſome effect upon the manners and cuſtoms of the natives. They imagine that the dreſs which the Hindoos now wear, the turban, the jummah, and long drawers, is an imitation of that worn by their Mahomedan conquerors. The ancient dreſs of the Indians, as deſcribed by Arrian, Hiſt. Indic. c. 16. was a muſlin cloth thrown looſely about their ſhoulders, a muſlin ſhirt reaching to the middle of the leg, and their beards were died various colours; which is not the ſame with that uſed at preſent. The cuſtom of ſecluding women, and the ſtrictneſs with which they are confined, is likewiſe ſuppoſed to have been introduced by the Mahomedans. This ſuppoſition is in ſome meaſure confirmed by the drama of Sacontala, tranſlated from the Sanſkreet. In that play, ſeveral female characters are introduced, who mingle

gle in ſociety, and converſe as freely with men, as women are accuſtomed to do in Europe. The author, we may preſume, deſcribes the manners, and adheres to the cuſtoms of his own age. But while I mention this remark, it is proper, likewiſe, to obſerve, that, from a paſſage in Strabo, there is reaſon to think, that, in the age of Alexander the Great, women in India were guarded with the ſame jealous attention as at preſent. "When their princes," (ſays he, copying Megaſthenes,) "ſet out upon a public hunt, they are accompanied by "a number of their women, but along the road in which "they travel, ropes are ſtretched on each ſide, and if any man "approach near to them he is inſtantly put to death." Lib. xv. p. 1037. A. The influence of European manners begins to be apparent among the Hindoos who reſide in the town of Calcutta. Some of them drive about in Engliſh chariots, ſit upon chairs, and furniſh their houſes with mirrors. Many circumſtances might be mentioned, were this the proper place, which, it is probable, will contribute to the progreſs of this ſpirit of imitation.

NOTE III. p. 262.

It is amuſing to obſerve how exactly the ideas of an intelligent Aſiatic co-incide with thoſe of the Europeans on this ſubject. "In reflecting," ſays he, "upon the poverty of "Turan [the countries beyond the Oxus] and Arabia, I was "at firſt at a loſs to aſſign a reaſon why theſe countries have "never been able to retain wealth, whilſt, on the contrary, it

5 "is

" is daily increaſing in Indoſtan. Timour carried into Turan " the riches of Turkey, Perſia, and Indoſtan, but they are " all diſſipated; and, during the reigns of the four firſt Ca- " liphs, Turkey, Perſia, part of Arabia, Ethiopia, Egypt, and " Spain, were their tributaries; but ſtill they were not rich. " It is evident, then, that this diſſipation of the riches of a " ſtate, muſt have happened either from extraordinary drains, " or from ſome defect in the government. Indoſtan has been " frequently plundered by foreign invaders, and not one of its " kings ever gained for it any acquiſition of wealth; nei- " ther has the country many mines of gold and ſilver, and " yet Indoſtan abounds in money and every other kind of " wealth. The abundance of ſpecie is undoubtedly owing to " the large importation of gold and ſilver in the ſhips of " Europe, and other nations, many of whom bring ready " money in exchange for the manufactures and natural pro- " ductions of the country. If this is not the cauſe of the " proſperous ſtate of Indoſtan, it muſt be owing to the peculiar " bleſſing of God." Memoirs of Khojeh Abdul-kurreem, a Caſhmeerian of diſtinction, p. 42.

NOTE IV. p. 267.

THAT the monarchs of India were the ſole proprietors of land, is aſſerted in moſt explicit terms by the ancients. The people (ſay they) pay a land-tax to their kings, becauſe the kingdom is regal property. Strabo, lib. xv. p. 1030. A. Diod. Sicul. lib. ii. p. 153. This was not peculiar to India. In all the great monarchies of the Eaſt, the ſole property of land ſeems to be veſted in the ſovereign as lord paramount. According to Chardin, this is the ſtate of property in Perſia, and lands were let by the monarch to the farmers who cultivated them, on conditions nearly reſembling thoſe granted to the Indian Ryots. Voyages, tom. iii. p. 339, &c. 4to. M. Volney gives a ſimilar account of the tenure by which lands are held in one of the great provinces of the Turkiſh empire. Voy. en Syrie, &c. tom. ii. p. 369, &c. The preciſe mode, however, in which the Ryots of Indoſtan held their poſſeſſions, is a circumſtance in its ancient political conſtitution, with reſpect to which gentlemen of ſuperior diſcernment, who have reſided long in the country, and filled ſome of the higheſt ſtations in government, have formed very different opinions. Some have imagined that grants of land were made by the ſovereign to villages or ſmall communities, the inhabitants of which, under the direction of their own chiefs or heads-men, laboured it in common, and divided the produce of it among them in certain proportions. Deſcript. de l'Inde, par M. Bernouilli, tom. ii. 223, &c. Others maintain, that the property of land has been transferred from the crown to hereditary officers of great eminence and power, denominated *Zemindars*, who collect the rents from the Ryots, and parcel out the lands among them. Others contend, that the office of the Zemindars is temporary and miniſterial, that they are merely collectors of revenue, removeable at pleaſure, and the tenure by which the Ryots hold their poſſeſſions is derived immediately from the ſovereign. This laſt opinion is ſupported with great ability, by Mr. Grant, in an Inquiry into the Nature of Zemindary Tenures in the landed Property of Bengal, &c. This queſtion ſtill continues to be agitated in Bengal, and ſuch plauſible arguments have been produced in ſupport of the different opinions, that although it be a point extremely interesting, as the future system of British finance in India appears likely to hinge, in an essential degree, upon it, persons well acquainted with the state of India, have not been able thoroughly to make up their minds upon this subject. Capt. Kirkpatrick's Introd. to the Institutes of Ghazan Khan. New Asiatic Miscell. N° II. p. 130. Though the opinion of the Committee of Revenue, composed of persons eminent for their abilities, leans to a conclusion against the hereditary right of the Zemindars in the soil, yet the Supreme Council, in the year 1786, declined, for good reasons, to give any decisive judgment on a subject of such magnitude. This note was sent to the press before I had it in my power to peruse Mr. Rouse's ingenious and instructive Dissertation concerning the landed property of Bengal. In it he adopts an opinion contrary to that of Mr. Grant, and maintains, with that candour and liberality of sentiment which are always conspicuous where there is no other object in view but the discovery of truth, that the Zemindars of Bengal possess their landed property by hereditary right. Did I possess such knowledge, either of the state of India, or of the system of administration established there, as would be requisite for comparing these different theories, and determining which of them merits the preference, the subject of my researches does not render it necessary to enter into such a disquisition. I imagine, however, that the state of landed property in India might be greatly illustrated by an accurate comparison of it with the nature of feudal tenures; and I apprehend that there might be traced there a succession of changes taking place, in much the same order as has been observed in Europe, from which it might appear, that the possession of land was granted at first during pleasure, afterwards for life, and at length became perpetual

and

and hereditary property. But even under this laſt form, when land is acquired either by purchaſe or inheritance, the manner in which the right of property is confirmed and rendered complete, in Europe by a Charter, in India by a *Sunnud* from the ſovereign, ſeems to point out what was its original ſtate. According to each of the theories which I have mentioned, the tenure and condition of the Ryots nearly reſemble the deſcription which I have given of them. Their ſtate, according to the accounts of intelligent obſervers, is as happy and independent as falls to the lot of any race of men employed in the cultivation of the earth. The ancient Greek and Roman writers, whoſe acquaintance with the interior parts of India was very imperfect, repreſent the fourth part of the annual produce of land as the general average of rent paid to the ſovereign. Upon the authority of a popular author who flouriſhed in India prior to the Chriſtian æra, we may conclude that a ſixth part of the people's income was, in his time, the uſual portion of the ſovereign. Sacontala, Act V. p. 53. It is now known that what the ſovereign receives from land varies greatly in different parts of the country, and is regulated by the fertility or barrenneſs of the ſoil, the nature of the climate, the abundance or ſcarcity of water, and many other obvious circumſtances. By the account given of it, I ſhould imagine that, in ſome diſtricts, it has been raiſed beyond its due proportion. One circumſtance with reſpect to the adminiſtration of revenue in Bengal merits notice, as it redounds to the honour of the Emperor Akber, the wiſdom of whoſe government I have often had occaſion to celebrate. A general and regular aſſeſſment of revenue in Bengal was formed in his reign. All the lands were then valued, and the rent of each inhabitant and of each village aſcertained.

A regular gradation of accounts was eſtabliſhed. The rents of the different inhabitants who lived in one neighbourhood being collected together, formed the account of a village; the rents of ſeveral villages being next collected into one view, formed the accounts of a larger portion of land. The aggregate of theſe accounts exhibited the rent of a diſtrict, and the ſum total of the rents of all the diſtricts in Bengal formed the account of the revenue of the whole province. From the reign of Akber to the government of Jaffeer Ali Cawn, A. D. 1757, the annual amount of revenue, and the modes of levying it, continued with little variation. But in order to raiſe the ſum which he had ſtipulated to pay on his elevation, he departed from the wiſe arrangements of Akber; many new modes of aſſeſſment were introduced, and exactions multiplied.

NOTE V. p. 269.

I SHALL mention only one inſtance of their attention to this uſeful regulation of police. Lahore, in the Panjab, is diſtant from Agra, the ancient capital of Indoſtan, five hundred miles. Along each ſide of the road between theſe two great cities, there is planted a continued row of ſhady trees, forming an avenue, to which (whether we conſider its extent, its beauty, or utility in a hot climate) there is nothing ſimilar in any country. Rennel's Memoir, p. 69.

NOTE VI. p. 272.

WE cannot place the equitable and mild government of Akber in a point of view more advantageous, than by contraſting it it with the conduct of other Mahomedan princes. In no country did this contraſt ever appear more ſtriking than in India. In the thouſandth year of the Chriſtian æra, Mahmud of Ghazna, to whoſe dominion were ſubjected the ſame countries which formed the ancient kingdom of Bactria, invaded that country. Every ſtep of his progreſs in it was marked with blood and deſolation. The moſt celebrated pagodas, the ancient monuments of Hindoo devotion and magnificence, were deſtroyed, the miniſters of religion were maſſacred, and with undiſtinguiſhing ferocity the country was laid waſte, and the cities plundered and burnt. About four hundred years after Mahmud, Timur or Tamerlane, a conqueror of higher fame, turned his irreſiſtible arms againſt Indoſtan, and, though born in an age more improved, he not only equalled, but often ſo far ſurpaſſed the cruel deeds of Mahmud, as to be juſtly branded with the odious name of the "Deſtroying Prince," which was given to him by the Hindoos, the undeſerving victims of his rage. A rapid but elegant deſcription of their devaſtations may be found in Mr. Orme's Diſſertation on the Eſtabliſhments made by the Mahomedan conquerors in Indoſtan. A more full account of them is given by Mr. Gibbon, vol. v. p. 646. vol. vi. p. 339, &c. The arrogant contempt with which bigotted Mahomedans view all the nations who have not embraced the religion of the prophet, will account for the unrelenting rigour of Mahmud and Timur towards the Hindoos, and greatly enhances the merit of the tolerant ſpirit and moderation with which Akber governed his ſubjects. What impreſſion the mild adminiſtration of Akber made upon the Hindoos, we learn from a beautiful letter of Jeſſwant Sing, Rajah of Joudpore, to to Aurengzebe, his fanatical and perſecuting ſucceſſor. "Your "royal anceſtor, Akber, whoſe throne is now in heaven, con-"ducted the affairs of this empire in equity and firm ſecurity "for the ſpace of fifty-two years, preſerving every tribe of "men in eaſe and happineſs; whether they were followers of "Jeſus, or of Moſes, of David, or of Mahomed; were they "Brahmins, were they of the ſect of Dharians, which denies "the eternity of matter, or of that which aſcribes the exiſtence "of the world to chance, they all equally enjoyed his counte-"nance and favour; inſomuch that his people, in gratitude "for the indiſcriminate protection which he afforded them, "diſtinguiſhed him by the appellation of *Juggut Grow*, Guar-"dian of Mankind.——If your Majeſty places any faith in "thoſe books, by diſtinction called divine, you will there be "inſtructed, that God is the God of all mankind, not the "God of Mahomedans alone. The Pagan and the Muſſul-"man are equally in his preſence. Diſtinctions of colours are "of his ordination. It is He who gives exiſtence. In your "temples, to his Name, the voice is raiſed in prayer; in a "houſe of images, where the bell is ſhaken, ſtill He is the "object of adoration. To vilify the religion and cuſtoms of "other men, is to ſet at naught the pleaſure of the Almighty. "When we deface a picture, we naturally incur the reſentment "of the painter; and juſtly has the Poet ſaid, "Preſume not "to arraign or to ſcrutinize the various works of Power Di-"vine." For this valuable communication we are indebted to Mr. Orme. Fragments, notes, p. xcvii. I have been aſſured by a gentleman who has read this letter in the original, that the tranſlation is not only faithful but elegant.

2 NOTE

NOTE VII. p. 282.

I HAVE not attempted a deſcription of any ſubterraneous excavations but thoſe of Elephanta, becauſe none of them have been ſo often viſited, or ſo carefully inſpected. In ſeveral parts of India, there are, however, ſtupendous works of a ſimilar nature. The extent and magnificence of the excavations in the iſland of Salſette are ſuch, that the artiſt employed by Governor Boon to make drawings of them, aſſerted that it would require the labour of forty thouſand men for forty years to finiſh them. Archæologia, vol. vii. p. 336. Looſe as this mode of eſtimation may be, it conveys an idea of the impreſſion which the view of them made upon his mind. The Pagodas of Ellore, eighteen miles from Aurungabad, are likewiſe hewn out of the ſolid rock, and if they do not equal thoſe of Elephanta and Salſette in magnitude, they ſurpaſs them far in their extent and number. M. Thevenot, who firſt gave any deſcription of theſe ſingular manſions, aſſerts, that for above two leagues all around the mountain nothing is to be ſeen but Pagodas. Voy. part iii. ch. 44. They were examined at greater leiſure and with more attention by M. Anquetil du Perron, but as his long deſcription of them is not accompanied with any plan or drawing, I cannot convey a diſtinct idea of the whole. It is evident, however, that they are the works of a powerful people, and among the innumerable figures in ſculpture with which the walls are covered, all the preſent objects of of Hindoo worſhip may be diſtinguiſhed. Zend-aveſta. Diſc. Prelim. p. 233. There are remarkable excavations in a mountain at Mavalipuram near Sadras. This mountain is well known on the Coromandel coaſt by the name of the *Seven Pagodas*. A good deſcription of the works there which are magnificent and of high antiquity is given. Aſiat. Reſearches, vol. i. p. 145, &c. Many other inſtances of ſimilar works might be produced if it were neceſſary. What I have aſſerted, p. 282. concerning the elegance of ſome of the ornaments in Indian buildings, is confirmed by Colonel Call, chief engineer at Madras, who urges this as a proof of the early and high civilization of the Indians. "It may ſafely be pronounced," ſays he, "that no part of the world has more marks of anti-"quity for arts, ſciences, and civilization, than the peninſula "of India, from the Ganges to Cape Comorin. I think the "carvings on ſome of the Pagodas and Choultries, as well as "the grandeur of the work, exceeds any thing executed now-"a-days, not only for the delicacy of the chiſel, but the ex-"pence of conſtruction, conſidering, in many inſtances, to "what diſtances the component parts were carried, and to "what heights raiſed." Philoſophical Tranſactions, vol. lxii. p. 354.

NOTE VIII. p. 285.

INDIA, ſays Strabo, produces a variety of ſubſtances which dye the moſt admirable colours. That the *Indicum*, which produced the beautiful blue colour, is the ſame with the *Indigo* of the

the moderns, we may conclude not only from the reſemblance of the name, and the ſimilarity of the effects, but from the deſcription given by Pliny in the paſſage which I have quoted in the text. He knew that it was a preparation of a vegetable ſubſtance, though he was ill-informed both concerning the plant itſelf, and the proceſs by which it was fitted for uſe, which will not appear ſurpriſing when we recollect the ſtrange ignorance of the ancients with reſpect to the origin and preparation of ſilk. From the colour of Indigo, in the form in which it was imported, it is denominated by ſome authors, *Atramentum Indicum*, and *Indicum Nigrum*, Salmaſ. Exercit. p. 180, and is mentioned under the laſt of theſe names, among the articles of importation from India. Peripl. Mar. Erythr. p. 22. The colour of the modern Indigo, when undiluted, reſembles that of the ancient Indicum, being ſo intenſely coloured as to appear black. Delaval's Experim. Inquiry into the Cauſe of the Changes of Colours, Pref. p. xxiii. The *Gum Lacca*, uſed in dying a red colour, was likewiſe known to the ancients, and by the ſame name which it now bears. Salmaſ. Exercit. p. 810. This valuable ſubſtance, of ſuch extenſive utility in painting, dying, japanning, varniſhing, and in the manufacture of ſealing-wax, is the production of a very minute inſect. Theſe inſects fix themſelves upon the ſucculent extremities of the branches of certain trees, and are ſoon glued to the place on which they ſettle, by a thick pellucid liquid which exudes from their bodies, the gradual accumulation of which forms a complete cell for each inſect, which is the tomb of the parent, and the birth-place of its offspring. This glutinous ſubſtance, with which the branches of trees are entirely covered, is the Gum-lacca. An account of its formation, na-

Z z ture,

ture, and uſe, is given in the Philoſ. Tranſ. vol. lxxi. part ii. p. 374. in a conciſe, accurate, and ſatisfactory manner. Cteſias ſeems to have received an account tolerably diſtinct of the inſect by which the Gum-lacca is produced, and celebrates the beauty of the colour which it dyes. Excerpta ex Indic. ad calc. Herodot. Edit. Weſſeling, p. 830. *Indian Dyers* was the ancient name of thoſe who dyed either the fine blue or the fine red, which points out the country whence the materials they uſed were brought. Salmaſ. Ib. p. 810. From their dying cotton-ſtuffs with different colours, it is evident that the ancient Indians muſt have made ſome conſiderable proficiency in chemical knowledge. Pliny, lib. xxxv. c. ii. § 42. gives an account of this art as far as it was known anciently. It is preciſely the ſame with that now practiſed in callico-printing.

NOTE IX. p. 295.

As Sanſkreet literature is altogether a new acquiſition to Europe, Baghvat-Geeta, the firſt tranſlation from that language, having been publiſhed ſo late as A. D. 1785, it is intimately connected with the ſubject of my inquiries, and may afford entertainment to ſome of my readers, after having reviewed in the text, with a greater degree of critical attention, the two Sanſkreet works moſt worthy of notice, to give here a ſuccinct account of other compoſitions in that tongue with which we have been made acquainted. The extenſive uſe of the Sanſkreet language is a circumſtance which merits particular attention.

"The

" The grand ſource of Indian literature," (ſays Mr. Halhed, the firſt Engliſhman who acquired the knowledge of Sanſkreet,) " the parent of almoſt every dialect from the Perſian gulf to " the China ſeas, is the Sanſkreet, a language of the moſt ve- " nerable and unfathomable antiquity; which, although, at " preſent, ſhut up in the libraries of Brahmins, and appropri- " ated ſolely to the records of their religion, appears to " have been current over moſt of the Oriental world; and " traces of its original extent may ſtill be diſcovered in almoſt " every diſtrict of Aſia. I have been often aſtoniſhed to find " the ſimilitude of Sanſkreet words with thoſe of Perſian and " Arabic, and even of Latin and Greek; and thoſe not in " technical and metaphorical terms, which the mutuation of " refined arts and improved manners might have occaſionally " introduced, but in the ground-work of language, in mo- " noſyllables, in the names of numbers, and the appellations of " ſuch things as would be firſt diſcriminated on the immediate " dawn of civilization. The reſemblance which may be ob- " ſerved in the characters on the medals and ſignets of various " diſtricts of Aſia, the light which they reciprocally reflect " upon each other, and the general analogy which they all bear " to the ſame grand prototype, afford another ample field for cu- " rioſity. The coins of Aſſam, Napaul, Caſhmeere, and many " other kingdoms, are all ſtamped with Sanſkreet characters, " and moſtly contain alluſions to the old Sanſkreet mythology. " The ſame conformity I have obſerved on the impreſſion of " ſeals from Bootan and Thibet. A collateral inference may " likewiſe be deduced from the peculiar arrangement of the " Sanſkreet alphabet, ſo very different from that of any other

" quarter of the world. This extraordinary mode of combi-
" nation ſtill exiſts in the greateſt part of the Eaſt, from the
" Indus to Pegu, in dialects now apparently unconnected, and
" in characters completely diſſimilar; and it is a forcible argu-
" ment that they are all derived from the ſame ſource. Another
" channel of ſpeculation preſents itſelf in the names of perſons
" and places, of titles and dignities, which are open to general
" notice, and in which, to the fartheſt limits of Aſia, may be
" found manifeſt traces of the Sanſkreet." Preface to the Grammar of the Bengal Language, p. 3. After this curious account of the Sanſkreet tongue, I proceed to enumerate the works which have been tranſlated from it, beſides the two mentioned in the text.—1. To Mr. Wilkins we are indebted for *Heeto-pades* or *Amicable Inſtruction*, in a ſeries of connected fables, interſperſed with moral, prudential, and political maxims. This work is in ſuch high eſteem throughout the Eaſt, that it has been tranſlated into every language ſpoken there. It did not eſcape the notice of the Emperor Akbêr, attentive to every thing that could contribute to promote uſeful knowledge. He directed his Vizier, Abul Fazel, to put it into a ſtyle ſuited to all capacities, and to illuſtrate the obſcure paſſages in it, which he accordingly did, and gave it the title of, *The Criterion of Wiſdom*. At length, theſe fables made their way into Europe, and have been circulated there with additions and alterations, under the names of Pilpay and Eſop. Many of the Sanſkreet apologues are ingenious and beautiful, and have been copied or imitated by the fabuliſts of other nations. But in ſome of them the characters of the animals introduced are very ill ſuſtained; to deſcribe a tyger as extremely devout, and practiſing

tiſing charity, and other religious duties, p. 16. or an old mouſe well read in the *Neetee Saſtras*, i. e. Syſtems of morality and policy, p. 24.; a cat who read religious books, p. 35, &c. diſcovers a want of taſte, and an inattention to propriety. Many of the moral ſayings, if conſidered as detached maxims, are founded upon a thorough knowledge of life and manners, and convey inſtruction with elegant ſimplicity. But the attempt of the author to form his work into a connected ſeries of fables, and his mode of interweaving with them ſuch a number of moral reflections in proſe and in verſe, renders the ſtructure of the whole ſo artificial that the peruſal of it becomes often unpleaſant. Akber was ſo ſenſible of this, that, among other inſtructions, he adviſes his Vizier to abridge the long digreſſions in that work. By theſe ſtrictures it is far from my intention to detract in the ſmalleſt degree from the merit of Mr. Wilkins. His country is much indebted to him for having opened a new ſource of ſcience and taſte. The celebrity of the Heeto-pades, as well as its intrinſic merit, notwithſtanding the defects which I have mentioned, juſtify his choice of it, as a work worthy of being made known to Europe in its original form. From reading this and his other tranſlations, no man will refuſe him the praiſe, to which he modeſtly confines his pretenſions, "of having drawn a picture which we ſuppoſe to be a "true likeneſs, although we are unacquainted with the origi-"nal." Pref. p. xiv.—2. In the firſt number of the New Aſiatic Miſcellany, we have a tranſlation of a celebrated compoſition in the Eaſt, known by the title of the *Five Gems*. It conſiſts of ſtanzas by five poets who attended the court of Abiſſura, King of Bengal. Some of theſe ſtanzas are ſimple and

and elegant.—3. An ode tranſlated from Wulli; in which that extravagance of fancy, and thoſe far-fetched and unnatural conceits, which ſo often diſguſt Europeans with the poetical compoſitions of the Eaſt, abound too much. The editor has not informed us to whoſe knowledge of the Sanſkreet we are indebted for theſe two tranſlations.—4. Some original grants of land, of very ancient dates, tranſlated by Mr. Wilkins. It may ſeem odd, that a charter of legal conveyance of property ſhould be ranked among the literary compoſitions of any people. But ſo widely do the manners of the Hindoos differ from thoſe of Europe, that as our lawyers multiply words and clauſes, in order to render a grant complete, and to guard againſt every thing that may invalidate it, the *Pundits* ſeem to diſpatch the legal part of the deed with brevity, but, in a long preamble and concluſion, make an extraordinary diſplay of their own learning, eloquence, and powers of compoſition, both in proſe and in verſe. The preamble to one of theſe deeds is an encomium of the monarch who grants the land, in a bold ſtrain of Eaſtern exaggeration: "When his innumerable army "marched, the heavens were ſo filled with the duſt of their feet "that the birds of the air could reſt upon it." "His elephants "moved like walking mountains, and the earth, oppreſſed by "their weight, mouldered into duſt." It concludes with denouncing vengeance againſt thoſe who ſhould venture to infringe this grant: "Riches and the life of man are as tranſient as drops "of water upon a leaf of the lotus. Learning this truth, O "man, do not attempt to deprive another of his property." Aſiatic Reſearches, vol. i. p. 123, &c. The other grant, which appears to be ſtill more ancient, is not leſs remarkable. Both

2 were

were found engraved on plates of copper. Ib. p. 357, &c.— 5. The tranflation of part of the Shafter, publifhed by Colonel Dow, in the year 1768, ought perhaps to have been firft mentioned. But as this tranflation was not made by him from the Sanfkreet, but taken from the mouth of a Brahmin, who explained the Shafter in Perfian, or in the vulgar language of Bengal, it will fall more properly under notice when we come to inquire into the ftate of fcience among the Hindoos, than in this place, where we are endeavouring to give fome idea of their tafte in compofition.

NOTE X. p. 303.

As many of my readers may be unacquainted with the extravagant length of the four æras or periods of Indian chronology, it may be proper to give an account of them from Mr. Halhed's Preface to the Code of Gentoo Laws, p. xxxvi.

1. The *Suttee Jogue* (or age of purity) is faid to have lafted three million two hundred thoufand years, and they hold that the life of man was extended in that age to one hundred thoufand years, and that his ftature was twenty-one cubits.

2. The *Tirtah Jogue* (in which one third of mankind was corrupted) they fuppofe to have confifted of two million four hundred thoufand years, and that men lived to the age of ten thoufand years.

3. The

3. The *Dwapaar Jogue* (in which half of the human race became depraved) endured one million ſix hundred thouſand years, and the life of man was then reduced to a thouſand years.

4. The *Collee Jogue* (in which all mankind are corrupted, or rather leſſened, for that is the true meaning of *Collee*) is the preſent æra, which they ſuppoſe ordained to ſubſiſt four hundred thouſand years, of which near five thouſand are already paſt, and the life of man in that period is limited to one hundred years.

If we ſuppoſe the computation of time in the Indian chronology to be made by ſolar or even by lunar years, nothing can be more extravagant in itſelf, or more repugnant to our mode of calculating the duration of the world, founded on ſacred and infallible authority. Some attempts have been made by learned men, particularly by M. Bailly, in a very ingenious diſſertation on that ſubject, to bring the chronology of the Hindoos to accord ſomewhat better with that of the Old Teſtament; but, as I could not explain the principles upon which he founds his concluſions, without entering into long and intricate diſcuſſions foreign from the ſubject of this Diſſertation, and as I cannot aſſent to ſome of his opinions, I ſhall reſt ſatisfied with referring to his Aſtron. Indienne, Diſc. Prelim. p. lxxvii. and leave my readers to judge for themſelves. I am happy to obſerve that a Memoir on the Chronology of the Hindoos will be publiſhed in the Second Volume of the Tranſactions of the Society of Bengal, and I hope that ſome

ſome learned member of that body will be able, from his acquaintance with the languages and hiſtory of the country, to throw light upon a ſubject which its connection with religion and ſcience renders extremely intereſting. From one circumſtance, however, which merits attention, we may conclude, that the information which we have hitherto received concerning the chronology of the Hindoos is very incorrect. We have, as far as I know, only five original accounts of the different Jogues or æras of the Hindoos. The firſt is given by M. Roger, who received it from the Brahmins on the Coromandel coaſt. According to it, the Suttee Jogue is a period of one million ſeven hundred and twenty-eight thouſand years; the Tirtah Jogue is one million two hundred and ninety-ſix thouſand years; the Dwapaar Jogue is eight hundred and ſixty-four thouſand. The duration of the Collee Jogue he does not ſpecify. Porte Ouverte, p. 179. The next is that of M. Bernier, who received it from the Brahmins of Benares. According to him, the duration of the Suttee Jogue was two million five hundred thouſand years; that of the Tirtah Jogue one million two hundred thouſand years; that of the Dwapaar Jogue is eight hundred and ſixty-four thouſand years. Concerning the period of the Collee Jogue, he, likewiſe, is ſilent. Voyages, tom. ii. p. 160. The third is that of Colonel Dow, according to which the Suttee Jogue is a period of fourteen million of years; the Tirtah Jogue one million eighty thouſand; the Dwapaar Jogue ſeventy-two thouſand; and the Collee Jogue thirty-ſix thouſand years. Hiſt. of Hindoſt. vol. i. p. 2. The fourth account is that of M. Le Gentil, who received it from the Brahmins of the Coromandel coaſt, and as his information was acquired in the ſame part of India, and derived from the ſame ſource with that of M. Roger, it agrees with his in every particular. Mem. de l'Academ. des Sciences pour 1772, tom. ii. part i. p. 176. The fifth is the account of Mr. Halhed, which I have already given. From this diſcrepancy, not only of the total numbers, but of many of the articles in the different accounts, it is manifeſt that our information concerning Indian chronology is hitherto as uncertain as the whole ſyſtem of it is wild and fabulous. To me it appears highly probable, that when we underſtand more thoroughly the principles upon which the factitious æras or Jogues of the Hindoos have been formed, that we may be more able to reconcile their chronology to the true mode of computing time, founded on the authority of the Old Teſtament; and may likewiſe find reaſon to conclude, that the account given by their aſtronomers of the ſituation of the heavenly bodies at the beginning of the Collee Jogue, is not eſtabliſhed by actual obſervation, but the reſult of a retroſpective calculation. Whoever undertakes to inveſtigate farther the chronology of the Hindoos, will derive great aſſiſtance from a Memoir of Mr. Marſden on that ſubject, in which he has explained the nature of their year, and the ſeveral æras in uſe among them, with much ingenuity and preciſion. Philoſ. Tranſact. vol. lxxx. part ii. p. 560.

NOTE XI. p. 311.

In the public buildings of India, we find proofs and monuments of the proficiency of the Brahmins in ſcience, particularly of their attention to aſtronomical obſervation. Their religion

ligion enjoins, that the four ſides of a Pagoda ſhould face the four cardinal points. In order to execute this with accuracy, they take a method deſcribed by M. le Gentil, which diſcovers a conſiderable degree of ſcience. He carefully examined the poſition of one of their Pagodas, and found it to be perfectly exact. Voy. tom. i. p. 133, &c. As ſome of their Pagodas are very ancient, they muſt have early attained ſuch a portion of knowledge as was requiſite for placing them properly. On the ceilings of Choultrys, and other ancient edifices, the twelve ſigns of the zodiac are often delineated; and, from their reſemblance to thoſe which are now univerſally uſed, it is highly probable that the knowledge of theſe arbitrary ſymbols was derived from the Eaſt. Colonel Call has publiſhed a drawing of the ſigns of the zodiac, which he found on the ceiling of a Choultry at Verdapettah, in the Madura country. Phil. Tranſact. vol. lxii. p. 353. I have a drawing of them in my poſſeſſion, differing from his in ſome of the figures, but I cannot ſay in what particular place it was found. Sir Robert Barker deſcribes an obſervatory at Benares, which he viſited A. D. 1772. In it he found inſtruments for aſtronomical obſervation, of very large dimenſions, and conſtructed with great ſkill and ingenuity. Of all theſe he has publiſhed drawings. Phil. Tranſact. vol. lxvii. p. 598. According to traditionary account, this obſervatory was built by the Emperor Akber. The view which Sir Robert took of it was an haſty one. It merits a more attentive inſpection, in order to determine whether it was conſtructed by Akber, or erected in ſome more early period. Sir Robert intimates, that none but Brahmins who underſtood the Sanſkreet, and could conſult the aſtrono-

3 A 2 mical

mical tables written in that language, were capable of calculating eclipſes. P. Tieffenthaler deſcribes, in a very curſory manner, two obſervatories furniſhed with inſtruments of extraordinary magnitude, at Jepour and Ougein, in the country of Malwa. Bernouilli, tom. i. p. 316. 347. But theſe are modern ſtructures.

INDEX.

INDEX.

A

ABUL FAZEL, minister to Akber, sovereign of Indostan, publishes the Ayeen Akbery, 273. and Heeto-Pades — — 356

Acesines, a city built on that river by Alexander the Great — 191

Æras of Indian chronology, explained, 359. remarks on — 360

Africa, general idea of the continent of, and of its trade, 145. origin of the slave trade — — 166

Agathemerus, his account of the island of Saprobana, 76. his character of Ptolemy the geographer — 212

Agathodæmon, illustrates the geography of Ptolemy, by maps — 213

Akber, sovereign of Indostan, his character — 272. 349

Albuquerque, Alphonso, the Portugueze admiral, seizes the island of Ormus, 139. his operations in the Red Sea, 140

Alexander the Great, his extensive views respecting India, 12. his expedition to India, 13. his war with Porus, 15. how reduced to relinquish his enterprize, 16. his measures for opening a maritime communication with India, 17. his account of India confirmed by modern observations, 20. his political views in exploring that country, 22. his measures to unite his European and Asiatic subjects, 24. consequences of his death, 28. the sufferings of his army from the periodical rains, 184. his surprize at the tides of the Indian ocean, 188. cities built by him in India, 191. 193. intended a survey of the Caspian sea — 206

Alexandria, long the chief seat of commerce with India, 12. the light-house on the Pharos erected by Ptolemy Lagus, 35. mode of conducting the silk trade at that port, 55. the Venetians trade there for silk, 114. and the Florentines, 117. is subjected to the Turks — — 142

Allahabad, the modern name of the ancient city of Palibothra, 30. account of this city by Megasthenes, 32. remarks on Major Rennel on this subject — — 196

America, discovered by Christopher Columbus, 132. the East India trade a continual drain from its silver mines, 165. origin of the slave-trade, 166. contrast between the natives of America and of India when first discovered, 167. the trade of Europe with each compared, 170. was obliged to be colonized, in order to be improved, 170. supplies Europe with its products, in return for manufactures 171

Antiochus

I N D E X.

Antiochus the Great, his inroad into India 199

Antoninus, Marcus, emperor, notices of an embaſſy ſent by him to the emperor of China — — 71

Antwerp, greatly enriched by becoming the ſtaple of the Hanſeatic league 128

Arabians, anciently great dealers in ſpices from the Eaſt, 52. great alterations affected in their manners by the religion of Mahomet, 92. they conquer Egypt and Perſia, *ib.* a view of their commercial navigation, 94. are the firſt who mention porcelane and tea, 96. derived the knowledge of the mariner's compaſs from Europe, 227. make no ſcruple to plunder the caravans travelling to Mecca — 246

Ariſtotle, his political advice to Alexander the Great, 23. his juſt deſcription of the Caſpian ſea, 205. doubted the expediency of commerce in a well-regulated ſtate — 208

Aromatics, why much uſed by the ancients, 51

Arrian, character of his Hiſtory of the Indian expedition of Alexander the Great, 19. his account of the commerce of the ancients, 56. inquiry into his geographical knowledge of India, 59. is the firſt ancient writer who had any knowledge of the Eaſtern coaſt of the great peninſula of India, 61. his account of Alexander's Indian fleet corroborated, 186. character of his Indian Hiſtory, 187. his account of the Caſpian ſea, 204. his Periplus compared with modern names and ſituations 211. 218

Arts and Sciences, where firſt cultivated, 2

Aſbeſtos, its extravagant price among the Romans — — 208

Aſtronomy, teſtimonies of the great proficiency of the Indoſtans in 302

Augſburg, greatly enriched by becoming a mart for Indian commodities 128

Auguſtus, emperor, reduces Egypt to a Roman province — 41

Ayeen Akbery, account of the intercourſe of the Eaſt Indians by water from, 186. See *Sanſkreet* literature.

B

Babelmandeb, derivation of the name 200

Bactria, riſe of the kingdom of, and its acquiſitions in India, 33. is overwhelmed by the Tartars 34. 199

Baghvat-Geeta, the pure theology taught in that poem — 327

Bailly, M. his examination into the antiquity of aſtronomy in India 306

Bank of Venice, the firſt eſtabliſhment of that kind formed in Europe 241

Barygaza, a conſiderable emporium on the coaſt of ancient India, its ſituation aſcertained — — 57

Baſſora, the city of, founded by the Caliph Omar — 93

Benares, the peculiar ſeat of Indoſtan ſcience and literature, 310. account of the obſervatory there 363

Berenice, the city of, founded to facilitate the trade between Alexandria and India — — 36

Bernier, M. his account of the Indian chronology — 361

Boddam, Eaſt India ſhip, remarkable ſpeedy voyage of, from Portſmouth to Madras 207

Brahmins, in India, their ſacred rights and high privileges, 265. inquiry into the ſtate of ſcientific knowledge among them, 296. their religious hierarchy and worſhip, 311. their great learning taught them a theology ſuperior to the popular ſuperſtition, 325. their doctrines coincide with the tenets of the Stoical School, 331. ſtudiouſly concealed religious truths from the people 334

Bruce, the inſight his travels afford into the maritime expeditions of king Solomon — — 9

Bruges, made the ſtaple of the trade of the Hanſeatic league, 120. is greatly enriched — — 128

Baron Sunker, a claſs among the Hindoos, deſcribed — 339

Byzantine hiſtorians, a character of 102

Caſſa,

I N D E X.

C

Caffa, the great trade carried on there 232

Cairo, account of the caravan that travels from thence to Mecca 245

Calicut, reception of Vasco de Gama in that country — 135

Call, colonel, his general opinion of the antiquity of arts and sciences in India 352

Camel, the valuable properties of that animal, 3. is peculiarly formed for traversing sandy deserts — 242

Candahar, under what name known to Alexander the Great — 14

Canton, in China, a factory settled there by the early Arabs — 95

Cape of Good Hope, circumstances that led to the discovery of a passage to India that way, 133. is said by Herodotus to have been passed by some Phenician ships, 153. importance of the discovery of this passage by the Portugueze — — 173

Caravans, the origin of, 3. were protected and encouraged under the Roman dominion, 70. great commercial use of, in the East, 144. account of the caravans which visit Mecca, 245. a considerable slave-trade carried on by the African caravans — 247

Caspian sea, erroneous opinion of the ancient geographers concerning, 39. 204. by whom first described in modern times 205

Casts, or orders of society among the native Gentoos, described, 258. remarks on the policy and tendency of this arrangement, 259. their peculiar names, ranks, and offices described 338

Cathay, the ancient name of China 122

Ceylon, supposed to be the island described by ancient geographers under the name of Taprobana, 77. Christian churches planted there by Persian missionaries, 97. is visited by Marco Polo the Venetian — 122

Chardin, Sir John, his testimony that the Orientals derived the use of the mariner's compass from the Europeans, 227. his account of the trade of Caffa 232

Chillambrum, description of the pagoda there — — 282

China, the only country from whence the Romans obtained silk, 55. through what medium they received it, 59. how the silk-worm was conveyed from thence to Europe, 88. is traded to by the Arabians, 95. first mention of porcelane and tea, 96. the Christian religion propagated there by Persian missionaries, 97. how the silk of, was conveyed to Constantinople, after the Greeks were excluded from the port of Alexandria, 98. estimate of the Chinese practice of navigation, 226. how the number of Mahometans increase in China, 230. a commercial intercourse, by land, opened between that country and Russia, 249. amazing exportation of tea from, to Europe — 252

Chronology, Indian, the four æras of, 359. remarks on — 360

Cleopatra, value of her famous pearl ear-rings — — 54

Colchos, the antient pearl fishery there, still carried on by the Dutch 60

Colours, Indian, for dying, account of 352

Columbus, his views in that voyage by which he discovered America, 132. his reliance on the authority of Marca Polo, the Venetian traveller, 238. See *Gama*.

Commerce, the extension of, abated the hostile sentiments which actuated one nation against another, 120. unfavourable opinion of Plato concerning 207

Common law, the origin of, traced 270

Comorin, Cape, is accurately described by Arrian — — 60

Compass, mariner's, was unknown by the ancient Chinese and Arabs 227

Constantinople, taken and plundered by the crusaders, 110. subversion of the Latin empire there, 112. is conquered by the Turks, and made the seat of their government — 123

Conveyancing, specimen of the ancient Indian style of — 358

S

Coromandel

Coromandel coaſt, the inhabitants of, always great traders —— 85
Coſmas Indicopleuſtes, ſome account of, and of his Chriſtian topography, 84. his account of the iſland of Taprobana 85
Cotton manufactures, evidence of their not being common among the Romans 211
Cruſades to the Holy Land, the origin of, traced, and their commercial effects, 104. the cruſaders acquired the policy and arts of the people whom they ſubdued, 107. brought different nations acquainted with each other 120

D

Damaſcus, account of the caravan that travels from thence to Mecca 246
Damaſk, the name of that ſpecies of ſilk manufacture, whence derived 126
Dandulo, Andrew, character of his Venetian Chronicle —— 231
D'Anville, M. his opinion as to the courſe purſued in the trading voyages of king Solomon's ſhips, 9. his corrections of Ptolemy's geography of India, 66. corroborates Nearchus's account of India, 190. his geography of India controverted by M. Goſſellin 216
Darius, the ſon of Hyſtaſpes, king of Perſia, his reſearches into, and conqueſts in India —— —— 10
Deccan, the ancient Dachanos of Arrian 219
Delta of the Indus, the general ſtate of the weather there —— 185
Diamonds, not ſo highly eſteemed by the Romans as pearls — 208
Diodorus Siculus, his hiſtory of the Indian expedition of Seſoſtris examined 180
Dow, colonel, account of his tranſlation of the Shaſter, 298. 359. his account of the Indian chronology 361
Dowlatabad, the ſame with the ancient Tagara —— —— 211
Du Halde, his deſcription of a peculiar ſpecies of ſilk — — 210
Dutch ſtates, became the firſt rivals of the Portugueze in the trade to India 163
Dyes, Indian, the excellence of 352

E

Eaſt, the regions of, where arts and ſciences were firſt cultivated, 2. the intercourſe between different countries how firſt carried on, 3. the firſt maritime communication with, from the Weſt, 5. See *India*.
Eclipſes, how calculated by the Brahmins of India —— 305
Egypt, ancient prejudice of the inhabitants againſt any intercourſe with foreigners, 5. how the Egyptians became a commercial people, 6. the city of Alexandria built, 12. the ſeat of government fixed there by Ptolemy Lagus, 35. intercourſe between the city of Berenice and India, 36. its opulence derived from its commerce with the Eaſt, 38. is reduced to a Roman province, 40. manner of conducting the ſilk trade at the port of Alexandria, 55. conqueſt of, by the Arabs, 92. the Venetians reſort to Alexandria for ſilk, 114. and the Florentines, 117. commercial view of the countries, 126. is ſubdued by the Turks, 142. how the Indian trade has been conducted through that country at different times — 200
Elagabalus, the firſt Roman emperor who wore ſilk —— 54
Elephanta, iſland, account of the ancient pagoda there —— 278
Ellore, general account of the pagodas there —— —— 351
Æſop's fables, the origin of, traced 356
Ethics, ſtate of, in India 299
Europe, a review of the ſtate of, at the time of the ſubverſion of the Greek empire, 123. extenſive operation of the commercial genius of, 167. the Europeans receive the products of America, and ſupply it with manufactures, 171. the exportation of ſilver to India, how beneficial to Europe, 172. importance of the diſcovery of the paſſage to India round the Cape of Good Hope 173

6 *Faquirs*

INDEX.

F

Faquirs of India, unite trade with devotion in their pilgrimages, 106. 232. brief account of — 341

Figures, arithmetical, originally derived from India — 301

Five Gems, an ancient Sanskreet poem, account of — — 357

Florence, rise of the state of, by manufactures and the banking business, 116. a commercial treaty concluded with Egypt, 117. summary of the instructions to their ambassadors to the Soldan 235

G

Gama, Vasco de, his voyage from Lisbon to India — — 134

Ganges, account of that river by Major Rennel — — 195

Genoa, motives that stimulated the Genoese to assist in subverting the Latin empire at Constantinople, 112. the great advantages they derived from this measure, 113. character of the Genoese government, 114. the Genoese expelled from all their Grecian settlements by the Turks, 123. character of, by Nicephorus Gregoras — 233

Gentil, M. le, his account of the Indian chronology — 361

Gentoos, see *Brahmins*, and *Hindoos*.

Gibbon, Mr. the Roman historian, testimony in favour of his accuracy 223

Gossellin, M. character of his geography of the Greeks analyzed — 216

Greeks, their national pride at the time of Alexander the Great, 23. how they attained the breeding of silk-worms under the emperor Justinian, 88. are shut out from the port of Alexandria by the Mahometan Arabs, 92. the Greek empire conquered by Mahomet II. 123. how they were deprived of Bactria, 199. origin of the ancient mythology of — 317

Gum Lacca, natural history of, and its uses in manufacture — 353

H

Halhed, Mr. his account of the Sanskreet literature — — 355

Hanno, commanded the only voyage for discovery undertaken by any of the ancient states in the Mediterranean 250

Hanseatic league, formed, and the staple fixed at Bruges — 120

Hastings, Mr. governor-general of Bengal, his attention to forming a code of Hindoo laws — — 273

Heeto-Pades, or Amicable Instruction, an ancient Sanskreet composition, account and character of — 356

Herodotus, affirms the Cape of Good Hope to have been passed by some Phenician vessels, 153. his history of Sesostris examined, 180. his unsatisfactory account of the tides in the Red Sea, 189. his just description of the Caspian sea 205

Hindoos, that people exactly described in the account of the Indian expedition of Alexander the Great, 21. their inflexible adherence to their religion, and casts, 229. their four orders, or casts, described, 258. remarks on the policy and tendency of this popular arrangement, 259. their high antiquity, and nature of their institutions, 274. character of their judicial code, 275. state of sciences among them, 296. their religious tenets and practices, 311. the names, ranks, and offices of their several casts described — 338

Hiram, king of Tyre, assists king Solomon in his naval undertakings 8

Hippalus, captain of an Egyptian vessel, avails himself of the monsoons, in sailing from the Arabian gulf to the Malabar coast — — 48

Hipparchus, the first who attempted to make a catalogue of the stars 63

History, authentic, the period of, extremely limited, 1. is minute in the records of blood, but silent as to the progress of useful arts — 47

Hydaspes, river, a numerous fleet raised there by Alexander the Great 17

Hyphasis, river, the utmost limit of Alexander the Great's progress in India 16

3 B *Jenaub,*

I N D E X.

J

Jenaub, a city built on that river by Alexander the Great — 191

Jenkinson, Anthony, the first modern traveller who gives a just description of the Caspian sea — 205

Jeswont Sing, his letter to Aurengzebe, containing a character of sultan Akber 349

Jewels, their great use, and high estimation among the ancients — 53

Jews, when they effected a commercial intercourse with India, 8. inquiry into the maritime commerce of king Solomon, 9. their commercial effort limited to his reign — — 10

India, the first naval communication with, from the West, 5. the trade of the Phenicians with, how conducted, 7. naval expedition of the Persians to, 10. conquests of Darius Hystaspes in, 11. Alexandria; for many centuries the chief seat of trade with, 12. expedition of Alexander the Great to, 13. flourishing state of the country at that time, 15. Alexander's voyage down the Indus, 17. political state of the country at that time, 20. Alexander's views in this expedition, 22. expedition of Seleucus, the successor of Alexander, 29. embassy of Megasthenes to, 30. conquests of the Bactrian princes in, 33. remains afterward undisturbed by Europeans, until the Cape of Good Hope was doubled by the Portugueze, 34. a commercial intercourse established with Egypt, 35. how Rome was supplied with Eastern commodities, 44. advantage taken of the monsoons, in sailing from the gulf of Arabia to the Malabar coast, 48. its commodities articles of luxury, 50. spices and aromatics, 51. precious stones, 53. silk, 54. general view of its exports and imports, 56. comparison between the ancient and modern trade with India, 58. D'Anville's corrections of Ptolemy's geography of, 66. the trade by caravans protected and encouraged by the Romans, 70. the inhabitants of the Coromandel coast always great traders, 83. the account given of India by Cosmas Indicopleustes, 85. the Romans rivalled in the India trade by the Persians, 86. the Italian states engage in the India trade, 101. account of the India trade by Marino Sanudo, 118. comparative view of the India trade, as carried on by different nations at different times, 125. a direct voyage to India effected by the Portugueze, 134. the staple of the Portugueze trade, established at the city of Malacca, 137. a commercial empire established in the East, by the Portugueze, 143. how it came to pass, that the discovery of a direct navigation to India was reserved for modern times, 150. the conduct of ancient and modern navigators to the East, compared, 154. the prices of Indian commodities greatly reduced by the opening a direct communication with India, 156. the India trade a continual drain of American silver from Europe, 164. contrast between the state of the natives of India and America, when first discovered, 167. the trade of Europe with each, compared, 170. the silver exported to India contributes to enrich instead of impoverishing Europe, 172. importance of the discovery of the passage to India round the Cape of Good Hope, to Europe, 173. examination of the improbabilities attending the supposed expedition of Sesostris to India, 179. remarks on the weather there, 185. remarks on the naval expedition of Nearchus, 188. peculiarities in the Indian tides, 189. aversion of the natives of the East to the sea, 192. Major Rennel's account of the river Ganges, 195. endeavours to ascertain the situation of the ancient city of Palibothra, 196. how the Indian trade has been carried on through Egypt at different times, 200. erroneous descriptions of the Caspian sea by ancient writers, 204. Deccan, the ancient Dachanos of Arrian, 219. the use of the mariner's compass learned by the Easterns from the Europeans, 227. the

the Gentoos inflexible in their religion, 229. computed number of Mahometans in India, 230. extensive circulation of Eastern goods by the caravans, 248. the natives of India the earliest known people who were civilized, 257. their division into casts, 258. the perfection of Indian manufactures accounted for, 261. the general tenure of land there, 266. character of the Hindoo code of laws, 275. general account of the pagodas, 277. fortresses, 284. mechanic arts, 285. literature, 287. their sciences, 295. their religious tenets, 311. origin of superstition, 315. the pure theology of the Brahmins, 325. general reflections formed on the preceding review of the Eastern nations, 334. the manners and customs of the natives influenced by the Mahometan and European intruders, 342. account of the Sanskreet literature, 354. the Heeto-Pades, 356. the Five Gems, 357. Ode from Wulli, 358. specimen of Indian conveyancing, *ib.* the four æras of Indian chronology, explained — — 359

Indicum of the ancients, the same with modern Indigo — 352

Indus, river, passed by Alexander the Great, 14. his voyage down that river 17

Institutions of India, the permanency of, accounted for — — 261

Interest of money, the most exact standard of commercial profits, 129. chronological review of — *ib.*

Joanna of Navarre, her exclamation at the wealth of the city of Bruges 239

Italy, rise of the commercial states of, 100. they import the productions of India, 101. the profits they reaped from the crusades, 108. See *Venice*, *Genoa*, &c.

Itineraries of the Roman empire, how formed — — 213

Julius Cæsar, his magnificent present to Servilia, the mother of Brutus, 54. his ignorance of the British tides, 189. a general survey of the whole Roman empire undertaken by him 213

Justin, observations on his account of the progress made by Seleucus in India 194

Justinian, emperor, how he introduced the silk-worm into the Greek empire 88

L

Land, the general tenures of, in India, 266. 344. specimen from an ancient grant of — — 358

Latitudes, how ascertained by the ancient geographers, 78. were more readily determined by them than longitudes 81. 219

Lawyers, European, the style of, compared with that of the Eastern Pundits 358

Leibnitz, his account of the instructions given to the Florentine ambassadors to the Soldan of Egypt — 235

Logic and Metaphysics, state of, in India 297

Longitudes of places, how determined by ancient geographers — 79. 221

M

Magellan, effects a passage to the East Indies Westward from America 162

Mahabarat, an ancient Indian epic poem, account of, 288. extracts from 297. 299. 327

Mahmoud of Gaznah, the vast fleet that opposed his invasion of India 186

Mahomet, rapid spread of his religion, and the great effects produced by it, 91. contributed greatly to extend the commerce of Asia and Africa 146

Mahomet II. emperor of the Turks, subdues the Grecian empire — 123

Mahudel, M. his proofs of the ignorance of the ancients as to the nature of silk 210

Malabar coast, probable derivation of its name, 85. how mentioned by the Arabian writers — 96

Malacca, the city of, rendered the staple of the trade carried on in the East, by the Portugueze — 137

Maldive Islands, probable derivation of their name — 85

I N D E X.

Man, a review of his progreſs in ſocial life — — 263
Manufactures, Indian, the perfection of, accounted for — 261
Maps, none known prior to thoſe formed to illuſtrate Ptolemy's geography 78
Marco Polo, the Venetian, account of his travels, 121. objections to his relations — — 236
Marſeilles, opens a trade with Conſtantinople for Indian commodities 103
Maſſoudi, the Arabian, his account of India — — 225
Mecca, the temple there viſited as well by commercial as by devout pilgrims, 105. the pilgrimages to, contributed greatly to facilitate trade, 146. account of the caravans which viſit the temple there 245
Medici, Coſmo di, a Florentine merchant, negotiates a commercial treaty with Egypt, in favour of his countrymen 117
Mediterranean ſea, the chief ſeat of ancient commerce — 152
Meghaſthenes, his embaſſy from Seleucus, king of Macedonia, to India, 30. his account of India — 31
Mocenigo, doge of Venice, in the fifteenth century, his account of the naval ſtrength of that republic — 242
Monkiſh annaliſts, a character of 102
Monſoons, the firſt application of them in voyages to India — 48
Moſes, the books of, the moſt ancient and genuine record of the early ages of the world — — 1
Muſiris, a port on the coaſt of Malabar, frequented by ancient navigators in the Indian trade — 48
Mythology of the Greeks, the natural origin of — — 317

N

Nadir Shah, general review of his Indian expedition — — 185
Nagara of Ptolemy, its latitude according to D'Anville — — 73
Navigation, origin of, traced, 4. where firſt cultivated, 5. how introduced among the Egyptians — 6
Nearchus, commands the naval expedition of Alexander the Great down the Indus, 17. remarks on — 188
Nicephorus Gregoras, his character of the Genoeſe at Conſtantinople 233
Niebbuhr, his evidence in favour of the European origin of the mariner's compaſs — — 228

O

Omar, caliph, founds the city of Baſſora, 93
Ormus, the iſland of, ſeized by the Portugueze — — 139

P

Pagodas of India, general account of, 277. 351. are placed with aſtronomical preciſion — — 362
Palibothra, endeavours to aſcertain the ſituation of that city — 196
Palmyra, by whom, and on what occaſion built, 45. its ſtupendous ruins, 46. its preſent ſtate — 47
Panjab, progreſs of Alexander the Great through that country — 15
Papyrus, occaſion of its being diſuſed for writing on — 231
Parchment, when firſt uſed for the record of charters and deeds — 231
Pariars, the moſt contemptible race of men in India — 229. 339
Patna, evidences of its not being the ancient city of Palibothra — 197
Pearls, their high eſtimation among the Romans, 53. were dearer than diamonds — — 208
Pera, the chief ſuburb of Conſtantinople, granted to the Genoeſe on the ſubverſion of the Latin empire there, 112. the Genoeſe expelled by the Turks 123
Perſia, how the commerce between that country and India was conducted, 38. vigorous cultivation of the India trade, 86. the ſilk trade engroſſed by the Perſians, 87. their extortions introduce the ſilk-worm to Europe, 88. is conquered by the Arabs, 92. Neſto-

I rian

rian churches planted there, 97. amount of the revenue of the Persian monarchs from Herodotus, 183. instances of their ancient aversion to the sea — — 192
Phalanx, Macedonian, how formed by Alexander the Great — 25
Phenicians, how they opened a commercial intercourse with India, 7. are said by Herodotus to have passed the Cape of Good Hope — — 153
Philosophy, the cure for superstition 322
Pilgrimages to the Holy Land, undertaken as well from commercial as from pious motives, 105. account of the pilgrimages to Mecca — 245
Pilpay's fables, the origin of, traced 356
Plato, his political objections to commerce in a well regulated commonwealth 207
Pliny the elder, his slender knowledge of India, 62. his account of the island of Taprobana, 75. observations on his account of the progress of Seleucus in India — — 195
Pomponius Mela, his account of the island of Taprobana, 75. and of the Caspian sea — — 204
Porcelane, the first mention of, by Arabian travellers — — 96
Portugal, circumstances that led the Portugueze to the discovery of the Cape of Good Hope, 133. vigorous exertions of the Portugueze to cultivate the Eastern trade, 137. they aim at a monopoly of the trade to the East, 139. establish a commercial empire in the East, 143. their activity in exploring the Eastern countries, 154. they drive the Venetians out of the European markets, by reducing the prices of India goods, 157. how they remained so long in the exclusive possession of the India trade, 161. are rivalled at length in the Indian ocean by the Dutch, 163. and by the English, *ib.* repulse the efforts of Solyman the Magnificent, to drive them from India, 175. their intercourse with infidels licenced by a Papal bull — — 234
Porus, opposes the progress of Alexander the Great in India, 15. remains steady to the Macedonian interest 29
Potosi, the discovery of the silver mines of, the first permanent source of wealth derived by Spain from America 169
Ptolemy, the geographer, estimate of his scientifical knowledge, 63. established geography upon its proper principles, 64. his accounts of the continent of India examined, 65. his geography of India corrected to modern times by M. D'Anville, 66. instances of his exactness, 73. his account of the island of Taprobane, 76. his character, by Agathemerus, 212. his geographical errors, 214. from what materials he composed his geography of India 221
Ptolemy Lagus, establishes the seat of the Egyptian government at Alexandria, and erects the light-house on the Pharos 35
Ptolemy Philadelphus, projects a grand canal to facilitate the intercourse between Egypt and India, 35. founds the city of Berenice — — 36
Pultanah, the ancient Plithania of Arrian, 211

R

Ramuzia, detects the geographical errors of Ptolemy — 214
Raynal, Abbe, character of his history of the East and West Indies 173
Red Sea, derivation of the name, and the different applications of it by the ancients and the moderns — 190
Religion and superstition, discriminated 313
Renaudot, M. his translation of the Eastern voyage of two Mahometans, from the Arabic, vindicated from the charge of imposition — 224
Rennel, Major, his illustrations of the Indian expedition of Alexander the Great, 18. his account of the river Ganges, 195. remarks on his account of the situation of the city of Palibothra, 196. his opinion of the Egyptian navigation examined — — 202
Rhinocolura, the ancient port of communication between Phenicia and India 7
Roger, M. his account of the Indian chronology — 361
Rome, rise of the power of, 40. how supplied with Indian commodities, 44. its

its imports from thence, articles of luxury, 50. ſpices, 51. precious ſtones, 53. ſilk, 54. remained ignorant of the nature or production of ſilk, 55. how the breeding ſilk-worms was introduced into the Eaſtern empire, 88. conſequences of the Roman empire being diſſolved by the Barbarians, 119. how the itineraries of the empire were formed — — 213
Ruſſia, a commercial intercourſe by land opened between that country and China 249
Ryots of Indoſtan, inquiry into the tenure by which they hold their poſſeſſions 345

S

Sacontala, an ancient Indian dramatic poem, account of — 290
Sacotecas, the mines of, in Mexico, importance of the diſcovery of, to Spain 169
Saint Croix, Baron de, obſervations on his Critique des Hiſtoriens d'Alexandre le Grand — 193
Samarcand, by what name known to Alexander the Great, 13. its latitude, as aſcertained by D'Anville 73
Sandracothis, an Indian prince, his revolt againſt, and treaty with, Seleucus king of Macedonia — 29
Sanſkreet literature, a new acquiſition, 354. Mr. Halhed's account of 355
Sanudo, Marino, his account of the Venetian trade with India in the fourteenth century — — 118
Sciences and Arts, where firſt cultivated, 2. a view of the ſtate of, in India 296
Scylax of Caryandra, his naval expedition to India, 10. gives fabulous accounts of the country, 11. why his voyage is not mentioned by Arrian 187
Seapoys, modern, eſtabliſhed upon the ſame principle with the phalanx of Perſians formed by Alexander the Great 25
Seleucus, the ſucceſſor of Alexander, his expedition to India, 29. obſervations on — — 194
Selim, ſultan, the conqueror of the Mamelukes, his attention to the advantages of the Indian commerce 174
Semiramis, the vaſt fleet that oppoſed her invaſion of India — 186
Sera Metropolis, of Ptolemy, its latitude according to D'Anville — 73
Seringham, deſcription of the pagoda there 282
Seſoſtris, king of Egypt, the firſt who rendered the Egyptians a commercial people, 6. improbabilities attending his ſuppoſed expedition to, and conqueſt of, India — — 179
Shaſter, ſome account of 298. 359
Sielediba, account given of this iſland, by Coſmas Indicopleuſtes — 85
Silk, its high eſtimation among the Romans, 54. the trade for, engroſſed by the Perſians, 87. ſilk-worms obtained and cultivated by the Greeks, 88. account of the Venetian and Florentine trade for ſilk, 114. ignorance of the ancients as to its production, 210. why diſliked by the Turks 211
Silver, is continually drained from Europe to carry on the Eaſt India trade, 165. Europe, how enriched by this exportation — — 172
Sinæ Metropolis, of Ptolemy, endeavours of M. D'Anville to aſcertain its ſituation 69
Slave-trade, modern, the origin of, 166. is largely carried on by the African caravans — — 217
Solomon, king of Judea, inquiry into his maritime commerce, 9. builds Tadmor in the deſert — 45
Solyman the Magnificent, his efforts to drive the Portugueſe from India 174
Soul, deſcription of, from the Mahabarat 297
Spain, how that country happened to have the advantage and honour of diſcovering America, 132. gold and ſilver the only profitable articles they firſt found in America, 169. are obliged to colonize in order to improve their diſcoveries 170
Spices, and aromatics, why much uſed by the ancients, 51. vaſt modern conſumption of them — 160
Strabo, his obſcure knowledge of India, 61. his account of the iſland of Taprobane, 74. denies that Seſoſtris ever entered

13

entered India, 182. evidences of his slender knowledge of India, 202. his account of the Caspian sea, 204. how he justifies his neglect of Hipparchus, 212. his free exposition of ancient theology, 332. his account of the ancient dyes — 352

Sumatra, the island of, visited by the early Arabians — — 95

Superstition and religion, discriminated, 313. origin of superstition, 314. progress of, 318. picture of Oriental superstition, 319. philosophy fatal to 322

Sylla, vast quantities of spices consumed in his funeral pile — 51

T

Tadmor in the desert, by whom built, and for what purpose, 45. its stupendous ruins, 46. its present state 47

Tamerlane, his judicious choice of the season for his Indian campaign 185

Taprobane, Strabo's account of that island, 74. Pliny's account of it. 75. Ptolemy's account, 76. appears to be the island of Ceylon, 77. account given of this island by Cosmas Indicopleustes 85

Tatta, great drought there, 185. vast numbers of vessels for water-carriage there — — 186

Tea, has within a century become a necessary of life in many parts of Europe, 252. amazing annual importation of *ib.*

Tea-tree, first mention of, by Arabian travellers — — 96

Tides of the Indian ocean, peculiarities in 189

Trade, how at first conducted between different countries, 3. between Egypt and India, 35. exports and imports of India — 51

Transmigration of souls, the Eastern doctrine of, explained — 330

Turks, their scruples against the wearing of silk — 211

Tyre, the best account of the commercial transactions of that city, to be found in the prophet Ezekiel — 183

V

Venice, first rise of, as a commercial state, 100. Constantinople taken, in conjunction with the crusaders, 109. the Venetians engage largely in the trade and manufacture of silk, 110. the Latin empire in the East subverted, 112. the Venetians supplanted in the trade with Constantinople by the Genoese, 114. they settle a trade with Alexandria, 115. account of the Venetian trade with India in the fourteenth century, 118. travels of Marco Polo, 121. their trade extended by the Turks subduing the Greek empire, 123. remarks on their trade for Indian goods, 125. evidences of the great wealth they acquired by this trade, 129. alarm taken at the direct voyage to East India, by Vasco de Gama, 136. measures prosecuted by the Venetians to check the progress of the Portugueze in the East, 140. the Portugueze supplant them in the European market, by reducing the prices of India goods, 157. of the great extent of their trade, 240. the bank of Venice the first formed of any in Europe, 241. amount of the Venetian naval strength in the fifteenth century — 242

Ulug Beg, his astronomical tables 73

Virgil, a good natural historian, as well as a descriptive poet — 210

Volney, M. his account of the camel, 244. and of the caravan from Damascus to Mecca — — 246

W

Wilford, lieutenant, his examination of Arrian's Periplus by modern names and situations — — 211

Wilkins, Mr. account of his translation of the Heeto-Pades — 356

Wulli, character of an ode translated from 358

Z

Zemindars, their office in the government of Indostan — — 345

THE END.

ERRATA.

Page	10.	line *antepen.*	*for* exclufive	*read* extenfive.
	11.	—— 21.	*for* people	*read* nations.
	87.	—— *antepen.*	*for* the kingdom	*read* their kingdom.
	183.	—— 1.	*for* fhall	*read* will.
	197.	—— 9.	*for* great veneration	*read* great devotion.
	246.	—— 5.	*for* Khizeh	*read* Khojeh.
	259.	—— *pen.*	*for* feems	*read* feem.
	260.	—— 2.	*for* tends	*read* tend.